MW00988275

I *LOVE* GEORGIA

Also by Patrick Garbin:

Then Vince Said to Herschel...
About Them Dawgs!
The 50 Greatest Plays in Georgia Bulldogs History
Historic Photos of University of Georgia Football

I
LOVE
GEORGIA

PATRICK GARBIN

TRIUMPH
BOOKS

Copyright © 2012 by Patrick Garbin

No part of this publication may be reproduced, stored in a retrieval system, or transmitted in any form by any means, electronic, mechanical, photocopying, or otherwise, without the prior written permission of the publisher, Triumph Books LLC, 814 N. Franklin St., Chicago, Illinois 60610.

Library of Congress Cataloging-in-Publication Data

Garbin, Patrick, 1975–
    I love Georgia, I hate Florida / Patrick Garbin.
      p. cm.
    ISBN 978-1-60078-723-2
    1. University of Georgia—Football—History. 2. Georgia Bulldogs (Football team)—History. 3. University of Florida—Football—History. 4. Florida Gators (Football team)—History. 5. Sports rivalries—United States. I. Title.
    GV958.G44G369 2012
    796.332'630975—dc23

                                   2012005148

This book is available in quantity at special discounts for your group or organization. For further information, contact:

Triumph Books LLC
814 North Franklin Street
Chicago, Illinois 60610
(312) 939-3330
www.triumphbooks.com

Printed in U.S.A.
ISBN: 978-1-60078-723-2
Design and editorial production by Prologue Publishing Services, LLC
Photos courtesy of AP Images unless otherwise indicated

To my heart and soul—my two young children, Trip and Rebecca. If not on the road to eventually becoming Georgia Bulldogs like your mommy and daddy, no matter where life takes you, as long as you don't become Florida Gators...

CONTENTS

FOREWORD

A LOT OF PEOPLE TALK ABOUT my game against Florida as a junior in 1988 because that was the year I was All-America, which led to my being drafted into the NFL. I had a good game against the Gators that season. However, to honor Patrick Garbin's incredible commitment to and expertise concerning the University of Georgia football program, I felt it best to reflect on my very *first* memory of the Georgia-Florida game during my years "between the hedges."

Before entering UGA in the summer of 1985, I didn't really know what to expect as a young, bright-eyed country boy from North Carolina. But immediately the spirit of Georgia football became ingrained in me. From my teammates, coaches, and fans, I learned right away that the Georgia-Florida game was *the* game.

During my freshman year, I was warned several times to be prepared for the change of atmosphere during the week of the game. I was told it's a regular season bowl game. The week of training was very intense, the pace of practice picked up, and there was a sense of urgency. Practices were longer, harder, and more physical in the trenches. The coaches were tougher on us. They made sure that any mistakes made on the practice field were corrected. This was the case not one time, not two times, but 10 times.

Freshman Tim Worley's 89-yard touchdown against Florida in 1985 tied a school record for longest run from scrimmage and sealed an upset victory over the top-ranked Gators. Photo courtesy of Wingate Downs

Travel day to Jacksonville was almost like a Christmas parade. As we left the campus, we saw fans following the bus, rooting us on as we approached the airport. We saw fans at the airport cheering, "Goooooooo Georgia Bulldogs" and "Go Dawgs...sic 'em!" Experiencing that as a freshman was like a five-year-old kid getting everything he wanted on his birthday—with all his friends there. The butterflies in my stomach were swarming. I was so nervous. All I could do in front of all of those fans was show my pearly whites and be grateful to be a Georgia Bulldog.

The city of Jacksonville was electrifying the night before the game. Although we weren't allowed to interact with the fans and their activities, we were still able to see and feel—from our hotel rooms—the energy from the thousands of people who had traveled there just to see us play. All night long, inside and outside the hotel, it seemed like all I heard was, "Go Dawgs!" By bedtime, it was like a serenade that pumped me up. I felt the pressure, responsibility, and honor of being on a grand stage, and I loved it!

Fullback Keith Henderson and I were always roommates on the road. Our freshman year, we started our own tradition of making sure we were asleep by a certain time, well rested, awake at a certain time, on time for morning meetings, and not eating any red meat on the day of the game. Instead, we ate pasta and omelets in order to stay light, so we could run faster.

The game day meal for the 1985 game was uneventful because the team was much more laid back than normal. The reason for this was because the team knew what it came to do, and we weren't stressed at all. We were barely ranked in the top 20, while Florida was the No. 1 team in the nation. The Gators had more to lose than we did. We knew no one expected us to win, although the team felt we were destined to do so.

By the time the game rolled around, we were ready to go. We knew our assignments. Tailback Lars Tate and fullback David McCluskey started the game, and Keith and I rotated in and out every other series. We stuck to what Georgia football does best—come right at you and run the ball down your throat. You can try to stop us if you can. Come to find out, Florida couldn't.

In the first quarter, we were smacking the Gators in the mouth. We realized after the first couple of minutes that we could play with those guys and beat them if the team stayed true to the game plan on offense and defense.

Keith and I noticed right away that the Georgia fans became louder—and the Florida fans became quieter—every time he or I touched the ball. I assume this is because each time we got a carry, we gained positive yardage. Florida had not encountered a running attack like ours all year long. Midway into the first quarter and with the game scoreless, Keith popped one for a touchdown of more than 70 yards. A simple fullback dive straight up the middle had instantly changed the game. When Keith scored, I became even more intense and just wanted the ball. I adopted the mind-set that I was playing in my final Georgia-Florida game—not my first. So, every opportunity I got to run the ball or to block, I wanted to have an impact.

Mike Cavan was our running backs coach. He was rotating all four of us based on the climate of the game and the momentum each of us gained throughout. By the fourth quarter, we were up 17–3. The Florida fans were in absolute shock and awe, and so were the Gators players and coaches. I could see the frustration on the faces of the defensive players.

Then we drove the dagger in even deeper. There's no mercy in the Georgia-Florida game.

I was blessed to have a big play with just under four minutes left. Florida had just driven inside our 10-yard line, but John L. Williams fumbled. Georgia linebacker Steve Boswell recovered the fumble on the 8-yard line. We ran another fullback dive play with Keith which gained three yards. On second-and-seven from the 11-yard line, I ran a toss sweep to the right. The blocking was perfect. What sealed the deal for me was when Keith blocked a defensive back out of the way, allowing me to turn upfield. From there, all I could see was the opposing end zone, and there was no way I was getting caught on the run.

The 89-yard touchdown play remains very near and dear to my heart. Not just because it still is tied for the longest touchdown run in the history of UGA football, but because it sealed a 24–3 win over Florida and, in a way, our legacy as a team. We were—and still are—the only Bulldogs football team to ever beat a No. 1 ranked opponent, and we did it with a total team effort.

When I was inducted into the Florida-Georgia Hall of Fame in 2007, I was asked by someone, "Could you hear the crowd while you were running for that long touchdown against the Gators in 1985?" Honestly, at first, all I heard was my own breathing. I didn't hear the crowd until I crossed the goal line and slowed down. That's when I finally heard uncontrollable cheering and, for really the first time, realized how much the Bulldog Nation loved its Georgia Bulldogs...especially when we beat the Florida Gators!

Go Dawgs!

—Tim Worley

INTRODUCTION

LET'S BE HONEST. Simply stated, the Bulldog Nation hates the Florida Gators, and their fans cannot stand our team. The Georgia-Florida football rivalry has a long, storied history at the neutral site of Jacksonville filled with fights and arrests, harsh ridicule, and lots of cocktails—whether consumed or thrown at others—while featuring two of the more prominent college football powers, and two of the most passionate fan bases in all of sports (one of which is often identified by its wearing of jean shorts, might I add, but more on that later).

This is a rivalry in which the two teams cannot even agree on when the series began. Georgia first faced a "University of Florida" team in 1904; however, the Gators disregard the game as a true contest since they were not located in Gainesville at the time (coupled with the fact they were trounced 52–0 by Georgia).

The hatred between the two schools has often spilled over from the stands onto the playing field, especially decades ago, when on a few occasions it took more than merely the game's referees to break up the hostility. For example, following the ending of the 1967 game, a brawl ensued between the Bulldogs and Gators players. Fans soon joined in the mêlée, and then some coaches even got involved before the fight was finally broken up by the police.

"That was something," said Florida assistant coach Gene Ellenson after the game. "I saw [Georgia assistant] Erskine Russell laying down on top of one of our boys. He was trying to protect our boy from [his own] players."

Over the years, the on-field fighting has lessened, but make no mistake about it, the hatred between the Bulldogs and Gators and their respective fans persists. In 2010 an online poll asked Georgia fans which of the Bulldogs' four biggest rivals did they "hate" the most. The results overwhelmingly pointed to Florida (72 percent), followed by Georgia Tech (20 percent), Auburn (4 percent), and Tennessee (4 percent).

Personally, my hate for the Gators began as a young child some time during the early to mid-1980s after I observed a photo in a newspaper or magazine of tailgating Florida fans in Jacksonville from the year before. Two of the pictured Gators were holding signs which read, "Dawgs Lick Themselves" and "Guck Feorgia." My parents wouldn't translate the latter expression to me, but I would soon find its true meaning from where I learned all the "four-letter" words—kids at school—and I was instantly incensed. How could opposing fans display such disrespect and animosity?!? Until then, I had regarded the Florida football team similarly to that of Vanderbilt, Kentucky, or the like—just another opponent Georgia had defeated every year since I could remember. However, I would soon realize that the Gators, their obnoxious fans, and the bitter rivalry they had with my Bulldogs were a far, far cry than that of the lesser programs, like the Commodores, Wildcats, etc.

Several years later, on my first trip to the Georgia-Florida game, I was exposed to window signs from countless cars of fans also heading to Jacksonville or its surrounding area. For those of you who have made the trip, especially traveling the 150-plus boring miles of Interstate 16 between I–75 and I–95, you know exactly what I'm talking about.

Barbara Dooley once told me of a trip she made on this same stretch of highway during the 1970s while husband Vince was Georgia's head coach. En route to the game, she noticed a car ahead of her traveling party's which appeared to have a human leg dangling from the back of its trunk. Immediately, Barbara and her friends sped up to see what the circumstances were with the car. As they approached, although the car was filled with Florida fans, they were relieved to find that the dangling leg was not a human's but rather looked to belong to a mannequin. Barbara also noticed that accompanying the dummy's leg (and the "dummies" in the car) was a sign that read: "We've got Barbara Dooley in the trunk!"

On my first venture south to what I had heard was celebrated as the World's Largest Outdoor Cocktail Party, the signs I recall declared, "Florida Eats Boogers" and "Gators Suck Snot." Apparently, I wasn't the only Bulldogs fan who loathed the Gators—a hate that was increasing even more, considering the Gators had started to win some games in the series. At the time, Georgia had lost three of the previous seven meetings with Florida. Worse, the last game had been a 38–7 thrashing at the hands of a new Gators head coach who seemed to know what it took to consistently defeat the Bulldogs.

From Steve Spurrier's first season in 1990 through 2003, except on two occasions when the Georgia-Florida game was played on the schools' campuses, Bulldogs fans, including yours truly, would annually enjoy what is considered the Cocktail Party—St. Simons Island, Jekyll Island, Amelia Island, the Jacksonville Landing, the RV Village south of the stadium, etc.—and then witness a Gators victory over our team every single year (except in 1997). For many Bulldogs fans, including yours truly again, those were some long, depressing, headache-filled drives back home from Jacksonville the following day.

THE GATORS' "FIRST" GEORGIA-FLORIDA GAME

The erroneous Gator Nation argues the first Georgia-Florida football game was not played in 1904, like the Bulldogs accurately contend, but took place 11 years later in 1915. Since this game was the first between the two schools played in the city of Jacksonville and its result was similar to the 1904 contest, anyway—an absolute Georgia rout—we'll humor the Gators and recount what they believe was the first meeting in the storied rivalry.

Entering the November 6 game, the *Florida Times-Union* notably said, "It is hoped that the attendance and spirit manifested at the game will be sufficient to warrant the staging of an annual Georgia-Florida game as the big football event each season in Jacksonville."

It would take another nearly 20 years, but the newspaper would eventually get what it desired when the big football event began being held in Jacksonville on an annual basis.

The 1915 contest was played at Barrs Field. This was the city's first municipal recreation field which was primarily used for baseball games and today is known as J.P. Small Memorial Stadium. From the field, an enormous parade crawled south down Durkee Avenue as reportedly every owner of an automobile in the city and surrounding area had decorated their cars either red and black or orange and blue for the grand occasion.

As far as which school would likely win the game, the *Atlanta Constitution* certainly had its viewpoint: "When the University of

After the Gators drubbed the Dogs in 1994 and 1995, conditions were even worse as there was no Cocktail Party to drown our sorrows. The first year, Bulldogs fans were stuck in the godforsaken city of Gainesville until we could escape the next morning after the defeat. The following year, we witnessed Spurrier's Gators score 52 points in our sacred Sanford Stadium and then watched as our beautiful town of Athens was

Georgia football authorities were arranging their football schedule for this season they picked out Florida as a pretty soft thing to put in between their Auburn and Tech games."

The "soft" Gators surprisingly held the Red and Black scoreless through the first quarter. Finally, in the second quarter, Georgia scored off an inadvertent error—the old "fumblerooski" play of sorts—when a halfback fumbled at Florida's 5-yard line, but alert right tackle Bright McConnell scooped up the bobble and lugged across the goal line for a touchdown.

By the final quarter, Georgia held a commanding 32–0 lead. The stars for the Red and Black had been plenty, but halfback E.H. Dezendorf particularly stood out, passing for a 70-yard touchdown and rushing for a 15-yard score.

The final points of the contest came on a momentous first in the rivalry: John Coleman drop-kicked a field goal from Florida's 30-yard line when goal posts were situated on the goal line, scoring three points for the Red and Black and the first field goal in the series' history. Only eight minutes into the final stanza, the game was called supposedly due to "darkness"; however, the one-sided 39–0 score likely had some bearing on the decision.

Despite Georgia's dismantling of the Gators, players and alumni of both teams met on better terms following the game for the rivalry's first unofficial Cocktail Party—a dinner and smoker on the 10th floor of the Seminole Hotel.

GEORGIA

engulfed with a bunch of celebrating Florida fans. Georgia senior strong safety and current Florida head coach Will Muschamp, who ended his playing career against the Gators with no victories in four tries, described the sentiments of many Bulldogs following the loss in 1994: "It hurts to play in such a great rivalry and never get a win. It's real frustrating. It's something that will live with me for the rest of my life."

For Bulldogs fans since 1990, the Georgia-Florida series has been nothing but, as Muschamp said, *real* frustrating. As I write this book, although the Bulldogs are fresh off a 24–20 win over the Gators in Jacksonville, they have lost 18 of the last 22 games in the rivalry through 2011.

And because of the recent domination of the series by Florida, we hate the Gators even more—much more—especially considering we're constantly reminded by their obnoxious fans of their dominance.

However, whenever I'm reminded of this or begin to actually believe that the Bulldogs are enduring some sort of two-decade-long "Jacksonville Jinx," as it has been called, I recall a one-time annual ritual of sorts by one of the very few Gators I do admire, even though I never met the individual.

My wife's grandfather, a graduate of the University of Florida in the late 1930s, passed away long before I even knew my wife. But from everything I've ever heard, my wife's "Papa," despite being a Gator, was quite an admirable man. During the 1970s and 1980s, it was the Bulldogs who dominated the rivalry. My wife and her family distinctly recall Papa's reaction after seemingly each of the Georgia-Florida games during that period. He would always emerge after having witnessed his Gators getting beat, and seemingly every year without fail, he'd utter the same four words: "Those damn lucky Dogs..."

The story signifies that those damn lucky Gators of the last 20-plus years need reminding of how the Bulldogs won 15 of 19 games in the series from 1971 to 1989, including all but one during a 10-season stretch from 1974 to 1983. Even before then, the apparent "rivalry" was hardly one at all and the Gators were somewhat of a joke.

Prior to the 1919 game, a Tampa sportswriter made the bold prediction of a Florida upset over the Bulldogs and continued by telling his readers, "Now tilt back your head, open your mouth, and enjoy a big hearty laugh..." The writer's fearless forecast was way off the mark as Georgia won 16–0. From 1904 until 1927, the Bulldogs won the first seven games of the rivalry by a combined lopsided score of 244–9.

Through 1948, Georgia had built a commanding 22–4–1 advantage in the series. At the time, there were only two teams—Furman and Mercer—that the Bulldogs had faced in their history more than 15 times and had achieved more success against than the Gators. During this period, there were several occasions Georgia would not just rest a starter or two for the Florida game, but rest the entire starting 11, saving them for the more formidable competition toward the end of its schedule.

In 1949, when the Gators defeated the Bulldogs for the first time in nine years, University of Florida students were so thrilled with the rare victory, they printed a two-page "We Beat Georgia!!" spread in their yearbook. So sad, but true…

By 1983, "Wait Until Next Year" had become an annual Florida cheer after its meeting with Georgia at the Gator Bowl. Following the Bulldogs' 10–9 win over the Gators, a Jacksonville hotel manager and Florida fan was asked when her team was going to finally defeat Georgia: "You can't break tradition. The Gators just can't beat the Georgia Bulldogs."

In short, Georgia fans hate the Florida Gators for a variety of reasons, one of which is because our Bulldogs have lately had such a difficult time defeating them. However, the rivalry has been extraordinarily cyclical since it first began: the Gators owned the series from the mid-1950s until the mid-1960s and since the start of the 1990s, while the Bulldogs have been in control, well, nearly all the rest of the time.

The bottom line is Georgia holds a 48–40–2 advantage in the series entering 2012. And if indeed the Bulldogs have lately suffered through any sort of jinx, I guess it's the exact same curse the Gators have experienced on a number of occasions during the rivalry's history.

Above all, as quarterback Aaron Murray said following the Bulldogs' victory in 2011: "Everyone has been saying how lopsided the series with Florida has been over the years, but this team was 0–0 [against the Gators] going into this game. And now we're 1–0."

When I was approached by Triumph Books with the idea of authoring a "funny and irreverent" *Love/Hate* flip book on the

Georgia Bulldogs and an opposing school, I jumped at the opportunity. I am rather obsessed with UGA football, particularly its history. I'm not very funny, but if Florida was chosen as Georgia's hated team, I was absolutely confident I could make at least a strong attempt at being irreverent toward the Gators.

I wanted this book to be for Georgia fans and by Georgia fans in regard to our rivalry with the detested Gators, so I conducted dozens of interviews with members of the UGA football faithful: numerous fans and former players and coaches. What resulted was one voice from your average Georgia fan's point of view, speaking for a significant portion of the Bulldog Nation. We detail the Georgia games, players, traditions, coaches, etc., that we love and, conversely, the Florida games, players, traditions, coaches, etc., that we hate.

In a nutshell, the following pages are your handy manual as to why we love the Georgia Bulldogs and why we hate the Florida Gators. Although the book may offend some folks, we hope you find it informative (while sometimes the truth hurts).

Go Dawgs!

1
GAMES WE LOVE

DON'T GET ME WRONG, every win over hated Florida is one the Bulldog Nation cherishes, and there have been plenty of them—nearly 50.

Whether Georgia routed the Gators, upset them, kept the rival from winning a conference title, or used the victory to springboard the Bulldogs to a championship of their own, several of these wins stand out slightly more than the rest.

Whatever the reason, here is a countdown of the top 15 Georgia gridiron victories over Florida, all of which made the subsequent 12 months a little better and each Bulldogs-Gators Cocktail Party a little merrier.

No. 15a: 2011

GEORGIA	0	10	7	7	24
FLORIDA	7	10	3	0	20

The Bulldogs entered the 90th meeting of the rivalry in need of a victory in the worst way. A win over the Gators would give Georgia just its fourth in the series in 22 games since 1990, keep alive its SEC East title hopes, and likely secure the head

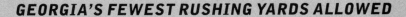

GEORGIA'S FEWEST RUSHING YARDS ALLOWED

	Yards	Opponent	Year
1.	−50	Kentucky	1999
2.	−49	VMI	1967
3.	−23	South Carolina	1971
4.	−21	Tennessee	2011
5.	−20	The Citadel	1958
6.	−19	Florida	2011

coaching position of Mark Richt, whose teams had faltered of late, particularly when facing Florida.

Trailing 17–3 late in the second quarter, Richt and his squad seemed destined to fall victim yet again to another comfortable Gators' win in Jacksonville. However, led by a few of the rivalry's freshest faces, Georgia rallied for one the largest comeback victories in the history of the series.

The second of two fourth-down touchdown passes by Bulldogs quarterback Aaron Murray tied the game in the third quarter. Florida retook the lead with a field goal, but Georgia responded with a shut-down defense and an unstoppable ground game to eventually seize an elusive 24–20 win over the Gators.

After gaining 194 yards of total offense and 10 first downs in the first half, Florida was held to 32 and one, respectively, in the final two quarters. Georgia sacked quarterback John Brantley six times, including four by linebacker Jarvis Jones, who was playing in his first Bulldogs-Gators game. Florida's minus-19 yards rushing was its fewest since netting minus-36 against Auburn in 2001, while Jones' four sacks were the most by a Bulldog since Charles Grant had the same number against Auburn in 2001.

Georgia true freshman Isaiah Crowell gained 81 yards on 18 carries and was complimented by junior Richard Samuel's 58 hard-earned yards on 17 rushes. Samuel, an all-but-forgotten third-string tailback, had his most carries since the 2009 season opener, including one which provided the winning margin—a four-yard touchdown run with 13:18 to play. From there, the Bulldogs continued to hold the Gators offense stagnant while Murray, Crowell, and Samuel ran out the clock for the victory.

MOST SACKS BY A GEORGIA PLAYER

	No.	Opponent	Year
Freddie Gilbert	5	Temple	1983
Freddie Gilbert	4	Florida	1981
Richard Tardits	4	TCU	1988
Mo Lewis	4	Ole Miss	1989
Charles Grant	4	Auburn	2001
Jarvis Jones	4	Florida	2011

GEORGIA

"I know it was just a ballgame, but it seemed like a lot more than that," Richt said following just his third win over Florida in 11 tries. "Just to see our players and fans celebrate, in this place especially, was awesome."

No. 15b: 1974

GEORGIA	7	2	0	8	**17**
FLORIDA	0	0	10	6	**16**

There was a time when it appeared the Gators, no matter how superior they may have seemed, simply put, just plain couldn't defeat Georgia, regardless of whether the Bulldogs resembled the weaker of the two teams. Such was the case in 1974.

Florida had started its season winning seven of eight games, was ranked sixth in the nation, and with an SEC championship a seemingly certainty, had already received a premature invitation to play in the Sugar Bowl. Georgia, on the other hand, was amid what would be one of the worst campaigns of the 25-year Coach Vince Dooley era.

The Bulldogs held a 9–0 halftime lead following a short touchdown run by Horace King—one of the first five African Americans given a football scholarship at Georgia—and a safety when Florida backup quarterback Jimmy Fisher slipped and fell in his own end zone. Clumsy Gator...

Starter Don Gaffney—the first African American quarterback at Florida—was reinserted and guided the Gators to a 10–9 advantage in the final quarter. However, the lead was short-lived as a second King touchdown and a two-point conversion put the Bulldogs back on top 17–10.

As he had done the year before in an 11–10 victory over Georgia, Gaffney led Florida to a touchdown in the final moments, scoring on a four-yard run with 28 seconds remaining. And, for the second consecutive year, Gators head coach Doug Dickey elected to go for the two points and the victory.

In 1973 a successful Gaffney two-point pass had defeated the Bulldogs, but a season later, a similar passing play fell low and wide of fullback Jimmy DuBose for an incompletion.

In the 17–16 Georgia victory, the Bulldogs gained only 263 total yards while allowing a staggering 420. "We stopped them and made the plays when we had to," said Dooley of his defense. "I guess you could say we just bled slowly."

You could also say, for the New Year's Day bowl–bound Gators, their sugar had turned sour by an undistinguished band of Bulldogs.

No. 14: 1959

GEORGIA	14	0	7	0	21
FLORIDA	0	2	0	8	10

From the end of Georgia's dominance during the 1940s until Coach Vince Dooley arrived in Athens in 1964, Bulldogs football endured mostly hardships for a period of 15 seasons. Unfortunately, during these difficult times for Georgia, Florida's play began to steadily improve after decades of dismal to mediocre performances.

Under head coaches Bob Woodruff and Ray Graves, the Gators defeated the Bulldogs 10 times over a span of 12 seasons, including in eight of nine meetings from 1955 through 1963.

Georgia's one "diamond in the rough" season during this period was its SEC title team of 1959, which won 10 of 11 games, including a thorough whipping of Florida reminiscent of the rivalry's days of old.

The Bulldogs jumped on the Gators early by grabbing a 14–0 first-quarter lead on two touchdown passes. The first was a

LONGEST SCORING PLAYS *IN* SERIES HISTORY

Rushing TD	UGA:	89 yards—Tim Worley (1985)
	UF:	90 yards—Ken McLean (1944)
Passing TD	UGA:	93 yards—Buck Belue–Lindsay Scott (1980)
	UF:	96 yards—Kerwin Bell–Rickey Nattiel (1984)
KO Return TD	UGA:	90 yards—Harry Woodruff (1904)
	UF:	99 yards—Jeff Demps (2011)
Punt Return TD	UGA:	50 yards—Joe Barchan (1919)
	UF:	68 yards—Hal Griffin (1947)
Int. Return TD	UGA:	100 yards—Charley Britt (1959)
	UF:	81 yards—Darren Hambrick (1994)
Field Goal	UGA:	51 yards—Kevin Butler (1983)
		51 yards—Steve Crumley (1987)
	UF:	56 yards—Caleb Sturgis (2009)

GEORGIA

halfback toss by Bobby Walden after receiving a pitch from quarterback Charley Britt. The second was a 35-yarder from Britt, who actually started over the SEC's leading passer at the time, Fran Tarkenton.

Playing in the rain and ankle-deep mud, Britt was a standout on defense, as well, intercepting a Dick Allen pass, deflected by teammate Pat Dye at his own goal line, and racing 100 yards for a third Georgia touchdown.

Earlier, perhaps Britt's biggest play came when he ran down lightning-fast receiver Bobby Joe Green from behind after a gain of 70 yards to Georgia's 2-yard line. From there, the Gators could not break the end zone in four plays and had to surrender the football.

When asked after the game how he was able to catch the speedy Green, Britt answered, "I heard he runs the 100 in 9.5, and I wanted to see how fast I would have to run to catch somebody that's that fast."

For the game, the only scores the Gators could muster were handed to them by the Bulldogs. A bad snap while Georgia was punting from its end zone resulted in a Florida safety. The Gators also returned an interception for a touchdown in the final quarter.

The following week, Georgia clinched its first SEC championship in 11 years with a victory over Auburn, due in large part to the play of...you guessed it, Charley Britt, who returned a punt for a touchdown.

Meanwhile, Florida would end its season with consecutive wins over rivals Florida State and Miami (Fla). Nevertheless, it didn't matter for Woodruff, whose fate had been sealed with the Gators' 21–10 loss to Georgia in Jacksonville. He was forced to resign at the end of the season.

No. 13: 1972

GEORGIA	0	0	0	10	**10**
FLORIDA	0	7	0	0	**7**

An unimpressive 1972 Georgia squad entered its annual show-down in Jacksonville far removed from the 11-win edition of the season before. The Bulldogs offense was inept, to say the least, and oddsmakers considered the team a slight underdog even though it had defeated the Gators by six touchdowns the year before.

After three quarters, Florida led Georgia 7–0, and in doing so, handed the Bulldogs its seventh consecutive quarter without scoring a single point. However, these Gators were coached by Doug Dickey—a head coach who would soon make a name for himself over the next several years for his bone-headed decisions and inadvertently becoming a generous friend of the Bulldogs.

Entering Georgia territory with possession of the ball in the final quarter, Dickey inexplicably called for All-SEC back Nat Moore to throw a halfback pass. Moore's "pass," if you want to call it that, was an ugly one as it wobbled into the waiting arms of Bulldogs senior Buzy Rosenberg, who was lined up at linebacker for the first time of his collegiate career.

On second down from Florida's 44-yard line, quarterback Andy Johnson launched a long touchdown pass to Rex Putnal, who nearly did not make the trip because of an injury. Kim Braswell's extra point tied the game.

The Gators had the ball on their own 30-yard line with about two minutes remaining and a 7–7 tie looking like a certainty. That is, until quarterback Chan Gailey, a surprise starter for the game, gave the Bulldogs another gift by losing a fumble.

Three plays netted nine yards, and with less than a minute remaining, Braswell came on to attempt a game-winning 37-yard field goal. Although almost as ugly as Moore's pass, the kick just snuck over the crossbar, clearing it by a mere half yard, and the Bulldogs escaped with the most unlikely of victories.

After the loss, Gators linebacker Ralph Ortega, an eventual All-American but apparently not the sharpest tack in the box, remarked, "It's weird...right now I feel like we won the game." Teammate Gailey would eventually give even more to the Bulldogs, losing all six games when he faced Georgia as Georgia Tech's head coach from 2002 to 2007.

No. 12: 1983

GEORGIA	3	0	0	7	**10**
FLORIDA	6	3	0	0	**9**

The Bulldogs entered their annual meeting with the Gators in an unfamiliar situation. They were Herschel Walker–less for a Florida game for the first time in four years and an underdog for a regular season game, regardless of the opponent, also for the first time in nearly four years. In addition, Georgia was not favored to defeat the Gators for the first time since 1977.

Nevertheless, the game resulted as many before had, as Florida, which actually appeared to be the better team, flat-out choked and lost for the sixth consecutive time.

Trailing 9–3 late in the third quarter, Georgia began from its own 1-yard line, having gained just 97 total yards to that point, compared to the Gators' 318, but still only trailing by less than a touchdown.

Engineered by senior quarterback John Lastinger, the Bulldogs slowly moved 99 yards in 16 plays, burning 7:26 off the

THE DRIVES

Prior to Georgia's game-winning drive against Florida in 1983, the Bulldogs had executed "The Drive" against the Gators in 1981. Three years before that, "The Drive" secured a victory in 1978. There were three game-clinching offensive possessions by Georgia against Florida in a span of only six years, all lasting at least 14 plays, burning roughly seven to eight minutes off the clock, and each dubbed "The Drive" by the media.

1978 *Started*: Georgia's own 25-yard line, leading 24–22 with 6:56 to play
Result: Georgia runs out clock on Florida's 16-yard line and wins 24–22
Drive: 14 plays, 59 yards in 6:56
Big Play: Fullback Ronnie Stewart picks up a first down on fourth-and-1 from Florida's 18-yard line

clock, and capped by a Barry Young one-yard scoring run. On the drive, Georgia converted two of three critical third-down plays while the one third down that wasn't converted, the Dogs picked up the first down on the subsequent fourth-down play.

Kevin Butler's extra point gave Georgia a one-point lead, but there was plenty of time remaining. Of course, this was a "jinxed" Gators program the Bulldogs were facing…

In the final minutes, a celebratory smoke bomb was hurled from the Gator Bowl stands onto the playing field. With it, Florida's opportunity to finally defeat Georgia had once again gone up in smoke. In their last 10 meetings, the Bulldogs had

1981 *Started*: Georgia's own 5-yard line, trailing 21–20 with 10:16 to play

Result: Tailback Herschel Walker runs for one-yard touchdown; Georgia leads 26–21 with 2:31 to play

Drive: 17 plays, 95 yards in 7:45

Big Play: On third-and-8 from Florida's 47-yard line, quarterback Buck Belue completes 17-yard pass to receiver Lindsay Scott

1983 *Started*: Georgia's own 1-yard line, trailing 9–3 with 5:44 left in third quarter

Result: Fullback Barry Young runs for one-yard touchdown; Georgia leads 10–9 with 13:18 to play

Drive: 16 plays, 99 yards in 7:26

Big Play: On second-and-10 from Georgia's own 30-yard line, QB John Lastinger completes a 25-yard pass to TE Clarence Kay, plus Florida is penalized for 15 yards

GEORGIA

defeated the Gators nine times, in seven of which Florida had the lead during the fourth quarter.

When asked why it seemed the Bulldogs had a mystique about them while the Gators seemed jinxed, senior tight end Clarence Kay vividly responded, "Character. You've got to have the character, baby," he said to a newspaper reporter. "You tell the printer that tomorrow. Character."

No. 11: 1954

GEORGIA	7	7	0	0	**14**
FLORIDA	0	7	6	0	**13**

After 32 meetings, the annual Bulldogs-Gators game finally meant more to *both* schools than just bragging rights and the partying. In the past, only one squad—routinely, Georgia—was playing to continue a quest for a conference title. In 1954, however, the Dogs and Gators entered the game positioned at second and third, respectively, in the 12-member SEC standings.

Besides shooting for a championship, Georgia was also seeking revenge. After absolutely dominating the series from the start, the Bulldogs proved there was a first time for everything and dropped consecutive games to Florida in 1952 and 1953 by a combined 51–7 score.

Florida fumbled the ball on the game's first play from scrimmage, which was recovered by Georgia's John Bell at the Gators' 45-yard line. On a critical third-down play, Roy Wilkins, who was playing with two injured ankles, caught a 28-yard pass from Jimmy Harper. Shortly thereafter, Harper scored on a quarterback sneak. Florida tied the game but soon the Bull-dogs offense was on the move again. Bob "Foots" Clemens' touchdown run gave the squad a 14–7 advantage over the favored Gators at halftime.

In the third quarter, a Harper errant pass was intercepted and returned 67 yards to Georgia's 7-yard line. Two plays later, Bob Davis rushed for a score. However, in Florida's attempt to tie the game, Wilkins, bum ankles and all, leapt in front of Ed Bass' all-important extra-point attempt and blocked it.

The game ended with the Bulldogs running out the clock fol-lowing a Gators turnover—one of five on the day for Florida, compared to just one for Georgia. Notwithstanding, perhaps the most important statistic of the game: Bulldogs 2-of-2 on point-after kicks, Gators 1-of-2.

Alas, by season's end there would be no championship for either team (not even a winning record for Florida, we might add), just bragging rights for the Bulldogs. Georgia would have to wait five years for its next SEC championship while Florida needed almost four entire decades for its first.

No. 10: 1976

GEORGIA	7	6	14	14	**41**
FLORIDA	14	13	0	0	**27**

In the first Georgia-Florida meeting when both teams entered ranked in the top 10, the Bulldogs benefitted from a "dumb" fourth-down call that generated momentum and, for the third consecutive season, dashed the Gators hopes of an SEC title.

A commanding 14-point Florida halftime lead was cut in half in the third quarter following a touchdown pass from Georgia quarterback and eventual head coach, Ray Goff.

Midway through the third quarter while maintaining a 27–20 lead, Florida faced fourth-and-1 from its own 29-yard line. That's when Doug Dickey, the Gators' foolhardy head coach, decided to strike once again with a gamble against the Bulldogs. And, like the few times before, Dickey's gamble backfired.

Florida's decision to go for the first down seemingly shocked everyone but the Bulldogs. As television play-by-play man Keith Jackson wondered aloud if Georgia would come after the Gators' punt or try to set up a return, Florida lined up in its offensive formation. Analyst Ara Parseghian exclaimed, "Oh, they're going for it…. Looka' here!"

Running back Earl Carr took a pitch and circled to his left only to be pulled down around his collar short of the first down by cornerback Johnny Henderson. Six plays later, a short touchdown run by fullback Al Pollard and successful point-after try tied the game.

In the final quarter, it was all Bulldogs, who scored two touchdowns on runs by Goff. Goff was named the game's offensive MVP, completing all five of his passes, including two for touchdowns, while rushing for 124 yards and three more scores.

Following the game, with even his own players questioning the coach's gamble on fourth down, Dickey admitted, "I made some dumb calls." A Jacksonville newspaper agreed in its Sunday edition, titling a piece covering the game, "Fourth and Dumb."

No. 9: 1964

GEORGIA	0	0	0	14	**14**
FLORIDA	0	7	0	0	**7**

As Georgia warmed up prior to its kickoff against Florida in 1964, much of the Bulldogs' student section in the Gator Bowl began chanting something not heard in quite a while by the UGA football squad: "Damn good team, damn good team, damn good team…"

Following an SEC title in 1959, Georgia recorded a 16–20–4 combined mark over the next four seasons. What's worse, this included an unfathomable 0–4 record against the Gators.

A young Coach Vince Dooley arrived in Athens and promptly turned around the team's misfortunes as the Bulldogs entered Jacksonville with a respectable 4–2–1 record. However, next on the schedule were the mighty and ninth-ranked Gators, who had been dubbed by Alabama's Paul "Bear" Bryant as the strongest team he had ever faced. Furthermore, the Florida team was even recognized by its own coach, Ray Graves, as "the finest team in Florida's history."

Early on, it appeared Coach Graves was quite possibly correct in his assessment. Sophomore quarterback Steve Spurrier drove the Gators 83 yards to a second-quarter touchdown and a 7–0 lead. Florida threatened to score a couple other times prior to halftime but came up empty. However, with the Gators defense holding Georgia to just 40 total yards and one first down the entire first half, it seemed Florida was in no need of any additional scoring.

The second half was another story as the Bulldogs began to run the ball with ease against perhaps an over-confident Florida defense. Fred Barber's two-yard touchdown run and Bobby Etter's extra point tied the game with 13:11 remaining.

For whatever reason, Graves replaced Spurrier for senior Tom Shannon, and the new Gators quarterback lost a fumble on his first snap. In six plays, Georgia gained 16 yards and faced fourth down from Florida's 5-yard line. Dooley then called for something that had been successful just six times in the history of the series and not since 1952—a field goal.

On the field-goal try, the snap was low, which holder Barry Wilson then bobbled. Nevertheless, the football rolled perfectly to place-kicker Etter, who scooped it up without hesitation and raced around the left end for a touchdown. It was the first rushing attempt since before high school by Etter, who was listed at a scant 150 pounds but was said to actually weigh more like 135.

Ironically, after not missing a single point-after try during the season, the sophomore kicker and game's hero missed the ensuing conversion. However, the Gators, who evidently had started to unravel, were offside, and Etter's second try was good.

Not good was the Gators' attempt to answer the opposition. A final-moment desperation heave by a reinserted Spurrier was intercepted, and Florida's "finest team" lost to a "damn good team."

For the Gators during the Coach Dooley era, losses in Jacksonville were something they would need to become accustomed to.

No. 8: 1942

GEORGIA	28	7	27	13	**75**
FLORIDA	0	0	0	0	**0**

A listing of the most-cherished victories over the despised Gators would not be complete without a good old-fashioned butt-whupping or two. Lord knows the Bulldogs received their fair share from some Spurrier-coached teams of the 1990s, but none of those were as bad—not even close—as the 75–0 beating Georgia handed Florida in 1942.

Coach Wally Butts' undefeated and No. 1–ranked Bulldogs lived up to their billing, gaining 593 yards of total offense while allowing a paltry 156. Eventual Heisman Trophy winner Frank Sinkwich rushed for 71 yards and two touchdowns on 10 carries, while completing five of nine passes for 112 yards and two scores.

Sinkwich's backup, sophomore sensation Charley Trippi, was just as effective, rushing for 80 yards and two touchdowns on six carries, completing two of three passes for 72 yards, including one for a touchdown, while adding an interception return for another score.

The late insertion of Frank Riofski, a seldom-used third-string center, was reportedly the highlight of the victory. With the Gators trailing 69–0 from their own 1-yard line, William Mims dropped back and passed out of his own end zone. Riofski intercepted the pass—one of seven Florida interceptions, compared to just six pass completions—and returned the errant throw 10 yards for the game's final points.

Seemingly, almost every Bulldog was involved in the dismantling of Florida.

"The biggest mistake of the [Georgia] cheerleaders this year was in not going to the Florida game," quipped the UGA student newspaper the *Red and Black*. "Coach Butts would have played them at least a quarter each."

No. 7: 1904

GEORGIA	23	29	52
FLORIDA	0	0	0

The very first Georgia-Florida gridiron meeting undoubtedly should be mentioned, especially when it resulted in a 52–0 trouncing by the Red and Black, and even if the Gators don't want to recognize that it actually transpired.

The Florida Agricultural and Mechanical College of Lake City, also identified at the time as the "University of Florida," met Georgia at the neutral site of Macon's Central City Park. In front of approximately 700 spectators, Florida, dressed in blue and white, was held by Georgia, donned in red and black, on the first offensive possession of the series.

Less than four minutes into the ballgame, Georgia's Charlie Cox rushed for a touchdown, counting for five points at the time, and with that, the rout had begun. By halftime, the Red and Black had tacked on three more touchdowns, including a 90-yard kickoff return by 125-pound Harry Woodruff, the older brother of future Georgia star player and head coach George Woodruff.

GEORGIA-FLORIDA *BY THE* NUMBERS

Series Record:
  Georgia 48–40–2

Biggest Margin of Victory by Georgia:
  75 points (75–0 in 1942)

Biggest Margin of Victory by Florida:
  40 points (47–7 in 1996)

Longest Georgia Win Streak:
  Seven—twice (1904 to 1927, 1941 to 1948)

Longest Florida Win Streak:
  Seven (1990 to 1996)

Total Points Scored by Georgia:
  1,790 (19.9 per game)

Total Points Scored by Florida:
  1,483 (16.5 per game)

GEORGIA

Notably, the year before in a win over Auburn, Woodruff had returned a missed drop-kicked field goal for a 107-yard touchdown. (Until 1912, the official length of a football field was 110 yards.)

In the second half, Georgia was even more dominating, scoring five touchdowns for a grand total of nine for the game. Florida not only was held scoreless for the inaugural meeting, but the school from Lake City didn't even pick up a single first down.

The game was limited to two 15-minute halves instead of the common 30 minutes. If the Red and Black had been granted an entire 60-minute contest, they very well could have reached the century mark in points.

GEORGIA

THE FIRST STAR OF THE SERIES

Because of the University of Georgia's then-small enrollment, there was a time when, if a male student had an ounce of athleticism in his body, he could try out and likely make the school's football squad with little trouble. Such was the case of Charlie Cox—a distinguished high school baseball pitcher—upon his arrival at the university as a student in 1903.

Cox immediately became the Red and Black's starting left halfback and, against Tennessee in his first season, scored the game's only points on a 35-yard touchdown run in a 5–0 Georgia victory. As expected, Cox starred for UGA's baseball team in the spring and then for an Atlanta club team that summer. However, when he returned to school, it was time for Cox to give the sport of football a second try.

Three weeks after he was elected president of his class, the hope was that Cox would also lead the school to a momentous football victory in the very first Georgia-Florida game, like he had against Tennessee the year before. Now recognized as "famous alike in football and baseball circles," Cox would not disappoint anyone on October 8, 1904, except maybe the University of Florida.

The left halfback scored the series' first points on an eight-yard touchdown run, and by the end of the game, had tallied three more scores in the Red and Black's 52–0 blowout victory.

After 107 years and 90 games in the Georgia-Florida football series, only three men—all Bulldogs—have scored four touchdowns or more in a single game of the historical rivalry: Herschel Walker, Robert Edwards, and the first Bulldog to do so, baseball-turned-football star Charlie Cox.

The next day, the *Atlanta Constitution* declared, "The 52 went to the men from Athens and the goose egg was laid for the special benefit of the brave little men of the University of Florida."

Notice it said "little men."

No. 6: 2007

GEORGIA	14	7	7	14	**42**
FLORIDA	7	10	7	6	**30**

In 2007 few expected a Bulldogs victory in Jacksonville. Barely defeating Vanderbilt in its previous game, Georgia entered having struggled to achieve a 5–2 record. Florida, on the other hand, had the exact same record but was ranked among the nation's top 10, quarterbacked by the eventual Heisman Trophy winner, and a solid favorite of more than a touchdown to beat the Bulldogs for the 16th time in 18 years.

Following a Gators fumble on the opening series, Georgia's ground game, highlighted by Knowshon Moreno, ran with ease through the Florida defense. Moreno's one-yard dive into the end zone gave the Bulldogs their first lead in the series since the victory three years before in 2004.

Immediately following the touchdown, what was witnessed was certainly a first in the storied rivalry and likely in the history of organized football.

Suddenly, almost every Bulldog from their sideline emptied into the Georgia end zone for a touchdown celebration in a motivating demonstration of unity. At that point it was clear,

Georgia players celebrate Knowshon Moreno's first-quarter touchdown against Florida in the Bulldogs' upset victory over the Gators at Jacksonville Municipal Stadium on October 27, 2007. Photo courtesy of Getty Images

the 2007 Bulldogs were not going to be pushed around by the Gators as they had for most of the previous two decades.

For most of the game, the teams matched one another score for score. Florida quarterback Tim Tebow's touchdown run with 9:40 remaining reduced Georgia's lead to 35–30. The Bulldogs countered with an 11-play, 68-yard drive capped by another Moreno touchdown.

Enjoying one of the best rushing performances in the Georgia-Florida series, Moreno gained 188 yards and scored three touchdowns on 33 carries.

Trailing 42–30, Florida's last chance for a possible victory was squandered when it fumbled at the Bulldogs' 15-yard line with 2:23 left in the game.

Revealed in the book *Urban's Way*—a look at Gators coach Urban Meyer and Florida's 2007 season—Meyer stated that Georgia's end-zone celebration "wasn't right. It was a bad deal. And it will forever be in the mind of Urban Meyer and in the mind of our football team."

Beginning with its win over Florida, Georgia closed out its year performing like a completely different team, finishing with 11 victories and a No. 2 national ranking. On the contrary, Florida and its head coach apparently used the game as a reason to sulk in the off-season (and an excuse for Meyer to refer to himself in the third person).

No. 5: 1966

GEORGIA	3	0	7	17	**27**
FLORIDA	7	3	0	0	**10**

Led by "Superman" in 1966, Florida looked like it was finally going to capture its elusive SEC championship. The Gators were undefeated at 7–0, ranked seventh in the nation, and were led by quarterback Steve "Superman" Spurrier, who had defeated the Bulldogs in the final seconds the year before and was the frontrunner to win the Heisman Trophy.

Florida, looking every bit of having the country's seventh-best offense, took the opening kickoff and quickly drove 86 yards in eight plays to a 7–0 lead. Georgia place-kicker Bob Etter got the Bulldogs on the scoreboard with a field goal, but Florida's Wayne Barfield would answer with one of his own just before halftime.

In the second half, Spurrier was far from super, hurrying almost all of his pass attempts and often sacked. After throwing just two interceptions in 191 passes for the first seven-and-a-half games of the season, Spurrier was intercepted three times in just 15 attempts in the second half. The Gators' ground game didn't fair much better, netting just five yards after halftime.

Meanwhile, the Bulldogs scored on a second Etter field goal, two rushing touchdowns, and a 39-yard interception return by safety Lynn Hughes, who had helped defeat Florida and Spurrier two years before as Georgia's quarterback.

Following the Bulldogs' 27–10 upset victory, Jim Minter, of the *Atlanta Journal-Constitution*, noted a spirited Georgia fan, dressed in red and assuredly enjoying the World's Largest Outdoor Cocktail Party, who repeatedly shouted from the Gator Bowl stands, "Superman can be stopped!"

Spurrier had been stopped on that particular day, although he couldn't be stopped from taking home the Heisman Trophy about a month later. Nevertheless, the loss to Georgia ended Florida's chance for its first conference title, and it would be the Bulldogs instead taking home the SEC championship.

No. 4: 1997

GEORGIA	7	7	7	16	**37**
FLORIDA	0	3	14	0	**17**

How is it possible that two teams entered a game played at a neutral site with identical 6–1 records, and only separated by eight spots—No. 6 and No. 14—in the national rankings, yet one team was an overwhelming three-touchdown favorite to defeat the other?

For the Bulldogs, the reason was simply because of the results of the Georgia-Florida series since Steve Spurrier showed up again in Gainesville.

Beginning in 1990, Spurrier's first year as the Gators' head coach, through 1996, Florida was 7–0 versus Georgia, winning by an average margin of more than 26 points. In year No. 8 for Spurrier, another easy victory was expected yet again over the Bulldogs.

Even with a 14–3 lead at halftime, thanks to running back Robert Edwards, a victory over the defending national champion Gators still seemed a little farfetched. Sure enough, that 11-point lead soon turned to a three-point deficit in the third quarter. However, then the Gators, and not the Bulldogs like so many times in the recent past, began to crumble.

While Spurrier was playing "musical quarterbacks" with his fun 'n' gun offense, constantly rotating Doug Johnson, Noah Brindise, and Jesse "the Bachelor" Palmer from under center, the Bulldogs offense scored 23 unanswered points.

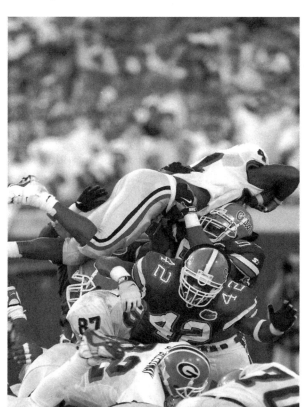

Georgia cornerback/ receiver/returner Champ Bailey goes up over a pile of Florida defenders in the Bulldogs' 37–17 win over the shocked Gators.
Photo courtesy of Getty Images

Edwards finished with 124 rushing yards and four touchdowns, Mike Bobo passed for 260 yards, while Hines Ward gained 85 receiving, 21 rushing, and even completed a pass for 27 yards.

In the end, it became apparent the oddsmakers simply had the wrong team favored by three touchdowns, while a bewildered Spurrier summed it up best: "Georgia's just a better football team than the mighty Gators."

No. 3: 1985

GEORGIA	7	10	0	7	24
FLORIDA	0	3	0	0	3

A choice story regarding the '85 Georgia-Florida game is how days before kickoff, certain that the top-ranked Gators were going to defeat the Bulldogs, the Jacksonville Gator Club actually printed and distributed flyers advertising a postgame victory party at the Jacksonville Coliseum immediately after Florida's expected win over Georgia.

One would think the Bulldogs were slumping into the Gator Bowl like the Gators had six years earlier—winless. Instead, Georgia had lost just one game all year, was ranked 15th in the UPI Poll, and was one of the best teams in the country in both running the ball and stopping the run.

Granted, the Gators were the No. 1–ranked team in the nation, according to the AP Poll (but had cheated and were placed on probation, so they were not ranked by the UPI). Quarterback Kerwin Bell was a Heisman Trophy candidate, the offensive line proclaimed itself as the "Great Wall of Florida," and the Gators had the 10th-best rushing defense in football.

Freshman Keith Henderson gashed the stout run defense early by galloping for a 76-yard touchdown in the first quarter. In the second quarter, the exact same play got the exact same result as Henderson bolted for a 32-yard touchdown. Holding a 17–3 lead late in the game, fellow freshman Tim Worley got in on the long-distance act, bolting for a school-record 89-yard touchdown run to seal the upset victory.

What happened to Florida's "great wall"? It crumbled as the Gators netted 30 yards on 28 rushes and Bell was sacked five times.

And perhaps the most astounding all-time statistic of the Georgia-Florida series: Bell actually passed for 408 yards. We assume it's the only time ever in the history of NCAA football that a player passed for 400+ yards, yet his team did not score a single touchdown.

After the game, although a victory over the Gators wasn't a total shock, a 21-point win was rather surprising. "I never thought we'd beat Florida 24–3," said Coach Vince Dooley. "Maybe [the Gators] were drained from the emotion of last week or bothered by the distractions of being No. 1."

Or maybe they were caught looking ahead to their postgame victory party at the Jacksonville Coliseum.

No. 2: 1975

GEORGIA	0	3	0	7	**10**
FLORIDA	7	0	0	0	**7**

Ask anyone aware of Georgia's upset victory over Florida in 1975, and the most common response will recount the "winning" touchdown—"Appleby to Washington. Eighty yards!" as was announced by legendary radio play-by-play man Larry Munson.

It is one of the greatest plays in Bulldogs history. Trailing 7–3 with possession of the ball at its own 20-yard line, Georgia ran the trickiest of trick plays as quarterback Matt Robinson handed the football to tight end Richard Appleby, who planted his feet and flung the ball to a streaking Gene Washington for an improbable 80-yard touchdown.

What often gets lost in the hoopla of the miraculous pass play was that there was still 3:12 remaining in the game, Florida would have possession of the ball two additional times, and the Gators actually attempted a field goal in the final seconds that would have tied the game.

Whereas "Appleby-to-Washington" was a tremendous and memorable play, it was Georgia's "Junkyard Dogs" defense that ultimately defeated the Gators.

Created by defensive coordinator Erk Russell, the Junkyard Dogs defensive unit was a group of small, inexperienced defenders given little chance to succeed. However, despite its shortcomings, the defense was quick, feisty, overachieving, and the primary reason the team trekked to Jacksonville with a surprising 6–2 record.

There were many who felt the Junkyard Dogs might have finally met their match in Florida's high-powered wishbone attack. The Gators had lost just once, were averaging approximately 30 points and 435 total yards per game, were ranked No. 11, and were double-digit favorites to defeat the Bulldogs.

Georgia allowed an early touchdown, but countered with a field goal, and then took a 10–7 lead following its improbable end-around touchdown pass.

JUNKYARD DOGS

The Junkyard Dogs defense of 1975 was perhaps at its best when it faced a formidable Florida wishbone offense. Georgia's bend-but-don't-break defensive unit allowed Florida only a single touchdown in a shocking 10–7 victory. An 80-yard end-around pass from Richard Appleby to Gene Washington might have provided the Bulldogs with the winning touchdown, but it was the Junkyard Dogs defense that, according to Coach Vince Dooley, "carried us all day."

Listed with their weight, class, and statistics for the 1975 season, the following are the starters and top reserves of the Junkyard Dogs:

Position	Starters	Weight	Class	Stats
LE:	Lawrence Craft	210	Jr.	57 tackles, 1 INT
LT:	Brad Thompson	230	Jr.	78 tackles

On the ensuing possession, the Gators reached Georgia's 36-yard line before a Dicky Clark sack of quarterback Don Gaffney caused a fumble. Following a Bulldogs punt, Florida was again on the move, driving all the way to the Bulldogs' 21-yard line. However, the Junkyard Dogs stiffened and forced Gaffney to throw three consecutive incomplete passes.

With 50 seconds remaining, Florida's David Posey, an eventual All-SEC place-kicker who made two 50-yard field goals in 1975, lined up for a 38-yard field goal try. His game-tying attempt missed badly, and Georgia again had knocked the Gators out of contention for an SEC title.

"What tickles me is that we're so small," said Clark following the game. "Florida thought we were some kind of joke when

Position		Weight	Class	Stats
RT:	Ronnie Swoopes	245	So.	52 tackles
RE:	Dicky Clark	205	Jr.	64 tackles, 1 INT
Sam LB:	Rusty Russell	195	Sr.	90 tackles
Mike LB:	Jim Griffith	210	So.	123 tackles, 1 INT
Will LB:	Ben Zambiasi	200	So.	148 tackles, 1 INT
LCB:	Bobby Thompson	185	So.	63 tackles, 4 INT
SS:	Bill Krug	205	So.	66 tackles, 2 INT
FS:	Johnny Henderson	185	So.	28 tackles, 1 INT
RCB:	David Schwak	175	Sr.	75 tackles
Position	Top Reserves	Weight	Class	Stats
T:	Jim Baker	215	Sr.	54 tackles
S:	Chip Miller	185	Sr.	46 tackles, 1 INT
LB:	Jeff Lewis	208	So.	29 tackles
CB:	Mark Mitchell	168	Jr.	9 tackles, 2 INT

GEORGIA

they lined up against us on that opening series. But I'll bet they are not laughing too hard right now."

No. 1: 1980

GEORGIA	7	7	6	6	26
FLORIDA	3	7	0	11	21

In early November 1980 the Bulldogs were on the doorstep of being in a position they hadn't been in 38 years as the No. 1–ranked team in the country. The opposing Gators were a far cry from their latest editions. Following a dreadful 0–10–1 season in 1979, Florida entered the game at 6–1 and ranked 20th in the nation. Less than two minutes into the contest, Herschel Walker took a pitch at Georgia's own 28-yard line and streaked for one of his patented long-distant touchdown jaunts. The freshman phenom finished with 238 rushing yards on 37 carries.

After a Gators field goal, the teams traded second-quarter touchdown passes. Georgia's Rex Robinson added two field goals in the third quarter, and the Bulldogs appeared to be primed for victory with a 20–10 lead entering the final stanza.

Featuring freshman Wayne Peace and unknown Tyrone Young, Florida responded with a potent fourth-quarter aerial attack. Following a James Jones touchdown, the Gators pulled to within two points on a Peace-to-Young two-point conversion. Young, a sophomore who had yet to catch a single pass while at Florida, made 10 receptions against the Bulldogs for 183 yards.

With just under seven minutes remaining, Brian Clark's field goal gave the Gators what seemed inconceivable only moments before—a lead and a good possibility to upset second-ranked Georgia.

Possible turned to most probable as the Bulldogs offense was backed up toward its own goal line with 1:35 to play. Trailing 21–20 from the 8-yard line, quarterback Buck Belue lost a yard on a scramble out of bounds. On second down, a Belue pass was dropped incomplete.

At this point, "Florida players were taunting us, saying, 'It's over,'" Belue would say later. The Gators defensive backs began doing the "Funky Chicken"—a celebratory dance that soon spread to other Florida players along the sideline.

While Florida evidently believed the game was over, Georgia realized it still had a play or two to save itself.

"Left 76"—a play designed to merely pick up a first down, instead turned into a 93-yard Belue-to–Lindsay Scott touchdown pass and the greatest single play in the history of Georgia Bulldogs football. And with it, the Gator Bowl instantly became unhinged.

Bodies were jumping and falling everywhere as seemingly a shower of beer and bourbon spread throughout the stands. In the celebration, one delighted Georgia fan grabbed a fresh face that had suddenly appeared next to him. "Hey, I'm a Gator!" screamed the female Florida student. "That's okay, I don't mind," replied the jubilant Bulldog.

Following Georgia's 26–21 victory, and with help from a Georgia Tech tie with top-ranked Notre Dame, the Bulldogs moved into the No. 1 national ranking—a position they would maintain for the next two months through the end of their memorable 1980 season.

Honorable Mention: 1996 Fiesta Bowl

NEBRASKA	6	29	14	13	62
FLORIDA	10	0	8	6	24

A general perception exists that fans of schools in the SEC will root for conference teams besides their own when facing nonconference opponents. In other words, in support of the conference, Bulldogs fans will pull for the Gators whenever Florida plays, say, Florida State, Miami (Fla.), in a bowl game, or the difficult nonconference slate of Southwestern Louisiana and Georgia Southern, as the Gators faced during their 1996 national championship season.

For many Bulldogs backers, nothing could be further from the truth. Some Georgia fans would only root for hated Florida if, and only if, the Gators football team faced a group of Taliban fighters.

Such was not the case in the Fiesta Bowl capping the 1995 football season. The Gators had been quite successful under the guidance of Coach Steve Spurrier and, after decades of mediocrity, had finally won the first few conference titles in their history. On January 2, 1996, a chance for Florida to capture its first football national championship emerged when the third-ranked Gators faced top-ranked Nebraska.

In the highly anticipated contest between supposedly evenly matched teams, Florida led the Cornhuskers 10–6 at the end of the first quarter. Most Georgia supporters hoped Nebraska could keep the game close and pull ahead by the end. We Bulldogs fans got much more than we ever desired as the Cornhuskers soon opened the flood gates.

Before one could blink, Nebraska was pounding the Gators in a sudden one-sided affair. The 10–6 Florida lead quickly turned to a 35–10 halftime advantage for the Cornhuskers. Leading 42–10, Nebraska quarterback Tommie Frazier kept the ball, broke a tackle, ran through four Gators defenders near midfield, and was off and racing to a 75-yard touchdown and arguably the most unbelievable run from scrimmage in the history of college football.

Nearly every chance he had to run up a score, Spurrier had done so while at Florida, particularly against Georgia in 1990, 1991, 1994, and in our own backyard of Sanford Stadium in 1995. Now, the tables had been turned, and Spurrier was getting a taste of his own medicine. And Bulldogs fans everywhere were loving it.

That's why the 1996 Fiesta Bowl is a must as an honorable mention for this list. Many more Gators humiliations to non-Bulldogs teams could have been included, but we weren't allowed the space.

"We've been on the good end of these scores, and now we're on the bad end," Spurrier said after the 62–24 loss. "We didn't come to the ballpark to play the best we could, and I'm embarrassed about that."

Embarrassed about being on the short end of a 38-point pummeling with a chance for the Gators' first national title at stake? We should say so.

2
PLAYERS WE LOVE

FROM THE COUNTLESS WALK-ONS who never appeared in a single game, to the most outstanding player in the history of the sport, Herschel Walker, every Bulldog is admired. It takes a special individual to strap on the red helmet, don the silver britches, and represent one of the greatest traditions in college football—a dream that so many of us have had, but so few have actually fulfilled.

The following is a chronological listing of the most celebrated Bulldogs, many of whom especially achieved success when facing the hated Gators.

BOB McWHORTER

Halfback Bob McWhorter played for the Red and Black during a 10-season hiatus (1905–1914) of the Georgia-Florida series, and it was a good thing for the Gators.

Whereas McWhorter is probably not necessarily the most outstanding Georgia football player of all time, he is arguably the school's most *valuable* in history. Consider in the six seasons prior to his arrival at Georgia in 1910, the Red and Black won just one-third of their games. From 1910 to 1913

GEORGIA

MOST TOUCHDOWNS SCORED

Career

61 Bob McWhorter (1910–1913)*

52 Herschel Walker (1980–1982)

37 Lars Tate (1984–1987)

35 Garrison Hearst (1990–1992)

Season

21 Garrison Hearst (1992)

20 Bob McWhorter (1910)*

20 Herschel Walker (1981)

18 Tim Worley (1988)

18 Knowshon Moreno (2008)

Game

7 Bob McWhorter (Gordon, 1910)*

6 Bob McWhorter (Alabama-Presbyterian, 1913)*

5 ½ Frank "Si" Herty (Mercer, 1892)**

5 Bob McWhorter (Locust Grove, 1910)*

5 Robert Edwards (South Carolina, 1995)

5 Washuan Ealey (Kentucky, 2010)

* Unofficial

** Herty's 5½-touchdown total against Mercer in 1892 is unofficial and includes a one-half touchdown when it was reported that, somehow, he and teammate Henry Brown scored one together.

with McWhorter nearly single-handedly carrying the team, Georgia had an astounding 25–6–3 overall record.

McWhorter scored 20 touchdowns in his first season of 1910, including 12 the first two games and 15 in 1911. Although playing much of his third year with an illness, he tallied 12 more. In the season-opening game of his final season in 1913 against Alabama-Presbyterian, McWhorter scored six touchdowns and had just as many rushes of 50 yards or longer. For his career, the halfback from Athens scored an unofficial school-record 61 touchdowns for 331 points. This is almost as many points as the entire Georgia team scored in the six seasons combined before McWhorter came to the school.

For the 1913 season, during a time when a southern player was rarely recognized, McWhorter was selected as an All-American by Parke H. Davis for the *New York Herald*. Each of the 10 other selections by Davis were from schools in the Northeast and Midwest.

The following fall, McWhorter entered the University of Virginia's law school. He would eventually return home to Athens, where he was a law professor at the university for 35 years. During this time, McWhorter also served as the mayor of the city from 1940 to 1947.

VERNON SMITH

Vernon "Catfish" Smith received his hard-earned nickname when he was on a fishing trip as a boy. After a playmate jokingly dared him to bite the head off a catfish, Smith grabbed the fish, jerked its whiskers a couple times, and with one snap, bit its head clear off, including the gills.

Playing the end position at Georgia, Smith was an excellent pass receiver and a deadly tackler. In 1929 he was the only sophomore named to the 11-member All–Southern Conference team. It was during that season Smith made a name for himself nationally when he scored every point in Sanford Stadium's dedication game. He scored a safety, a touchdown off a blocked punt, caught a touchdown pass, and kicked an extra point in Georgia's 15–0 historical victory over Yale.

Smith, who was called the game's greatest "money player" by the press, was considered one of the best ends in football by 1930. As both a junior and senior, he was again recognized as an All–Southern Conference member and became only the second consensus first-team All-American in Georgia football history in 1931.

Against Florida, Smith was a member of Bulldogs teams that were 1–1–1 against the Gators in games played at three different sites: Jacksonville's Fairfield Stadium, Savannah's Municipal Stadium, and Gainesville's Florida Field. At Florida Field on Halloween 1931, one of the greatest Georgia teams at that time defeated the Gators 33–6. Smith was constantly in the opposition's backfield, harassing standout passer A.L. Rogero, and kicked three extra points, as well.

For his Bulldogs career, Smith totaled seven touchdowns, converted 31 extra points, and scored two safeties. In 1979 Catfish was given a ceremonial salute at Sanford Stadium for his induction into the College Football Hall of Fame earlier that year. His heroics from the 1929 Yale game were recognized on the 50th anniversary of the venue's dedication.

BILL HARTMAN

Before playing under Harry Mehre in the head coach's final three seasons at Georgia from 1935 to 1937, fullback Bill Hartman starred at the preparatory Georgia Military College for soon-to-be Bulldogs coaching legend Wally Butts.

Hartman was recognized by Mehre as the best back he ever coached in his 10 years at UGA. The versatile Hartman was also an excellent punter and place-kicker, and ended his playing days as the Bulldogs' starting quarterback.

Entering the 1936 Georgia-Florida game, the underdog Bulldogs were given little chance to defeat the Gators. Fortunately for Georgia, the game saw the return of junior "Wild" Bill Hartman, who had been sidelined for five weeks with a leg injury. Hartman rushed for a touchdown in the second quarter of a 26–8 upset victory for the Bulldogs, which prompted Florida coach Josh Cody to declare, "The Georgia team of today is the greatest Georgia team I ever saw."

A year later in Jacksonville, it was the Bulldogs who were upset by a score of 6–0 by the Gators. Rushing for 106 yards and punting for roughly a 40-yard average, senior and Captain Hartman was one of Georgia's few bright spots against Florida. During the loss, the Bulldogs were decimated by a rash of injuries, causing Mehre to move a number of players to unfamiliar positions in the weeks that followed.

Georgia, losers of three of its previous four games, miraculously went undefeated in the final four contests of the 1937 season with Hartman at quarterback. The first-team All-SEC back's successful extra point against Tulane was the difference in a one-point victory. Hartman's 93-yard kickoff return for a touchdown against Georgia Tech two weeks later in a 6–6 tie is considered likely his most outstanding play as a Bulldog.

From 1939 to 1956, except for a stint in the military during World War II, Hartman was once again under old mentor Butts as Georgia's backfield coach. In 1972 head coach Vince Dooley persuaded Hartman to return to the school, coaching the punters and place-kickers as an unpaid volunteer coach and then as a graduate assistant through 1994.

FRANK SINKWICH

As a freshman at Georgia in 1939, Frank Sinkwich was once pointed out in a crowd by one Bulldogs assistant coach to another as the next possible gridiron star at the school. Spotting the large-hipped Sinkwich, walking awkwardly pigeon-toed, the latter assistant merely assumed the other was obviously joking. However, it was soon realized by all that the newcomer from Youngstown, Ohio, was no joke whatsoever.

As a standout on Georgia's freshman team of 1939, Sinkwich was described by the *Red and Black* this way: "If one man tackled 'That Man Sinkwich,' he carried him along over the line…and so on up to eleven. We have one thing to be thankful for—he's on our side!"

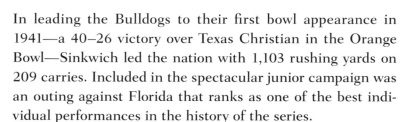

In leading the Bulldogs to their first bowl appearance in 1941—a 40–26 victory over Texas Christian in the Orange Bowl—Sinkwich led the nation with 1,103 rushing yards on 209 carries. Included in the spectacular junior campaign was an outing against Florida that ranks as one of the best individual performances in the history of the series.

In a 19–3 Georgia win, Sinkwich rushed for 142 yards on 31 carries and scored the game's only two touchdowns. Even a Gator knew an outstanding performance when he saw one as Frank Wright, Florida's public relations director, commented afterward, "A move should be started to disfranchise all Americans who think Sinkwich is not an All-American."

In scoring all but seven of the combined 22 points in the contest, the left halfback also pulled off a rare feat by successfully making a field goal. It was the first Georgia field goal versus the Gators since 1919. It would be another 12 years before another Bulldog made a field goal in a game against *any* opponent.

After finishing fourth in 1941, Sinkwich captured the Heisman Trophy as a senior, becoming the first player from the Southeast to win the award. During the 1942 season, to make room in the lineup for sophomore halfback Charley Trippi, Sinkwich was moved to fullback—the position he originally wanted to play when he first arrived at Georgia more than three years earlier. The halfback/fullback was responsible for a national-leading 26 touchdowns in 1942 and became the first player in history to gain 2,000 yards of total offense in a single season.

The powerhouse backfield of senior fullback Frank Sinkwich (21) and sophomore halfback Charley Trippi (62) pose on the field at Sanford Stadium in November 1942, the year that Sinkwich won the Heisman Trophy.

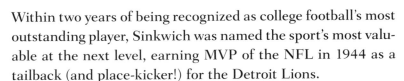

Within two years of being recognized as college football's most outstanding player, Sinkwich was named the sport's most valuable at the next level, earning MVP of the NFL in 1944 as a tailback (and place-kicker!) for the Detroit Lions.

MIKE CASTRONIS

Fittingly from Jacksonville, Mike Castronis was an all-state lineman at the River City's Andrew Jackson High. "Black Mike" originally wanted to attend his state school until Florida head coach Tom Lieb indicated he was too small to play for the Gators. One school's terrible mistake would become a blessing for Castronis—an eventual three-time All-SEC honoree—and the University of Georgia.

Entering the 1943 football season, the only players who remained on Georgia's depleted team were individuals too young for the massive draft of World War II or those not acceptable for military service. Of the 38 Bulldogs on the squad, only eight were 18 years or older, including the oldest, 21-year-old Castronis, who was elected team captain as just a sophomore.

Castronis had a kidney removed soon after enrolling in school and despite not being fit for the military, wore a special kidney pad allowing him to play football. Notwithstanding, he was considered one of the best blockers and fiercest tacklers in the South, although often underappreciated during his three seasons on Georgia's varsity.

"There's always one on every good team," said esteemed sportswriter Jack Troy on Castronis. "That is, a boy who knows his assignments so well and does such a thorough job in every game that he is taken for granted." In 1945 someone finally took notice of the senior Castronis when he was selected to the International News Service's 11-member All-America team.

Castronis, who often helped with area high school teams while attending Georgia, jumped immediately into the coaching profession after graduation. For 10 seasons, he was the head football coach for three different high schools, including undefeated Hartwell High in 1948 and state champion Hogansville High four years later.

Castronis returned to the Bulldogs in 1961, where he filled a variety of roles over the next quarter-century, including head freshman coach, health and P.E. instructor, director of intramurals, and advisor to UGA cheerleaders. Moreover, the one-time overlooked Castronis was considered a tremendous supporter of his university, its people, and a leader in the Athens community.

Castronis died of cancer in January 1987, and with his passing departed one of the most beloved Bulldogs of all time.

CHARLEY TRIPPI

While in high school in Pittston, Pennsylvania, standout athlete Charley Trippi had his mind set on attending Fordham University until he had a chance encounter with a "War Eagle." Harold "War Eagle" Ketron, who had captained Georgia's 1903 football team, operated Coca-Cola bottling plants in Pennsylvania and made an agreement with Trippi that if he attended the University of Georgia, there would always be a job waiting for him during the summers driving a Coca-Cola truck.

Soon afterward, Trippi became a Georgia Bulldog and starred on the freshman squad of 1941. Upon moving up to varsity as a sophomore, under normal circumstances, the gifted Trippi would have promptly been inserted into the starting lineup; however, there was an obstacle standing in his way—senior and eventual Heisman Trophy winner Frank Sinkwich, who played the same halfback position as Trippi.

Backing up Sinkwich, Trippi played sparingly in the first few games of the 1942 season until his playing time finally began to increase. In a 75–0 win over Florida, the sensational sophomore was responsible for four touchdowns, two rushing, one passing, and one via an interception return.

By the end of the year, Trippi was starting at halfback and Sinkwich had been moved to fullback. In a 9–0 victory over UCLA in the 1943 Rose Bowl, Trippi was named the game's most outstanding player, rushing for 115 yards, passing for 96, intercepting a pass, and punting for a 49.5-yard average.

Prior to the 1943 season, like most every other Bulldog who was 18 years and older, Trippi was sent overseas for military service, where he would serve in the Air Force for almost three years. In mid-October of 1945, Trippi was suddenly released from duty by the U.S. war department on a request by Georgia state senator (and UGA graduate) Richard B. Russell.

Returning to the Bulldogs four games into the season, Trippi faced yet another obstacle. Georgia had scrapped its old single-

TOP 5 RUSHING GAMES vs. FLORIDA

1. **Charley Trippi** | 239 yards | 1945
   25 rushes, 3 TDs | 34–0 (UGA)

2. **Herschel Walker** | 238 yards | 1980
   37 rushes, 1 TD | 26–21 (UGA)

3. **Herschel Walker** | 219 yards | 1982
   35 rushes, 3 TDs | 44–0 (UGA)

4. **Kevin McLee** | 198 yards | 1976
   30 rushes | 41–27 (UGA)

5. **Knowshon Moreno** | 188 yards | 2007
   33 rushes, 3 TDs | 42–30 (UGA)

GEORGIA

wing offense and was running the unfamiliar T formation. In his first two contests back as a Bulldog, Trippi struggled in consecutive losses to LSU and Alabama, gaining only a combined 49 rushing yards on 23 carries.

However, it would be Trippi's game in Jacksonville two weeks later that placed him back among college football's elite and still ranks as the greatest rushing performance in the long history of the Georgia-Florida series.

In a 34–0 win over the Gators in 1945, Trippi rushed for 239 yards and three touchdowns on 25 carries, prompting the *Atlanta Constitution* to declare, "If Florida players and partisans never see Charlie [sic] Trippi again it will be too soon."

Unfortunately for the Gators, they would see Trippi one more time. En route to a perfect 11–0 season in 1946, the Bulldogs and Trippi pummeled Florida for a third time. In Jacksonville, the senior and eventual runner-up for the Heisman Trophy rushed for 93 yards, threw for 126 on seven-of-seven passing, and was responsible for three touchdowns in a 33–14 Georgia victory.

In three games against Florida, Trippi rushed for 412 yards, averaged 8.1 yards per carry, scored eight touchdowns, including five rushing, and passed for two touchdowns in three Georgia victories by a 142–14 combined score.

An All-American on Georgia's baseball team as well, Trippi is still considered one of the greatest athletes in the history of collegiate sports. He played both professional baseball and football, including nine seasons with the NFL's Chicago Cardinals, and is one of just two Bulldogs currently enshrined in the Pro Football Hall of Fame.

JOHN RAUCH

Like most of Georgia's football stars from the 1940s and 1950s, John Rauch was also from outside the South. Although, instead of UGA, the Bulldog quarterback from Yeadon, Pennsylvania, almost wound up at another southern school, only to then nearly return home up North.

As a senior in high school, Rauch had decided he would attend the University of Tennessee until a visit to a Georgia practice and a run-in with head coach and chief Bulldogs salesman Wally Butts. Once Butts observed how the youngster threw a football and ran the Bulldogs' new T formation to near perfection, he quickly managed to talk Rauch into switching his allegiance by promising him he would start as Georgia's varsity quarterback as freshman.

Rauch agreed and would start all 11 games as a freshman in 1945; however, during the season, he had grown homesick for his hometown of Yeadon. In an attempt to sneak out of Georgia by train and return back home, Rauch told his teammates he was leaving to take some clothes to the local dry cleaners. However, his plan was foiled when lineman Mike Castronis inquired of an assistant coach, "Have you ever seen anybody carry their dry-cleaning in a suitcase?"

After quarterbacking Georgia to an undefeated season in 1946, Rauch entered his junior season no longer in the shadow of legendary halfback Charley Trippi and, for the first time, was the focal point of the Bulldogs offense.

In 1947 Rauch became one of the most efficient and productive quarterbacks in the game and the next Bulldogs offensive star of the 1940s, after Frank Sinkwich and Trippi, to have his way with the Gators. In a 34–6 Georgia victory over Florida, Rauch completed 12 of 20 passes for 133 yards and two touchdowns while also rushing for two touchdowns.

The game got so out of hand in the Gator Bowl, the fair-weather Florida fans began booing their very own Gators but, as the *Red and Black* stated, "It was really John Rauch's right arm that sent the Florida partisans back home saying, 'Wait 'til next year.'"

The next year in Jacksonville was the same result, as Rauch, who would be recognized in 1948 as a first-team All-American

FOR STARTERS...

In the 90-game history of the Georgia-Florida rivalry through 2011, 53 different players started at quarterback for the Bulldogs, including 20 who started just one game under center against the Gators but were victorious. In addition, only one Bulldogs quarterback, John Rauch, was 4–0 against Florida, and just one was 0–4.

Every Georgia quarterback to have ever started in the series is listed below following their starting record against the Gators:

4–0: John Rauch (1945–1948)

3–0: Buck Belue (1979–1981)

2–0: Charlie Treadaway (1934–1935), Ray Goff (1975–1976), John Lastinger (1982–1983)

2–1: Robin Nowell (1938–1940), James Jackson (1985–1987)

1–0: Harry Woodruff (1904), Dave Paddock (1915), E.H. Dezendorf (1916), Joe Barchan (1919), Sheldon Fitts (1920), Howell Hollis (1926), John Broadnax (1927), Willie Sullivan (1931), Leroy

and the SEC's Player of the Year, led the Bulldogs to their seventh consecutive win over the Gators and a second conference championship in three seasons.

Starting all 45 of his games at Georgia, Rauch finished with a 36–8–1 record as the Bulldogs' quarterback. His 36 wins as a starter would be an NCAA record for 30 years, an SEC record for nearly 50, and a school record until 2004.

FRAN TARKENTON

A homegrown talent, Fran Tarkenton was a four-sport star at Athens High School, where his prep achievements included

Young (1932), Byron Griffith (1933), Lewis Young (1936), Cliff Kimsey (1941), Ken Keuper (1942), Billy Hodges (1944), Mal Cook (1950), Lynn Hughes (1964), Mike Cavan (1968), James Ray (1971), Matt Robinson (1974), Wayne Johnson (1988)

1–1: Jimmy Harper (1954–1955), Andy Johnson (1972–1973), Jeff Pyburn (1977–1978), Greg Talley (1989–1990), Mike Bobo (1996–1997), Aaron Murray (2010–2011)

1–2: Zeke Bratkowski (1951–1953), Charley Britt (1957–1959), Kirby Moore (1965–1967), Matthew Stafford (2006–2008)

1–3: David Greene (2001–2004)

0–0–1: Donnie Hampton (1969)

0–1–1: Austin Downes (1929–1930)

0–1: H.F. Johnson (1928), Wallace Miller (1937), Ray Prosperi (1949), Bill Hearn (1956), Fran Tarkenton (1960), Paul Gilbert (1970), Todd Williams (1984), Hines Ward (1995), Joe Tereshinski (2005), Joe Cox (2009)

0–3: Larry Rakestraw (1961–1963), Quincy Carter (1998–2000)

0–4: Eric Zeier (1991–1994)

GEORGIA

quarterbacking the Athens Trojans to a Georgia state championship as a junior in 1955.

Upon his arrival at UGA, Tarkenton—a gifted drop-back passer and an excellent scrambler and runner—had combined skills that no other Bulldogs quarterback before him possessed. In 1957 he guided the school's freshman Bullpups team to an undefeated season.

Besides athletic prowess, Tarkenton undoubtedly had tremendous moxie, as well. During the season opener of 1958 against 11th-ranked Texas, Tarkenton made his varsity debut by substituting himself for quarterback Tommy Lewis. The daring move by the sophomore not only came without consulting Georgia coaches, but also occurred when Tarkenton believed a decision had been made for him to redshirt that year. The determined quarterback refused to be held out of a season, or even a single game, for that matter.

Although he played a reserve role for most of 1958, one of Tarkenton's best games as a Bulldog was against the Gators as a sophomore. Coming off the bench, he completed seven passes, including a touchdown, on 11 attempts for 100 yards (he totaled just 175 passing yards the entire year) in a 7–6 come-from-behind win by Florida.

Even though he didn't start any games as a junior in 1959, Tarkenton—the "passing" quarterback—was quick to relieve senior starter Charley Britt. In leading the SEC in passing, Tarkenton was a unanimous All-SEC selection. In addition, he led the Bulldogs to their first conference title in 11 years and the lone win over Florida in the nine games from 1955 to 1963.

In 1960, similarly to the season in general, Georgia was having a disappointing outing against the Gators, trailing 22–0 in the fourth quarter. Come to find out, Tarkenton had not slept at all the night before while suffering from asthma attacks, and the pills he took, according to the senior quarterback, "made me flighty during the game." But there was no quit in the courageous Tarkenton.

First, scrambling as far back as Florida's 30-yard line before reaching the end zone, Tarkenton scored on a four-yard touchdown run facing fourth-and-goal. On the play, he received a vicious hit to his hip by a Gators defender, causing the Bull-dogs quarterback to limp the rest of the game. Next, Tarkenton drove Georgia 53 yards to a touchdown in just four plays and the Bulldogs had reduced Florida's lead to only eight points.

However, with only a few minutes to play and Tarkenton barely able to move, Georgia ran out of steam and was eventually defeated 22–14. With no sleep, dizzy from medication, and often limping, Tarkenton completed 14 of 28 passes against the Gators for 145 yards. He would finish his final season of 1960 at Georgia ranking fifth in the nation in passing and was rec-ognized as second-team All-America by the Associated Press.

Demonstrating the same courage and determination he exhib-ited as a Bulldog, Tarkenton's tenure in the NFL lasted a remarkable 18 seasons. In producing likely the greatest NFL career by any former Georgia player, Tarkenton passed for more than 47,000 yards and guided three teams to Super Bowl appearances.

GEORGE PATTON

It's unfortunate that defensive statistics like tackles for loss, sacks, quarterback pressures, forced fumbles, etc., weren't kept until the late '70s/early '80s. If they had been tallied back in defensive tackle George Patton's day, he would have undoubtedly been the school record-holder for a number of these categories, if not all.

The "General" was a standout quarterback at Deshler High in Tuscumbia, Alabama, and was a signal caller for Georgia's B-Team in 1963 as a freshman. However, upon the arrival of new head coach Vince Dooley in 1964, Patton was promptly moved to tackle, where he would soon terrorize his former position, especially one particular Gators quarterback.

In Georgia's 14–7 upset of Florida in 1964, the Bulldogs forced three second-half fumbles after the Gators had fumbled for a total of three times in their first six-and-a-half games of the season. The most critical of these miscues was a Patton sack of Florida's Steve Spurrier behind the line in the final quarter, causing a lost fumble recovered by cornerback Doug McFalls.

As both a sophomore and junior, Patton received All-SEC recognition and was also selected first-team All-America in 1965. He was noted for constantly being in the opposition's backfield, and this may have never been more evident than the following year in Patton's final encounter with the Gators and Spurrier.

After Florida jumped out to a 10–3 third-quarter lead, Spurrier sputtered the rest of the way, and the undefeated Gators were upset 27–10. The primary reason for Florida and its sensational quarterback's second-half collapse was Patton's steady harassment of Spurrier—the so-called "Superman of Gator Land."

For his efforts against Florida, Patton was recognized as the U.S. Lineman of the Week by the Associated Press: "Patton led the defensive 'Dog line in crashing into the Gator backfield to terrorize Florida's running game and pressure All-American Steve Spurrier's passing."

We'll probably never know the exact number of times Spurrier was tackled for a loss by Georgia in the 1966 meeting, but apparently it was on at least six occasions, nearly all in the second half and most of them courtesy of the General. For Patton, and all defenders of his day, the only available statistic is if they ever happened to make an interception. And Patton was successful in this, as well—a combined four interceptions in 1965 and 1966, an extraordinary number for a defensive tackle.

In 1966 Patton finished 10th in the Heisman Trophy voting and again was named first-team All-America. In addition, he made a return to his old position in his final game as a Bulldog. In a 24–9 victory over SMU in the Cotton Bowl, Dooley inserted Patton at quarterback late in the decided game. In four plays under center, Patton attempted three passes and ran for a 16-yard quarterback keeper.

BILL STANFILL

Bill Stanfill, the Bulldogs' largest player at 6'5" and 225 pounds on the 1966 SEC title team, was the only non-junior or senior defensive starter that season. The right tackle was a primary reason for the team's exceptional effort in the second half against Florida that year, giving quarterback Steve Spurrier absolute fits in leading to Georgia's historic upset. Stanfill would later identify the 27–10 win over the Gators as his most memorable moment in football, yet the sophomore's Gator Bowl bliss as a Bulldog had only begun.

Against Florida in 1967, Stanfill harassed a second Gators quarterback—Larry Rentz—for much of the game. His biggest play was sacking the Florida signal-caller behind the line in the second quarter, causing a costly lost fumble in Georgia territory.

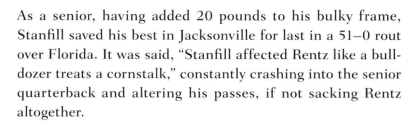

As a senior, having added 20 pounds to his bulky frame, Stanfill saved his best in Jacksonville for last in a 51–0 rout over Florida. It was said, "Stanfill affected Rentz like a bulldozer treats a cornstalk," constantly crashing into the senior quarterback and altering his passes, if not sacking Rentz altogether.

For the 1968 season, Stanfill was honored as a first-team All-SEC player for a third consecutive season while becoming just the sixth Bulldog to ever be recognized as a consensus first-team All-American. That year, he was also the recipient of the Outland Trophy and remains the only Georgia player to date ever to win the coveted award.

The 11th overall selection of the 1969 AFL-NFL Draft, Stanfill played eight seasons with the Miami Dolphins, averaging nearly eight sacks per year, and was named to the Pro Bowl on five occasions.

Besides being one of the Bulldogs' most beloved, Stanfill is still regarded as perhaps Georgia's greatest defensive player of all time. And specifically against despised Florida, he was an absolute three-year terror for two different Gators quarterbacks.

JAKE SCOTT

Jake Scott, whose life, history, and even whereabouts seems to have been surrounded by mystery for decades, remains unconditionally admired by the Bulldog Nation, although he has rarely been seen or heard from since his retirement from the NFL in the late 1970s.

Entering the 1967 season at Georgia and having yet to play a single down at the varsity level, safety/returner Scott was already billed as even better than the departing senior he was replacing in the starting lineup, All-American Lynn Hughes. Scott would more than live up to the hype surrounding him.

Vince Dooley has always said Scott was Georgia's most talented and gifted player, even more so than Herschel Walker, in the head coach's 25-year tenure. As a sophomore, he intercepted six passes, including one he returned for a 32-yard touchdown against Florida.

In the season opener of 1968 against Tennessee, Scott returned a punt 90 yards for a score. Against Kentucky in late October, he intercepted two passes, returning both for touchdowns. Four plays into the Florida game that season, Scott returned a punt 59 yards on a muddy Gator Bowl surface before he was finally brought down at the Gators' 5-yard line. His all-around play that day during a steady downpour prompted teammate Dennis Hughes to declare: "If there is a better safety man [than Scott], then somebody has Superman playing for them."

In his final season at Georgia, Scott was named the SEC's most outstanding player, but the "freest of free spirits" did not even attend the banquet to receive his award. Later, he abruptly left school after his junior year for the Canadian Football League for reasons only completely known by Scott himself.

The rumors and campus legends involving him are numerous—one favorite being that Scott inconceivably drove his motorcycle up a ramp to the top of UGA's basketball arena, and then drove back down the other side.

Although he played just two seasons, Scott intercepted 16 passes as a Bulldog—a school record that still stands. His four returns for touchdowns (three on interception returns, one via punt return) also stood alone as a Georgia record until recently broken by Brandon Boykin in 2011.

After years of aloofness, strained relationships, and a disinterested attitude, Scott was finally inducted into the College Football Hall of Fame in 2011. He had the support to be instated much sooner and on several occasions, but Scott never seemed to care. And from what we hear, remarkably, he actually did show up for this particular banquet.

HERSCHEL WALKER

It's difficult to express in just a handful of paragraphs why the legendary Herschel Walker is adored by Georgia fans. An entire book could effortlessly be written on his accomplishments alone as a Bulldogs football player. Heck, one was recently published merely on his apparent multiple personalities—but we digress.

What makes Herschel so admired goes well beyond his extraordinary play and tremendous achievements on the football field 30 years ago. He is and always has been a bona fide "Renaissance man" in the truest meaning of the term.

In high school, Herschel wrote poetry, was an award-winning Future Homemaker of America, and the valedictorian of his senior class. On a football field, he displayed a combination of speed, power, and size never before seen on a high school

Georgia tailback Herschel Walker, seen here in action against Georgia Tech, always saved his best for the Bulldogs' archrival Florida, gaining 649 yards and scoring eight touchdowns in just three games against the Gators.

gridiron, making him arguably the most highly recruited prep athlete ever at that time.

At Georgia, Herschel's impact was immediate; just ask former Tennessee safety Bill Bates. Just days prior to the 1981 Sugar

Bowl, he won a disco contest in New Orleans and then followed that up by being named the game's MVP. In a 17–10 win over Notre Dame for the national title, Herschel rushed for 150 yards and two touchdowns, while the rest of his team gained a grand total of minus-23 yards of total offense. Let me add, the freshman phenom's sensational performance was after separating a shoulder in the first series of the game.

After finishing runner-up for the Heisman Trophy as a sophomore in 1981, Herschel was the odds-on favorite to take home the award the following year. After eight games and entering the Florida contest in 1982, the junior tailback was still favored to win the award, but Stanford quarterback John Elway was reportedly in a close second place.

Against the Gators, Herschel had such a bad case of the flu, he wore a girdle under his uniform to keep from shivering in 62-degree Jacksonville weather. Regardless, no illness, Gators, or women's undergarments could stop Herschel that day as he rushed for 219 yards and three touchdowns on 35 carries in just over two-and-a-half quarters of play in a 44–0 Georgia victory.

"He may have gotten 300 yards," said coach Vince Dooley, meaning if he had played Herschel a little longer. "If he's not a Heisman Trophy winner, then none that have ever won it before are."

The following week at Auburn, Tigers fans attempted to poke fun at the superstar's girdle and manhood by hanging a sign from their stadium saying, "Herschel Eats Quiche." Herschel responded by making the Tigers eat their words, rushing for

177 yards and two touchdowns as the Bulldogs won their third consecutive SEC championship. A few weeks later, Herschel would indeed bring home the Heisman Trophy while Elway, likely sensing a landslide decision, didn't even show up for the award ceremony.

Speaking of which, one of the many reasons Dawgs fans feel Herschel is the greatest college football player of all time is his unequaled, respective string of Heisman Trophy finishes of third, second, and first in his three seasons of play. Incidentally, his third-place finish as a freshman in 1980 could very well have been a winning one if his 205-yard, three-touchdown performance against Georgia Tech in the regular season finale had been considered by voters (all ballots were due the day before the game).

Also, we strongly believe that if Herschel had stayed at Georgia for his senior season and not departed for the upstart USFL, he would have been the recipient of another Heisman in 1983, and the Bulldogs could have won their second national championship in four years.

Nearly 30 years after leaving Georgia, Herschel has continued his Renaissance-man ways. To name a few, he has successfully run a number of businesses, earned a black belt in karate, and competed in the 1992 Winter Olympics in the two-man bobsled. Along the way, in 15 USFL and NFL seasons, Herschel gained 25,283 all-purpose yards—the most by any player in the history of professional football.

Recently, Herschel began a career in mixed martial arts and, by the deadline of this manuscript, had defeated both of his

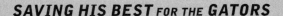
SAVING HIS BEST *FOR THE* GATORS

While at Georgia, Herschel Walker faced eight common opponents in all three of his seasons from 1980 to 1982. Walker's best was his three games against Florida, rushing for a combined 649 yards, averaging 5.5 yards per carry, and scoring eight touchdowns.

Opponent	Rush Yds.	Rush Avg.	TDs
FLORIDA	649	5.5	8
Vanderbilt	643	6.4	6
Georgia Tech	592	6.7	9
South Carolina	538	4.8	4
Ole Miss	458	6.0	4
Auburn	419	4.4	4
Kentucky	412	4.2	3
Clemson	252	4.1	0

opponents by TKO. This new role certainly seems in sharp contrast to when he once danced with the Fort Worth Ballet (and for any opposing fans, I'd keep any thoughts of "quiche" to yourself); however, when it comes to Herschel Walker, nothing surprises us any longer.

TERRY HOAGE

Even a Gator must admire Georgia's Terry Hoage—college football's absolute epitome of a true student-athlete, and something the University of Florida has certainly lacked in recent years. Scarcely recruited out of high school in 1980, the quarterback/defensive back from Huntsville, Texas, was signed by the Bulldogs only after a recommendation from a Georgia alumnus living in Texas.

As a freshman, Hoage hardly played during the regular season, recording just a single tackle. However, the newcomer made one of the biggest plays in the 1981 Sugar Bowl against Notre Dame for the national championship. With Georgia trailing the Fighting Irish 3–0, Hoage blocked a first-quarter field goal in his first appearance on the Bulldogs' field-goal defensive team.

Following a rumored near transfer to the University of Texas, Hoage started at roverback for the Bulldogs as a sophomore in 1981. As a junior the next season, he experienced one of the greatest campaigns ever by a Georgia defensive back, recording 101 tackles, 11 tackles for loss, 10 passes broken up, three caused fumbles, a blocked extra-point attempt, and a national-leading 12 interceptions.

In 1983 Hoage suffered through three different ailments throughout the year, including an ankle injury which caused him to miss the entire Florida game. During his senior season, Hoage was sidelined for three entire games, started just five, twice played out of position at safety because of injuries to teammates, and did not practice for an entire two months. Nevertheless, he still managed to record 60 tackles for the season and, in just a two-game span, blocked three field goals.

Despite the missed playing time, Hoage was so revered in 1983 and made such an impact when he did play that—get this—he finished fifth in the Heisman Trophy voting, even totaling seven first-place votes. In 77 years of the celebrated trophy through 2011, no individual who solely played the defensive back position had ever placed higher than Hoage's fifth-place finish. In addition, we'll make an educated guess and assume

GEORGIA

ONE-HIT WONDER

Entering the 1983 Florida game, the Bulldogs were without the services of All-America roverback Terry Hoage and facing one of college football's best passing games, quarterbacked by senior Wayne Peace and coordinated by Mike Shanahan. Against the Gators, Georgia's fears were heightened when Hoage's backup, John Little, was also lost to an ankle injury on the third play of the game. In stepped third-string roverback Gary Cantrell.

In nearly three whole seasons at Georgia, the junior Cantrell had hardly played and had not recorded a single tackle. Nevertheless, in a 10–9 win over Florida, he made eight tackles, broke up a pass in a crucial situation, and would be named the UPI's Southeast Defensive Player of the Week.

For the game, Peace and the Gators penetrated the Bulldogs' 25-yard line six times; however, Cantrell's defensive performance was a major reason why Florida scored only three field goals.

"A team can gain all the yards they want to," said Cantrell following the game, "but if they don't score, they don't win."

For his efforts, Cantrell was given the starting nod in Georgia's final two regular season games against Auburn and Georgia Tech. In the preseason of 1984 while competing with Little for the starting roverback position, it was the senior Cantrell suffering an injury—a damaged collateral knee ligament—causing him to miss the entire year. Before the start of the 1985 season and still with a year of eligibility remaining, Cantrell decided to leave the team altogether.

no player considered a non-starter, like Hoage in 1983, has finished as high in the award's voting.

Speaking of educated, Hoage graduated from UGA with a B.S. in genetics, finished with a 3.85 grade-point average, and was the recipient of scholarships from the NCAA and the National Football Foundation. Considered likely the only NFL player in history to major in genetics, Hoage played 12 seasons in the league for six different teams.

Today, Hoage owns and operates Terry Hoage Vineyards in Westside Paso Robles, California. The vintner has indicated one of his favorite wines is his "5 Blocks" Syrah Cuvee, appropriately named for the five blocked kicks he totaled at Georgia.

KEVIN BUTLER

Many newer Bulldogs fans may only know of Kevin Butler as the father of Drew Butler, Georgia's All-America punter who just ended his career in 2011 with a school-record punting average of 45.4 yards. However, for the older Georgia faithful, we remember Kevin as the most skillful of place-kickers before being accurate was somewhat the norm.

Following Georgia's national championship season of 1980, one of the Bulldogs' major concerns heading into the following year was how All-America place-kicker Rex Robinson was going to be replaced. The concern became even bigger when Butler, a true freshman from Stone Mountain, Georgia, missed his first field-goal attempt as a Bulldog in the season opener of 1981 against Tennessee—a mere chip shot of 26 yards. Regardless, Butler quickly recovered from the short miss and made all eight of the rest of his kicks (three field goals, five extra points) that day to set a then single-game UGA record of 14 points scored by a kicker.

From 1981 to 1984, Butler made 77 of 98 field goals, including 11 of 21 from 50 yards and beyond. In comparison, his overall field-goal percentage of nearly 80 percent, including more than 52 percent from 50 yards and beyond, far exceeded the accuracy during the same time period for all of major college football: 64.6 percent overall and 35.1 percent from 50 yards and more.

Butler's 353 career points at Georgia were a school record until broken almost two entire decades later by fellow Bulldogs place-kicker Billy Bennett. To date, Butler remains the most decorated Georgia kicker in history, earning All-SEC recognition for all four of his seasons and first-team All-America status in both 1983 and 1984. Perhaps above all, of the roughly 900 players in the College Football Hall of Fame as of 2011, Butler was the only sole place-kicker inductee.

For 13 seasons, from 1985 to 1997, Butler kicked in the NFL for two teams and scored 1,208 career points—the second-most in the league of all former Georgia players.

Notably, whether in the NFL or as a Bulldog, Butler wasn't your typical place-kicker, who often stands alone on the sideline, hardly talking to teammates, while waiting for the few times during a game he is called upon to kick.

No, Kevin Butler was a true team player, a vocal leader, and more than willing to hit the return man following one of his own kickoffs (and talk trash to the returner after his tackle). For those very reasons, along with the astonishing statistics and accomplishments, Butler remains one of the most admired Bulldogs of all time—even if he was "just a kicker."

TIM WORLEY

In his seemingly short time at Georgia, tailback Tim Worley didn't total the flashy career numbers as others or have the accomplished NFL tenure like some. However, when it comes to the Georgia-Florida series, few backs in this storied rivalry achieved as much as Worley.

A native of Lumberton, North Carolina, Worley originally planned to attend and play football at Oklahoma until his mother intervened, and the blue-chip recruit wound up signing instead with the University of Georgia—his fourth choice.

In his freshman season of 1985 Worley was second on the team with 627 rushing yards and first with 10 touchdowns scored. In Georgia's 24–3 victory over top-ranked Florida that season Worley carried the ball seven times for 104 yards, 89 of which came on a long fourth-quarter scoring run, tying the school record for longest rush from scrimmage, while securing the Bulldogs' shocking upset over the Gators.

In the fourth game of the 1986 season, Worley was lost for the year with a knee injury and ruled academically ineligible a year later in 1987. Entering his junior season of 1988, Worley was considered one of the most talented running backs in the history of the school but had little to show for it. That, however, would soon change.

Six games into the season, Worley was seventh in the nation in rushing and fourth in scoring despite not having started a single game as the backup to first-string tailback Rodney Hampton. Regardless, UGA began hyping Worley as a Heisman Trophy candidate in what was believed to be the first time a reserve had ever been promoted by a school for the trophy.

Printed on the Heisman "Here Comes Worley" media flier was a quote from Ole Miss head coach Billy Brewer, whose Rebels allowed the junior candidate 121 rushing yards and a touchdown rushing, passing, and on a kickoff return: "Tim Worley is the most physical and abusing runner we've seen in a long time. He has God-given ability you don't see in many running backs. We needed two weeks off just to get over Tim Worley."

About a month later, the Gators would have similar feelings, for a second time, regarding the gifted Worley.

Late in the game against Florida in 1988, Georgia was in an eerily similar position as exactly three years before: winning by about two touchdowns with only a few minutes remaining, far from the Gators' goal line, and in need of a big play to clinch another win in the Gator Bowl. And, just like in 1985, the Bulldogs handed the ball to Worley, who once again, ripped Florida's defense for a long touchdown run. In Georgia's 26–3 win, Worley rushed 22 times for 135 yards and two touchdowns, including a 51-yard scoring jaunt.

By the end of the 1988 season, there was no Heisman for Worley—not even a top-10 finish—but some remarkable accomplishments: 1,216 rushing yards, 18 touchdowns scored, two touchdowns passing, a 34.3 kickoff-return average, and

GEORGIA

RIVALRY HALL *of* FAMERS

In 1995 the Jacksonville Economic Development Commission created the Florida-Georgia Hall of Fame, which we prefer to call the "Georgia-Florida Hall of Fame." Every year, two Bulldogs and two Gators who left their mark on the football rivalry are selected. In 2011 the Georgia inductees were offensive lineman/linebacker Bill Saye (1953–1955) and linebacker John Brantley (1984–1987).

Native Athenian Saye was the hero of Georgia's lone victory over Florida during a seven-season stretch (1952–1958)—a 14–13 upset win in 1954. From his linebacker position, Saye recovered a critical late Gators fumble and intercepted two passes during the game—his only interceptions during his Bulldogs career. Actually, Saye intercepted three Florida passes, but one was disregarded after an official ruled the quarterback stepped over a sideline before he threw.

Brantley, from Wildwood, Florida, led the team in tackles for both of the Bulldogs' victories in 1985 and 1987. In Georgia's 24–3 upset over No. 1–ranked Florida as a sophomore, Brantley recorded seven tackles, one for a loss, and a quarterback sack. Two years later, the two-time All-SEC honoree tallied 14 tackles, including one for loss, in the Bulldogs' 23–10 win.

Since college, Brantley has remained and worked in the city of Athens, and fans certainly don't blame him; it would surely beat moving back home to a place like Wildwood.

first-team All-America recognition. Immediately following the season, Worley declared early for the NFL draft, where he would be the seventh overall pick.

Cut short by injury, ineligibility, and an early departure, Worley's Georgia career lasted just 26 regular season games. Still, he left the school as the Bulldogs' sixth all-time leading rusher. Even today, Worley's 78.4 career rushing yards per game currently rank sixth at Georgia behind Herschel Walker, Knowshon Moreno, Garrison Hearst, Robert Edwards, and one-time teammate Hampton. And besides winners Frank Sinkwich and Walker, along with Charley Trippi in 1946 and Hearst in 1992, to date, no other Bulldogs running back has made a run for the Heisman Trophy as late in a season as Worley did in 1988. In 2007 he was inducted into the Florida-Georgia Hall of Fame for his two performances against the Gators.

GARRISON HEARST

In the winter of 1990, the Bulldog Nation suddenly was in a frenzy. After a few years of subpar recruiting classes, producing mixed results on the football field, the Dawgs had finally landed a top-notch group of freshmen, and the head of the class was the No. 1 prospect in the state—Lincoln County tailback Garrison Hearst.

It would take some time for the newcomers to fully mature, like Hearst, but when they finally did, it was well worth the wait.

In 1990 Hearst was one of the few highlights of an inexperienced and injury-plagued team. While splitting time with junior Larry Ware, the freshman tailback rushed for a team-high

717 yards on a Bulldogs' squad which could muster only a 4–7 record—Georgia's worst season in nearly 30 years. In 1991, and again sharing the load with Ware, Hearst gained nearly 1,000 yards rushing as the Bulldogs returned to their winning ways with a 9–3 campaign.

As a junior in 1992, Hearst would become the workhorse in Georgia's backfield. The end result was one of the greatest seasons ever for a Bulldogs player during one of the better years for Georgia football in recent memory.

In the Bulldogs' 10–2 season, Hearst rushed for 1,547 yards, averaged almost seven yards per carry, was second on the team in receiving, and scored an SEC-record 21 touchdowns. For his efforts in 1992, Hearst remains one of only six different Georgia players in history to be recognized as a unanimous first-team All-American.

Disappointingly, Hearst finished third in the Heisman Trophy voting—a touchy subject for some Bulldogs fans. How one could finish behind a player who had inferior statistics playing for a 5–5–1 team while faced with Western Athletic Conference opposition—San Diego State's Marshall Faulk—and another who wasn't even close to being the best player on his own team—Miami (Fla.) quarterback Gino Torretta—is beyond us.

This just demonstrates that sometimes the voting for certain awards, even the most coveted, are cast as a lifetime-achievement honor and/or for those that are the most publicized, and not necessarily the most deserving—like Garrison Hearst in 1992.

ERIC ZEIER

Rarely does a program's offensive scheme suddenly change with the signing of a single player. But such was the case when Georgia landed the No. 1 quarterback prospect in the nation in the winter of 1991—Eric Zeier of Marietta, Georgia. The Bulldogs, who had averaged approximately 245 rushing yards and just 17 pass attempts per game during the decade of the 1980s, were instantly transformed from "Tailback U." to "Air Georgia" almost overnight.

"I want to work hard, I want to earn the respect of my team-mates," said Zeier after signing with Georgia. "I'm ready to be a Bulldog." What are cliché statements for some signees turned out to be absolute standards for Zeier.

When it was far from commonplace as today, Zeier enrolled early in college during his final year of high school. Allowed to practice in the spring, the incoming QB was welcomed with a newly installed pro-set offensive formation after Georgia had used the run-oriented I formation for 13 consecutive seasons.

In his first five games as a Bulldog in 1991, Zeier passed for 791 yards as the team's *second*-string quarterback. In his eighth game and third start, he threw for 302 yards on 19-of-23 passing against Kentucky—at the time, only the third 300-yard individual passing performance in Georgia history. By the end of the season, Zeier had thrown for more yards in a single year with nearly 2,000 than any Bulldog before him. Most importantly, the SEC's Freshman of the Year had been instrumental in Georgia's achieving a 9–3 record after going 4–7 the year before.

With the departure of running back Garrison Hearst by Zeier's junior season, the Bulldogs all but completely dumped their running game. In 1993 the quarterback passed for 3,525 yards and 24 touchdowns. In his final campaign of 1994, a season in which Georgia had fewer rushes than any team in Division I-A football, Zeier passed for another 3,396 yards and 24 touchdowns.

Admittedly, the legendary Zeier had little success against the Gators; he's the only Bulldogs quarterback with an 0–4 record as a starter in the rivalry. However, completing more than 56 percent of his passes in the four games for 1,078 yards, you can find little fault with Zeier's performances against Florida. We shudder to think what the losing margin of the four games would have been without him under center.

Upon his departure from Georgia, Zeier's 11,153 career passing yards was an SEC record and the third-most in the history of major college football. Finishing 10th in 1993 and seventh in 1994, he remains one of only three Bulldogs ever to finish in the top 10 of the Heisman Trophy's voting for more than one season.

After six seasons in the NFL with three different teams, "Air Zeier" joined the airwaves in 2007 as a color analyst on the Georgia Bulldog Radio Network.

ROBERT EDWARDS

Whether suffering through injuries, faced with unfamiliar circumstances, or enduring his own disappointing play, there is likely no other Bulldog, and very few players in general, who ever had to overcome as much adversity as Georgia's Robert Edwards.

After playing very little as a freshman in 1993, Edwards became the Bulldogs' starting right cornerback the next year. Recording 64 tackles, four interceptions, and a team-high seven passes broken up in 1994, the sophomore from Tennille, Georgia, had an admirable season for a first-time starter, that is, except for an unpleasant experience in Gainesville against the Gators.

Against Edwards' coverage, Florida wide receiver Chris Doering caught two touchdown passes in the first 10 minutes of an eventual 52–14 Gators' romp over the Bulldogs. The two Doering-against-Edwards scoring plays were recognized by the *Atlanta Journal-Constitution* as the game's "Best burn job."

In the spring of 1995, what began as only an experiment resulted in a team's solution when Edwards, who was being touted as a preseason all-star cornerback, was moved to Georgia's scat back position because of injuries to teammates. In perhaps the greatest individual offensive debut in Georgia history, the junior rushed for 169 yards on 30 carries, caught two passes for 42 yards, and scored a modern-school-record five touchdowns in a season-opening win over South Carolina. Edwards followed that up with 156 yards and two touchdowns on 15 carries against Tennessee, but was lost in the third quarter for the rest of the season with a fractured foot injury.

Coming off a medical redshirt season, there were high hopes for Edwards; however, he and the rest of first-year head coach Jim Donnan's Bulldogs would have little to enjoy in 1996.

Although he rushed for 800 yards and scored 10 touchdowns during Georgia's 5–6 campaign, Edwards was prone to fumbling the ball. Against Florida, he fumbled twice before halftime, giving Edwards a total of eight fumbles in just eight games, and he was indefinitely benched in the second quarter.

Edwards returned from the Bulldogs' sideline the following game at Auburn only when an injury benched his replacement, Patrick Pass. Running with vengeance, and finally holding onto the football, Edwards remarkably totaled 97 yards (60 rushing, 37 receiving) of Georgia's 100-yard total in four overtime periods and scored three touchdowns in a 56–49 upset of the Tigers.

As a senior in 1997, like two years before, Edwards was injured early in the season. However, after carrying the ball only a combined two times in Georgia's first three contests because of an ankle injury, a healthy Edwards managed six 100-yard rushing games during a 10–2 season for the Bulldogs.

In a 37–17 upset win over Florida that year, Edwards rushed for 124 yards and four touchdowns on 26 carries. The last of his series-record four rushing scores was a 37-yard fourth-quarter run, giving the Bulldogs a two-touchdown lead and delivering the knockout blow to the Gators.

Edwards' final touchdown, according to quarterback Mike Bobo, was the "the single-greatest feeling" the Bulldogs signal-caller ever had in his life. "When you consider what all [Edwards] has been through the past few years," said Bobo, "you can't imagine what that run did."

What that run did, after two previous forgettable outings against the Gators, was place one of the most injured but talented Bulldogs into Georgia-Florida football lore forever.

HINES WARD

In 1994 Hines Ward signed with Georgia out of high school as a blue-chip quarterback. However, with the Bulldogs featuring All-American Eric Zeier under center, along with worthy backups Mike Bobo and Brian Smith, Coach Ray Goff made the decision to promptly shift the incoming freshman from quarterback to the scat back position. Few could have guessed it was the first of several moves the versatile Ward would experience as a Bulldog.

After considering a redshirt season for Ward, Goff instead thrust the true freshman into action the first game of 1994. By the third game of the year, Ward was starting over senior and future NFL great Terrell Davis. In his first two starts at Georgia, Ward produced 100-yard rushing performances, including 137 yards against 11th-ranked Alabama.

Prior to the 1995 season, Ward was moved to receiver and delivered with a 100-yard receiving game in the Bulldogs' opener against South Carolina. Soon, injuries would decimate the team, and Ward returned to scat back. In the fifth game, he started at quarterback for the first time since high school, but then was moved back to the scat back position.

By the Florida game in 1995, Ward was again starting under center for Georgia. In an otherwise forgettable 52–17 loss to the Gators, the sophomore signal-caller shined. Ward passed for 226 yards and a touchdown and rushed for 65 yards, all while playing with a broken wrist. His wrist was so injured, in fact, Ward could not line up under center, but received snaps solely from the shotgun formation.

"[Adrenaline] kept me going, but on the sideline [my wrist] hurt like crazy," said Ward after the Florida game. "I just told the coaches to put me in and let's call the play."

Continuing to play through the injury, Ward ended the year as Georgia's lone legitimate quarterback and finished with an amazing 413-yard passing, 56-yard rushing performance versus Virginia in the Peach Bowl.

After seven starts at scat back and five at quarterback in two seasons, Ward started at split end for the Bulldogs in 1996, where he was a mainstay his final two years. In earning All-SEC recognition as both a junior and senior, Ward made a combined 107 receptions for 1,615 yards. In 1996 and 1997 the one-time quarterback even found time to complete three passes for 46 yards and a touchdown, including a key 27-yarder in a win over Florida as a senior.

For his Bulldogs career, including two bowl games, Ward totaled 2,087 receiving yards, 1,331 passing, and 1,202 rushing. In becoming what was believed to be the first player in NCAA history to gain 1,000 yards three different ways, the quadruple-threat also added nearly 1,000 on returns.

Since college, Ward has produced one of the best NFL careers of any Georgia player in history. Notably, playing for the Pittsburgh Steelers, the four-time Pro Bowler became the third

Bulldog to be named a Super Bowl MVP in a victory over the Seattle Seahawks in 2006.

By the way, the multitalented Ward also has sported some moves on the dance floor. Five years after Gator Emmitt Smith succeeded in doing so, Ward won ABC-TV's *Dancing with the Stars* in 2011 as a "celebrity" contestant.

Although he did win his season, we'd like to point out that Smith came in last place with the competition's judges at one point. Just goes to show, whatever a Gator can do, a Bulldog can do as well, if not better.

THE BAILEYS

Hailing from the small southern town of Folkston, Georgia, where "If you blink you'll miss it," according to Boss Bailey, the Bailey brothers—Ronald, Roland (Champ), and Rodney (Boss)—attended and played football at the University of Georgia over a stretch of 10 seasons from 1993 to 2002.

After redshirting as a freshman and playing sparingly in 1994, the elder Ronald started 28 games for the Bulldogs at right cornerback from 1995 through 1997. For his career, he recorded 133 tackles, broke up 15 passes, and intercepted five passes.

Champ, the most talented of the three, entered Georgia with the dream of one day starting with Ronald in the Bulldogs' defensive backfield. By the 10th game of the 1996 season, his dream came to fruition. When the Baileys started at Georgia's two cornerback positions against Ole Miss, it marked the first time brothers started for the Bulldogs in a game on the same

side of the ball since center Joe and tight end Wally Tereshinski did so 20 years before.

Not wanting Champ's extraordinary talent to go to waste, head
coach Jim Donnan had the sophomore in 1997, besides starting at left cornerback for the Bulldogs, returning kickoffs and
seeing time at wide receiver. By 1998, the triple-threat was
considered perhaps the most versatile and exciting player in
college football and a legitimate Heisman Trophy candidate.
In his junior and final season, Champ tallied 52 tackles, three
interceptions, 744 receiving yards, and 310 yards in total kick
returns, while averaging a whopping combined total of 87
defensive, offensive, and special-team plays per game.

Placing seventh in the award's voting in 1998, Champ remains
the last Bulldog to finish in the top 10 of a Heisman Trophy's
balloting through 2011. Chosen by the Washington Redskins,
he was also the seventh overall selection of the 1999 NFL Draft.

In Champ's last year at Georgia, his younger brother, Boss,
was a valuable reserve at the strong-side linebacker position
as just a true freshman. In 1999 Boss became the third Bailey
brother to regularly start as a sophomore. After suffering a
season-ending torn ACL on the team's first kickoff of 2000, he
returned the following year as a junior to become one of the
school's greatest linebackers in recent memory. In 2002 Boss
recorded 114 tackles, six sacks, three blocked kicks, and, just
like his brother Champ four years before, was recognized as a
first-team All-American.

Whereas Champ has gone on to play in 11 Pro Bowls through
2011—the most of any Bulldog ever in the NFL—both Ronald

and Boss' professional football careers were cut short because of injuries. Nevertheless, the brothers have continued to follow the path of one another back to the Classic City. In 2010 they opened Bailey's American Tavern along with an Athens-based trucking company, which fittingly employs the fourth of a long line of Bulldog Baileys—cousin Kenny, a tailback/defensive back at Georgia from 2000 to 2003.

DAVID GREENE

Off the top of our heads, Georgia fans can name roughly a dozen, maybe more, Bulldogs quarterbacks who certainly had more talent than our beloved David Greene—the school's starting signal-caller for the first four seasons of the Coach Mark Richt era. However, when it comes to the ultimate goal in athletics—winning—no quarterback in Georgia history, or all of college football, for that matter, was better than Greene.

Not highly recruited out of high school, Greene was promptly redshirted as a true freshman. Under newly hired Richt in 2001, he entered the following year with little fanfare, having just barely beat out a former walk-on just days prior to the season opener for the team's starting position.

Regardless, any doubts as to whether Greene was qualified for big-time SEC football were quashed in his fourth game as a Bulldog. Against sixth-ranked Tennessee, the redshirt freshman led an unranked Georgia team to a 26–24 upset victory on the road, including driving the Bulldogs 59 yards on four completions in the game's final 42 seconds for the game-winning touchdown.

From the momentous victory over the Volunteers through the next four seasons, Greene helped deliver one significant victory after another while guiding Georgia to its most successful four-year run in more than 20 years.

From 2001 to 2004, Greene was never recognized as an All-American and just once—in his sophomore season of 2002—was acknowledged as a first-team All-SEC honoree. Yet, joining Bulldogs legends John Rauch and Eric Zeier, he became just the third Georgia quarterback in history to lead the team in passing four consecutive years while his 11,528 career passing yards upon his departure from the school were an SEC record and the ninth-most in Division I-A history.

Leading up to the Florida game in 2004, the one victory that had eluded Greene in three attempts was one over the detested Gators. However, in his final attempt in Jacksonville, the senior quarterback played a near-perfect game, completing 15 of 23 passes for 255 yards, three touchdowns, and no interceptions, as Georgia, thanks in large part to Greene, defeated Florida 31–24 for the first time in seven years.

In four seasons as a Bulldog, and despite the presence of the acclaimed and multi-talented D.J. Shockley, Greene was Georgia's starting quarterback for every one of its 52 games. During his tenure, the Bulldogs captured their first SEC championship in 20 years, made a second trip to the conference title game, and won three consecutive New Year's Day bowls.

Moreover, despite not being the most talented of players, Greene was simply a tremendous leader and winner, who totaled a staggering 42 victories as a starting quarterback—an NCAA Division I-A record which stood until 2009.

DAVID POLLACK

Georgia's David Pollack is absolute proof that no matter the circumstances, with lots of hard work, heart, and determination, even a long shot can have tremendous success.

Pollack entered Georgia in 2001 not even ranked by some recruiting services among their top 100 incoming defensive linemen. Upon his arrival, Pollack was promptly moved to the fullback position, and only returned to the other side of the ball when injuries occurred along the Bulldogs' defensive line.

Pollack made such an impression during practices, where it was reported he would often sprint to workouts and then go full steam during sessions, the true freshman began the season as a top reserve. By early November, he was Georgia's starting left defensive tackle and finished 2001 on the All-SEC Freshman Team.

If you didn't know of David Pollack before, you certainly did by Georgia's SEC championship season of 2002. The sophomore, who had since moved to defensive end, recorded a school-record 14 sacks and was recognized as a consensus All-American. In addition, Pollack was named the SEC's Player of the Year—the first defender to be acknowledged since Auburn's Tracy Rocker 14 years before.

In his final two seasons of 2003 and 2004, Pollack was again selected as a first-team All-American, joining Herschel Walker as the school's only other three-time All-American, and received the Ted Hendricks Award both years as the nation's top defensive end. In 2004 he was also the recipient of the Lombardi Award (nation's top lineman) and Bednarik Award (nation's top defensive player). Pollack's 58½ total tackles for loss, 36 sacks, and 117 quarterback hurries from 2001 to 2004 remain Bulldogs career records.

The obscure recruit, who gave his all on every snap while often playing with pain, became the most decorated defensive player in Georgia football history after nearly becoming the team's starting fullback.

After being selected 17th overall in the 2005 NFL Draft by the Cincinnati Bengals, Pollack's football career abruptly ended when he suffered a broken neck during just his 16th professional game. Yet, exhibiting the same will and determination Bulldogs fans admired when he was at Georgia, Pollack again has persevered and is currently enjoying a successful career in broadcasting.

MATTHEW STAFFORD

In 2005 Matthew Stafford—a 6'3", 225-pound, strong-armed Texan, who was considered by some as the top prospect in the nation—spurned his native state to come to, of all places, Athens. Stafford would soon show why he had been so highly touted, displaying talent by a Georgia quarterback never witnessed by most Bulldogs fans.

Entangled in a four-quarterback race in the summer of 2006 for the starting position, Stafford would become Georgia's

*Georgia quarterback Matthew Stafford tucks the ball and runs between two
Florida defenders during the second quarter of the Bulldogs' 42–30 spanking
of the Gators on October 27, 2007, in Jacksonville.*

first-string signal-caller by the third game of his true freshman
season. During the year, after the Bulldogs had lost four of five
games, Stafford was one of the primary reasons for a prompt
turnaround, resulting in three consecutive wins, all against
opponents ranked 16th or higher in the nation.

After a 4–2 start to the 2007 campaign, Stafford engineered
seven straight victories, leading to a No. 2 final ranking for
Georgia. Included was a 42–30 upset victory over ninth-ranked
Florida, where Stafford went head-to-head with another

sophomore quarterback—Tim Tebow. While the soon-to-be Heisman Trophy winner was sacked six times and ineffective on the ground, Stafford passed for 217 yards and a then-career-high three touchdowns on just 18 attempts.

In his final season of 2008, Stafford threw for 3,459 yards—the second-most in school history at the time—and a school-record 25 touchdowns, while leading the team to a second-consecutive 10-wins-or-more season.

Besides posting some gaudy statistics while at Georgia, Stafford was, most importantly, a proven winner. In three seasons as a Bulldog, he registered a 27–7 record as a starter, including 11–4 against AP-ranked opponents and 7–3 in games decided by four points or less.

Selected by the Detroit Lions in 2009, Stafford became the fourth Bulldog to be chosen as the top pick of an NFL Draft. After two injury-filled seasons, the strong-armed talent proved he could win at any level, guiding the Lions to a 10–6 campaign and a playoff appearance in 2011 after the team had won just two games in 2008 and 2009 combined.

KNOWSHON MORENO

After redshirting as a true freshman in 2006, there was some doubt highly recruited Knowshon Moreno would play much even in his second year at Georgia. Returning for the Bulldogs in 2007 would be tailbacks Thomas Brown, Kregg Lumpkin, and Danny Ware—all seniors and each with at least 1,500 career rushing yards in 30 or more career games. Thus, it certainly seemed to most of the Bulldog Nation that newcomer

BULLDOGS ACTIVE IN THE NFL IN 2011

Player	Pos.	2011 Team	1st Season
Asher Allen	CB	Minnesota Vikings	2009
Geno Atkins	DT	Cincinnati Bengals	2010
Champ Bailey	CB	Denver Broncos	1999
Clint Boling	OG	Cincinnati Bengals	2011
Shaun Chapas	FB	Dallas Cowboys	2011
Chris Clemons	DE	Seattle Seahawks	2004
Thomas Davis	LB	Carolina Panthers	2005
Akeem Dent	LB	Atlanta Falcons	2011
Demarcus Dobbs	DE	San Francisco 49ers	2011
Kris Durham	WR	Seattle Seahawks	2011
Dannell Ellerbe	LB	Baltimore Ravens	2009
Darryl Gamble	LB	San Diego Chargers	2011
Robert Geathers	DE	Cincinnati Bengals	2004
Kedric Golston	DE	Washington Redskins	2006
A.J. Green	WR	Cincinnati Bengals	2011
Justin Houston	LB	Kansas City Chiefs	2011
Corvey Irvin	DT	Jacksonville Jaguars	2010
Tim Jennings	CB	Chicago Bears	2006

Moreno, hailing from Bedford, New Jersey, would primarily be watching from the sideline for yet another season.

When Ware declared early for the NFL draft, Moreno moved up to the third-string slot entering the 2007 season. After Lumpkin went down with an injury in the opening game, Moreno and Brown split carries through Georgia's first six contests, two of which resulted in losses. In the sixth game, Brown suffered a broken collarbone and would be sidelined for the next four weeks.

Charles Johnson	DE	Carolina Panthers	2007
Reshad Jones	DB	Miami Dolphins	2010
Sean Jones	S	Tampa Bay Buccaneers	2005
John Kasay	PK	New Orleans Saints	1991
Kregg Lumpkin	RB	Tampa Bay Buccaneers	2008
Mohamed Massaquoi	WR	Cleveland Browns	2009
Randy McMichael	TE	San Diego Chargers	2002
Prince Miller	DB	Buffalo Bills	2010
Knowshon Moreno	RB	Denver Broncos	2009
Paul Oliver	DB	San Diego Chargers	2008
Leonard Pope	TE	Kansas City Chiefs	2006
Dennis Roland	OT	Cincinnati Bengals	2008
Richard Seymour	DE	Oakland Raiders	2001
Matthew Stafford	QB	Detroit Lions	2009
Kiante Tripp	DL	Cleveland Browns	2011
Fernando Velasco	OL	Tennessee Titans	2009
Hines Ward	WR	Pittsburgh Steelers	1998
Danny Ware	RB	New York Giants	2007
Ben Watson	TE	Cleveland Browns	2004
Will Witherspoon	LB	Tennessee Titans	2002
Jarius Wynn	DE	Green Bay Packers	2009

GEORGIA

What once appeared like a small role, if any at all, for Moreno in 2007 had quickly turned into the redshirt freshman becoming the team's only legitimate tailback heading into the last half of the Bulldogs' schedule.

Moreno's performance over the next three games was absolutely astonishing as he averaged 29 rushes for more than 180 yards per contest. Included was a spectacular outing in a 42–30 win over Florida, where the fabulous freshman was nearly unstoppable, rushing for three touchdowns and 188 yards—

the fifth-most rushing yards by a Bulldog in the Georgia-Florida series.

Against Troy the following week, Moreno finished just four yards shy of becoming only the ninth different Georgia player in history to rush for 200 yards in a single game. In a win over the Trojans, he reached the 1,000-yard rushing mark for the season, only the second Bulldogs freshman in history, along with Herschel Walker, to succeed in doing so.

By season's end, Moreno had rushed for 1,334 yards and 14 touchdowns. Most importantly, he was perhaps the primary reason for Georgia's second-half resurgence to finish its season as the second-ranked team in college football after a 4–2 start.

As a sophomore in 2008, Moreno surpassed his lofty numbers from the season before, rushing for 1,400 yards, gaining nearly 400 receiving, and scoring 18 touchdowns. Honored by the American Football Coaches Association, he became the first Georgia running back in 16 years (Garrison Hearst, 1992) to be named first-team All-America.

Moreno declared early for the 2009 NFL Draft and was selected 12th overall by the Denver Broncos. In just two seasons at Georgia, the Bulldogs great from the Garden State, who once appeared like he might hardly see the field of play, emerged as the school's fourth-leading all-time career rusher (2,734 yards) and touchdown scorer (32) of the modern era.

AARON MURRAY

During Aaron Murray's first two seasons at Georgia in 2010 and 2011, there were many commendable qualities exhibited by the Tampa, Florida, native. Perhaps, the most evident quality by the Bulldogs quarterback was a fighting mentality.

There's not much more Georgia fans appreciate than a quarterback with a tough-as-nails approach to the game. Murray demonstrated this quality in the middle of his senior season in high school, when he broke his left leg while quarterbacking Plant High. Rightfully anxious at first, the highly touted recruit soon developed a relentless plan to return to the field by the state championship game that year. Less than two months after the injury, Murray's miraculous return culminated with victories in both the semifinals and finals of the state playoffs.

Murray decided to attend UGA over, among other schools, the University of Florida, primarily because the Bulldogs coaching staff was "all about getting to know me," according to the Georgia quarterback. (To his credit, it's certainly not surprising if then–Gators head coach Urban Meyer, who evidently had one foot out the door, was not willing to be personable with recruits.)

Entering the 2010 season, Georgia returned 10 of 11 starters on offense from the year before with only the starting quarterback not returning. Murray, a redshirt freshman, was given the starting nod for the first game of the year, becoming only the fourth Bulldogs freshman signal-caller since World War II to start a season-opening contest. As it turned out, Murray would be one of the few bright spots for Georgia as the one-time "question mark" had one of the greatest seasons ever by a Bull-dogs quarterback.

Even today, Georgia fans cringe at the thought of how much worse a 6–7 year in 2010 would have been without Murray under center.

The following year, the fans experienced the best of both worlds as again Murray put up gaudy numbers, but this time, the team as a whole succeeded, as well. The highlight of a 10-win and SEC East championship season may have been Georgia's 24–20 victory over Florida. The victory in Jackson-ville was especially satisfying for Murray, who, despite passing for 313 yards and three touchdowns in his initial return to his native state, had thrown three interceptions in an overtime loss to Florida in 2010.

While at home during that off-season, Murray endured friendly teasing from the Gators faithful—"You're Gator Bait and this-and-that," said Murray.

In the win over Florida in 2011, Georgia trailed 17–3 late in the second quarter before Murray passed for two touchdowns to tightly covered receivers, both coming on fourth-down plays. In leading the Bulldogs to only their fourth win over the Gators in the series' previous 22 meetings, Murray etched his name in Georgia-Florida lore while saving the same tiresome "Gator Bait" ridicule for at least another season.

"We just kept fighting," Murray said following Georgia's four-point win over Florida. "That's something we've done all year—keep fighting, fighting."

GEORGIA

HOW MURRAY MEASURES UP

The single-game and single-season school records Aaron Murray broke or tied during the 2010 and 2011 seasons are numerous. In the interest of space, here are a handful of Georgia *career* records entering 2012, most of which are within Murray's reach after quarterbacking the Bulldogs for only two seasons.

Here's to our revered quarterback, and the hope he sticks around for an entire four-season tenure to shatter even more records!

Rank	Category	Murray thru 2011	Needed to Break Record*
1st	Passing Efficiency	150.11	—
1st	Completion Percentage	60.0	—
3rd	Touchdown Responsibility	65	13
3rd	Passing Touchdowns	59	14
5th	Total Offensive Yards	6,468	4,803
5th	Pass Completions	447	403
6th	Passing Yards	6,198	5,331
11th	Wins by a Starting QB	16	27
16th	Rushing Yards by a QB	270	1,530

*For all but one of the records above—"Rushing Yards by a QB"— David Greene (2001–2004) is the current school record holder. Andy Johnson (1971–1973) is Georgia's current record holder for career rushing yards by a quarterback.

3

TRADITIONS WE LOVE

WHEN A FOOTBALL PROGRAM has experienced tremendous success over 120 years of existence, like Georgia's, it conceivably will have amassed its fair share of traditions. The beloved Bulldogs have one of the richest traditions in all of college football, but their biggest and most cherished individual tradition is one that's rather simple to grasp—*winning*. Beyond that comes a host of others too numerous to list, so here are some favorites.

BULLDOGS

In the early years of UGA athletics, although often referred to as the "Red and Black," the university's teams were without an official nickname. After adopting "Wildcats" to start its 1920 football campaign, Georgia was first introduced as the "Bulldogs" during the middle of that season by Atlanta sportswriters, or so the story goes. For years, Morgan Blake and Cliff Wheatley were credited with labeling the University of Georgia as the "Bulldogs" in 1920.

Actually, the football program was first associated with the current nickname as far back as 1901, when fans arrived in Atlanta for a game against Auburn with badges featuring a bulldog and the phrase, "Eat 'em, Georgia." Three years later, Athens photographer Frederick J. Ball was said to be the first to propose that the bulldog be the university's mascot. According to newspaper reports during 1911 and 1912, the baseball squad apparently became the first team at the school to actually be referred to by the press as "Bulldogs."

As far as the football squad, the nickname was evidently first used prior to the 1916 Georgia Tech game when a correspondent of the *Atlanta Constitution* stated that "the Georgia Bulldogs will face the Tech Yellow Jackets for the supreme contest of the season."

En route by train for a game in Charlottesville, Virginia, in 1920, a group of football players, coaches, and athletics director Dr. S.V. Sanford officially decided that "Bulldogs" would be the team's nickname, and the moniker has remained ever since.

Uga

(And please pronounce it correctly—*UH-guh*. We're often shocked how some folks have such a difficult time pronouncing such a simple name.)

For the school's inaugural football season of 1892, Georgia's first mascot was a goat named Sir William, while a bull terrier named "Trilby" followed a couple of years later. And although the nickname "Bulldogs" had been associated with the university since the early 1900s, a bulldog was not officially crowned mascot until just prior to kickoff of the 1938 Georgia Tech game, when "Count"—a "ferocious English bulldog" owned by Buck Elton of Atlanta—became the Georgia Bulldogs' first bulldog.

Over the next nearly 20 years, other English bulldog mascots followed, including Baldy, Mr. Angel, Butch, and Mike. Finally, in the home opener of the 1956 football season, the first "Uga" was unveiled at Sanford Stadium by owners Sonny and Cecelia Seiler, who actually had no intention of taking the dog to the game until persuaded by friends at a pregame party.

For more than 50 years until 2011, eight different Ugas served as the official mascot of the University of Georgia, while earning the distinction as one of the most acclaimed live mascots in all of sports. Wearing a spiked collar and normally a red jersey, Uga has his own student ID card, his own cheer— "Damn good dog"—access to an air-conditioned doghouse during games, has been featured in a number of magazines, and has even appeared in a couple of movies. Each mascot is a descendent of the original Uga I, and when the time comes to ascend into Bulldog heaven, each is buried within the confines of Sanford Stadium.

Uga is known to be outgoing, friendly, loving to children, and a true lap dog. "He certainly isn't a watchdog," Cecilia Seiler said of Uga II during the early 1970s. "Our house has been robbed twice, and both times Uga has been there."

However, one should never threaten Uga. Just ask Auburn's Robert Baker, who sauntered up to Uga V in 1996 and a chunk was nearly removed from the Tigers wide receiver.

Over the years, there have been a handful of second-stringers filling in for Uga when called upon. When Uga II became ill during the 1971 season, a brown-and-white replacement named "Bugga Lou" was quietly pressed into service for a 49–7

The original Uga (center, with collar), became the Georgia Bulldogs mascot in 1956. Here he gets a hug from booster Sheri Lyn Stewart on October 25, 1966, in Athens during his 11ᵗʰ and final season.

whipping over Florida. Despite the new mascot's brown color, hardly anyone noticed the change, including a local newspaper, which displayed a photo of the backup with the heading, "He's Uga, and He Spurred Bulldogs to a Win!"

Recently, filling in admirably for both Uga VII and VIII, replacement "Russ" was the interim mascot for the majority of the football team's games from 2009 through 2011. As of this book's deadline, the Bulldog Nation was hopeful for an unveiling in 2012 for the next beloved bulldog mascot—Uga IX.

LARRY MUNSON

Unless one has been part of the Bulldog Nation, it might be difficult to comprehend how a radio play-by-play man could be so admired by a particular fan base. If you don't understand, unlike many of us Dawgs fans, then you must have not had the pleasure of growing up listening to the legendary Larry Munson.

We are often reminded that Munson was on the radio for nearly two decades prior to becoming the "Voice of the Bulldogs." During that time, his radio duties included calling Wyoming football games, Vanderbilt football and basketball, and minor league baseball. He also worked as a disc jockey and hosted a fishing and hunting show.

The 1966 season was Munson's first at Georgia and the beginning of a voice that would be endeared by generations of Bulldogs followers. For the next 42 years, or until 2008, we listened to Munson while sitting in Sanford Stadium, including those who normally didn't wear headphones, and as we watched the Bulldogs on television—the only time we'd ever turn down the TV and listen to the radio at the same time. We were absolutely captivated by his dramatic delivery and an unabashed partisanship for the Bulldogs that Munson himself described as his "will to win."

Another Bulldogs legend, Herschel Walker, was asked what he first thought of when he heard the name *Larry Munson*: "That voice…[Munson] brings things to life like they're right there, and that takes a special talent."

Over the years, that voice had some of us actually believing that the Gator Bowl was rocking, "The girders are bending now," that there really was "Sugar falling out of the sky" at Auburn, and that the Bulldogs stepped on Tennessee's face with a hobnail boot *"and broke their nose! We just crushed their face,"* to name only a few among many others. These calls, some of which are decades old and have been heard countless times, still leave us with goose bumps, and even brings some to tears.

Besides having a stentorian voice, Munson was probably, more simply, one of us—a die-hard Georgia fan who backed his Bulldogs like few others. When the Jacksonville police force got a little out of hand with some of our fans following Georgia's upset win over Florida in 1985 (see chapter 7, "We Love the World's Largest Outdoor Cocktail Party"), Munson made it a point to interject over the airwaves, "[The cops] are kicking those fans! I can't believe it! Those people are just lying on the ground, and they're kicking them!"

As indicated, the man certainly had a flair for the dramatic and was a Bulldog through and through.

At 89 years of age and only three years removed from calling Georgia Bulldogs games, Larry Munson recently passed away on November 20, 2011. Although he will never be forgotten, Munson is certainly and dearly missed by many. We can just hear Munson right now, in a much better place, sitting in a broadcast booth that is absolute heaven, announcing to the masses to lend him an ear to "Get the picture." R.I.P., Larry.

BETWEEN THE HEDGES

Charles E. Martin, the one-time business manager for UGA's athletics department, had initially wanted to plant rose hedges around Sanford Stadium's field for the venue's opening in 1929 after first observing them at the Rose Bowl in Pasadena a few years before. However, when university horticulturalists indicated roses would not thrive in the Athens climate, Martin settled on privet hedges instead. Martin had no idea his compromise, accompanied by its distinguished catchphrase, would eventually become one of the most renowned traditions in southern college football.

TOP 5 LARRY MUNSON CALLS AGAINST THE GATORS

Appleby to Washington (1975)
Matt Robinson fakes, end-around to Appleby. Appleby's gonna throw a bomb! He's got a man open down on the far side! Complete! A touchdown!... Appleby to Washington. Eighty yards! Appleby! End-around! Just stopped, planted his feet and threw it! Washington, caught it, thinking of Montreal and the Olympics, and ran out of his shoes right down the middle. Eighty yards!

Ray Goff Rallies Dogs (1976)
The Gators had us down and out 27–13, but in this Gator Bowl where we broke their hearts last year, our guys ran behind that big quarterback from Moultrie and came back to win it 41–27.

Run, Lindsay, Run (1980)
Buck back, third down on the 8. In trouble. Got a block behind him. Gonna throw on the run. Complete to the 25! To the 30! Lindsay Scott! Thirty-five, 40! Lindsay Scott! Forty-five, 50! Forty-five, 40!

The original hedges were a far cry from the size they are today. For the stadium's inaugural game—a 15–0 victory over Yale on October 12, 1929—the hedges stood only one foot high. Ralph McGill of the *Atlanta Constitution* later recalled "slipping through the newly planted hedges at the new stadium that day—with just 30 seconds left to play—and whispering congratulations to [head coach] Harry Mehre."

With a current size of approximately 5′ tall by 5′ wide, there is no "slipping through" today's hedges. Although, whether a streaker or two from graduation ceremonies, students trying to

Run, Lindsay! Twenty-five, 20, 15, 10, five! Lindsay Scott! Lindsay Scott! Lindsay Scott!... I can't believe it. I broke my chair. A metal, steel chair with about a five-inch cushion. Well, the stadium fell down!... I didn't mean to beg Lindsay to run, but I had to.

Toss Sweep to Edwards (1997)
Dawgs up to the line, still more than six minutes. Toss sweep to Edwards, no blocking, but he got to the corner anyway. And he's goin' down to the corner over the 20, the 15, the 10, the 5, and he's down in the corner. TOUCHDOWN! He stayed in bounds, he tight-roped it. A sudden pitch to Edwards, who stayed inches inside, and Edwards just went 37 yards.... Edwards just went 37 yards and it's 30 to 17!

Don't Give Up! (2004)
We are back on the 15-yard line, third down. Gators in a 5, we're in an I. Fake, and he fires right down the middle! TOUCHDOWN! TOUCHDOWN! TOUCHDOWN! Fred Gibson caught a ball running right to left. Greene hit 'em, Greene hit 'em with a 15-yarder. He was barely in bounds on that back sideline—on that back line. 30–21! Don't give up!

G E O R G I A

get on the field to tear down the stadium's goal posts, or tight end Aaron White getting stuck after catching a touchdown pass against New Mexico State in 2011, a number of individuals have attempted to pass through Sanford's sacred hedges.

Not long after the hedges were unveiled, the saying "Between the Hedges" was introduced supposedly by Grantland Rice. The celebrated sportswriter is credited with the phrase by once declaring "that the Bulldogs will have their opponent between the hedges." Rice apparently made the expression some time during the 1930s, but not until the 1960s was it widely used by Georgia fans.

SILVER BRITCHES

When Wally Butts became head football coach at Georgia in 1939, he donned the Bulldogs in silver britches for the first time, beginning a tradition that has continued to this day.

During World War II, the striking pants evoked the popular battle cry of "Go, You Silver Britches," lasting through the Butts and successor Johnny Griffith eras until 1964. With the arrival of Vince Dooley that season at Georgia, the new head coach wanted to change the team's image—one that had suffered through three consecutive losing years—and that included the Bulldogs' uniform. The silver britches were suddenly transformed to white.

Sixteen years later, Dooley decided to reintroduce the silver pants for what would be fittingly Georgia's national championship season of 1980, and they have been sported by the Bulldogs ever since.

Since the silver britches were reinstituted by Dooley, the Bulldogs' preference in pants has been tinkered with at times. On several occasions from 1978 to 1988, Georgia wore red britches with its white jerseys for road games. Admirably, head coach Jim Donnan reintroduced white pants in 1999 for a few games after a 20-year hiatus in memory of deceased assistant coach Pat Watson. However, against Florida the year before, Donnan had tried to get cute and dressed the Bulldogs in a red top/black pants combination for the first time in school history. The end result was a 38–7 blowout loss to the Gators.

In 2009 Coach Mark Richt's Bulldogs not only decided not to wear the customary silver britches in Jacksonville, but dressed in a black helmet/black pants, Grambling State–like alternative uniform that most Georgia fans would soon like to forget. In a performance against Florida nearly as forgettable, the Bulldogs were hammered 41–17.

Accepted by most Bulldogs backers, Georgia's silver-less snafus against Florida in 1998 and 2009 just go to show that some traditions should never be changed. Don't mess with a good thing.

REDCOAT BAND

During halftime, a distinguished introduction can always be heard over Sanford Stadium's loudspeakers that every Bulldogs fan is accustomed to: "Keep your seats, everyone…the Redcoats are coming!" Considered by many to be the "heart" of the Bulldog Nation, the University of Georgia Redcoat Band has captivated audiences around the Southland and as far reaching as China in its more than 100 years of existence.

Established in 1905 as a section of the UGA Military Department, the university's first marching band was comprised of 20 military cadets. A year later, the band made its first non-military performance at, of all places, a Georgia baseball game against Clemson.

In the 1950s the "Georgia Marching Band" was transformed into the celebrated group that we know of today—the Redcoat Band. During that time, it had grown tremendously in size since its days as a military band, including the addition of dancers and, later, a flag line.

During the 1960s and 1970s, the Redcoats performed some of the most elaborate shows in marching-band history. At halftime of the 1978 Georgia-Vanderbilt game, the band performed its "Wedding Show," where a couple actually got married in a three-minute ceremony. A few years before, James Brown, the "Godfather of Soul," performed his song "Dooley's Junkyard Dogs" with the Redcoats for several shows over the course of a couple of football seasons, including a performance at the 1977 Georgia-Florida game that the site of the old Gator Bowl still has not forgotten.

In 2000 the 400-member band was the first from the Southeastern Conference to receive the prestigious Sudler Award for the "close historical relationship and outstanding contribution of intercollegiate Marching Bands to the American way of life." In 2005, during its 100th anniversary, the Redcoats became the first marching band ever to tour the country of China.

THE CHAPEL BELL

Located in the heart of UGA's Old North Campus, the Chapel Bell has been ringing following Bulldogs victories for more than 100 years. Ironically, the tradition began in 1901 after a Georgia football "moral victory" of sorts—a 0–0 tie against a heavily favored Auburn team. For more than 50 years, only university freshmen were supposed to ring the bell, and ordered to do so until at least midnight on each occasion.

The first significant damage to the Chapel Bell resulted in 1911, when it was cracked during a celebratory ringing. Roughly a decade later, jubilant students cracked the bell for a second time. Following the Bulldogs' victory over Notre Dame in the 1981 Sugar Bowl to capture the national championship, fans broke the rope on the bell. Finally, after Georgia's upset win over Florida in 2007, it was rung so hard by an enthusiastic crowd, the bell sprung from its moorings. The 173-year-old Chapel Bell was soon taken down for repairs, but would be housed in a new tower in time for the start of the 2008 football season.

Today, if one doesn't mind standing in line after another Georgia victory, anyone and all are welcomed to ring the Chapel Bell. And even Gators are gladly received in partaking in this longtime tradition of the Bulldogs.

4
COACHES WE LOVE

THE BEGINNINGS OF FOOTBALL at the University of Georgia, as for many southern schools, was an absolute revolving door of coaches. Most of the Red and Black's first dozen or so head coaches were young men from the North, not too far removed from their college days, who desired some coaching experience first in the South before returning home for a more prominent position.

In the first 18 seasons of football at Georgia (1892–1909), the program had 14 different head coaches and none for more than two years.

We often have to remind college football enthusiasts that perhaps the sport's greatest coach of all time got his start at Georgia. Even before the Florida Agricultural and Mechanical College in Lake City knew what football was, our university had landed 24-year-old Glenn "Pop" Warner from Cornell in 1895. In earning $34 per week for a 10-week contract, Coach Warner was so impressive in his initial season, he was granted a $6-per-week raise in his second year at the school.

In 1896 Warner guided Georgia to a 4–0 season; however, the perfect campaign was somewhat bittersweet for the Red and

Black. Within a month of the final game, Warner left Athens to return to Cornell for his next stop in an acclaimed coaching career that eventually totaled 44 seasons and 319 victories.

Of course, admired by the Bulldog Nation is the Georgia coach—if you'd call him that—to first defeat the hated University of Florida. Charles Barnard, who had been an All-America guard at Harvard, arrived at the university in 1904 to coach the football team. It was said that Barnard, weighing a strapping 200 pounds, was a better athlete than any of his own players and could out-sprint everyone on the squad except speedy halfback Harry Woodruff.

Nevertheless, what Barnard possessed in athleticism, he apparently lacked in coaching. During the season, players often complained the coach did not correct their mistakes and rarely gave instruction. Even with a head coach who reportedly cared more about playing cards with his players than their performances on the field, the Red and Black devastated Florida 52–0.

Before he could be run out of Athens, Barnard beat Georgia to the punch soon after the season ended, leaving for Washington, D.C., to become the head coach at George Washington University in 1905. There, he lasted for only a single season, which happened to result in a second straight losing year for "Coach" Barnard.

A decade later, in 1915, Florida had what it wrongly considers its first meeting with a Georgia football coach. Either way, that particular Red and Black head coach—Alex Cunningham—defeated the Gators, as well, and like Barnard before him, had an easy time doing so in a 37–0 decision.

Cunningham probably doesn't get the credit he deserves as one of the best head coaches in the history of the school. The innovative Vanderbilt alum implemented preseason practices starting a full two weeks prior to any other Georgia team. Once the games began, his frequent substitution of players was like few had ever seen in football at the time, especially in the South.

Before Cunningham's arrival in 1910, Georgia had achieved just seven winning seasons in its first 18 years of football. During the coach's eight-season tenure through 1919, the Red and Black had a winning campaign in every year except one.

In addition, when Cunningham left the university, it wasn't to venture north for a better coaching job like those before him. Instead, his departure was in order to serve his country in World War I, where he would eventually reach the rank of general in the U.S. Army.

The next head coach with any sort of extended stay at Georgia was Harry Mehre. From 1928 through 1937, the one-time pupil of Knute Rockne enjoyed eight winning seasons in 10 years, had a few near-misses of capturing a conference championship, and lost to Florida just three times in 10 games. Nonetheless, it had been nearly 20 years since the Bulldogs' last conference title of 1920 (and most teams were beating the Gators at the time, so that mattered little), so Mehre was forced to resign after a decade at the school.

To compete annually for a championship in the newly formed Southeastern Conference, Georgia was willing to force the resignation of a head coach who had been so successful, the school would eventually name a building on campus after him.

Some of us older Bulldogs might have found this treatment to be somewhat harsh; however, we realize Georgia eventually found the right man—a "Little Round Man"—for the job, and a more than acceptable replacement.

The football championships for Georgia would come soon thereafter, while having the upper hand over Florida would only continue.

WALLY BUTTS

After a successful 10-year coaching career on the high school level in the states of Georgia and Kentucky, Wally Butts became an assistant for the Bulldogs in 1938 under new head coach Joel Hunt. Hunt's tenure at Georgia lasted only a single season, but Butts had been such a standout assistant, and he was named his old boss' successor.

Butts, nicknamed "the Little Round Man" for his squatty stature, was personable, an excellent recruiter, and an innovator of offensive football. If you thought Steve Spurrier's "fun 'n' gun" offense at Florida took the SEC by surprise in the early 1990s, it didn't quite compare to how Butts' offensive attack took the conference by storm during the 1940s.

During the era of the three-yards-and-a-cloud-of-dust offense, Butts instructed his boys to throw the football all over the field and often. Notre Dame coaching legend Frank Leahy called Butts "football's finest passing coach," and for good reason. From 1940 to 1953, using players predominantly from distant areas like Ohio and Pennsylvania, Butts' offense ranked in the nation's top 10 in passing in 10 of 14 seasons.

With the innovative offense came success as Georgia played in its first bowl game—the 1942 Orange Bowl—in just Butts' third season. In the following season of 1942, the Bulldogs won their first SEC title and captured a consensus national championship, while halfback Frank Sinkwich was the recipient of the Heisman Trophy. Four years later, in 1946, Georgia was SEC champion yet again while finishing its season with a perfect record (11–0) for the first time since Coach "Pop" Warner's team 50 years before in 1896.

In 1948 Butts won another conference title—his third in only a seven-season span. The coach's success from 1941 to 1948, when the Bulldogs won nearly 80 percent of their games in eight seasons, was matched by few programs during that time and is one of the winningest eras in Georgia football history.

Admittedly, Butts and his Bulldogs endured some trying times in the last half of the coach's regime. From 1949 through the coach's final season of 1960, Georgia suffered six losing seasons and made only two bowl trips. However, in the midst of this 12-year period of mediocrity was what we call Butts' "diamond in the rough" campaign—the 1959 SEC title season.

Butts' next-to-last Georgia squad was forecast to do no better than the subpar Bulldogs teams before it. Nevertheless, quarterbacked by Fran Tarkenton, Georgia achieved a 10–1 record, presented the coach with his fourth conference championship, finished No. 5 in the nation, and defeated Missouri in the Orange Bowl.

In 22 seasons, from 1939 through 1960, Butts had a 140–86–9 overall record, including 5–2–1 in bowl games. Specifically, against the Gators, he was 12–9, including winning seven in a row from 1941 to 1948, when the Bulldogs' average winning margin was by nearly 30 points.

VINCE DOOLEY

Vince Dooley's success against the Gators and in the city of Jacksonville began more than a decade before his arrival at Georgia. As a senior quarterback and captain at Auburn in 1953, he led the Tigers to a memorable 16–7 win over Florida. Two months later, and playing in his final collegiate game, Dooley led Auburn in rushing and passing and was named the team's MVP for his performance against Texas Tech in the Gator Bowl.

From 1956 to 1963, Dooley was an assistant at Auburn (6–2 against the Gators), including the Tigers' head freshman coach his final three years. In December of 1963, much to everyone's astonishment, 31-year-old Dooley was named head football coach at the University of Georgia. He had been hand-picked for the job by athletics director Joel Eaves. Eaves had just arrived in Athens only a week and a half earlier after serving as Auburn's head basketball coach and, like Dooley, an assistant on the football team.

Evidently, Eaves knew of something in Dooley few others were aware of as most of the Bulldogs faithful wondered, "Vince who?" regarding the inexperienced and unknown new head football coach.

Coach Dooley first gained appreciation when he took the 1964 Bulldogs—a group that was forecast to be as dismal as the

Georgia head coach Vince Dooley is carried off the field by his team after their 24–9 victory in the Cotton Bowl over SMU in Dallas, Texas, on December 31, 1966. Dooley coached the Bulldogs to 201 victories over 25 years, 1964 to 1988.

proceeding three- and four-win Georgia teams from 1961 to 1963—and led them to a 7–3–1 record and a victory in the Sun Bowl. Notably, in the 15 previous seasons prior to Dooley's initial campaign, Georgia had achieved just five winning years and two trips to bowl games.

In 1966 Dooley won his first SEC championship and just two years later finished the 1968 regular season undefeated and captured his second conference title in just five seasons at Georgia.

The decade of the 1970s might have been a little turbulent, but the period did include a third SEC championship in 1976, several near-misses at a title, six bowl games (back when appearing in a bowl was nothing to sneeze at) and, better yet, a 7–3 record versus Florida. The decade might be primarily recognized, however, as the buildup to the greatest era in the history of Georgia football—the early 1980s.

In 1980 Dooley guided the Bulldogs to a perfect 12–0 record and the school's first undisputed national championship. In 1982 Georgia captured its third consecutive SEC title— Dooley's sixth in a 17-season span—and played for another national championship.

In 1983 opposing fans, especially Gators fans, predicted Georgia would accomplish little without the benefit of having Herschel Walker, who had just departed the team after three extraordinary seasons from 1980 to 1982. All the Herschel-less Bulldogs achieved was a No. 4 national ranking to go along with a 10–1–1 overall record. Included was a sweet 10–9 win over Florida, and less than two months later, a victory over Texas in the Cotton Bowl by the same exact score, robbing the Longhorns of a national title.

For all of his admirable coaching attributes, arguably, the greatest—and one Dooley would admit himself—was his ability to surround himself with a tremendous supporting staff. Together, Dooley and his Bulldogs won 201 games over 25 seasons from 1964 to 1988, appeared in 20 bowl games, and experienced just one losing year. In addition, perhaps there has been no other college football head coach more triumphant in the city of Jacksonville than Dooley, who had

COACHING RECORDS *IN THE* GEORGIA-FLORIDA RIVALRY

	Seasons	*Games*	*Record*
Georgia			
Charles Barnard	1904	1	1–0
Alex Cunningham	1910–1919	3	3–0
Herman Stegeman	1920–1922	1	1–0
George Woodruff	1923–1927	2	2–0
Harry Mehre	1928–1937	10	6–3–1
Joel Hunt	1938	1	1–0
Wally Butts	1939–1960	21	12–9
Johnny Griffith	1961–1963	3	0–3
Vince Dooley	1964–1988	25	17–7–1
Ray Goff	1989–1995	7	1–6
Jim Donnan	1996–2000	5	1–4
Mark Richt	2001–2011	11	3–8
Florida			
M.O. Bridges	1904	1	0–1

a 19–7–1 record in the River City: 17–7–1 against the Gators and 2–0 in Gator Bowls.

ERK RUSSELL

The absolute best of Coach Vince Dooley's aforementioned supporting staff was Erk Russell—Georgia's defensive coordinator from 1964 through 1980. Russell was not your run-of-the-mill assistant coach and is held in high regard by Bulldogs fans, still today, since his departure from the school more than 30 years ago and his passing in 2006.

Charles McCoy	1914–1916	2	0–2
Al Buser	1917–1919	1	0–1
William Kline	1920–1922	1	0–1
Tom Sebring	1925–1927	2	0–2
Charles Bachman	1928–1932	5	2–2–1
D.K. Stanley	1933–1935	3	0–3
Josh Cody	1936–1939	4	1–3
Thomas Lieb	1940–1945	5	1–4
Raymond Wolf	1946–1949	4	1–3
Bob Woodruff	1950–1959	10	6–4
Ray Graves	1960–1969	10	6–3–1
Doug Dickey	1970–1978	9	3–6
Charley Pell	1979–1983	5	0–5
Galen Hall	1984–1988	5	2–3
Gary Darnell	1989	1	0–1
Steve Spurrier	1990–2001	12	11–1
Ron Zook	2002–2004	3	2–1
Urban Meyer	2005–2010	6	5–1
Will Muschamp	2011	1	0–1

GEORGIA

Just four years after graduating from Auburn, where he remains the university's last four-sport letterman, Russell guided Grady High School (Atlanta) as its head football coach to a Georgia state championship in 1953. He was later an assistant with Dooley at Auburn from 1958 to 1962 and would eventually follow him to Athens for the start of the head coach's tenure at the University of Georgia in 1964.

In 17 seasons and 192 games at Georgia, Russell's defensive units allowed a paltry 13.9 points per contest, while yielding roughly the same average (13.8) in 17 games against Florida.

Perhaps no assistant in the history of college football was known for being as much as a motivator and communicator with his players than Russell. His distinct shaven bald head would often be bleeding during games since he frequently rammed it into his players' helmets during pregame drills for motivational purposes.

After Georgia upset Florida in 1964, Russell was so overwhelmed with emotion that he jumped up on a table and led a bedlam-filled Gator Bowl locker room to a repeated cheer of "DAMN GOOD TEAM!" Russell once noticed a Georgia Tech student trainer with a sweatshirt reading "G.T.A.A."—Georgia Tech Athletic Association. The defensive coordinator swapped the two middle letters and came up with a celebrated slogan for his own team—"G.A.T.A."—Get After Their Asses. Russell also devised the Bulldogs' big "TEAM," little "me" T-shirt, declaring that the individual player was always less significant than the entire team. Later on, he also created the rallying cry of "Tuck Yech," and, well, you can probably figure that expression out on your own.

ERK RUSSELL QUOTES WE LOVE

"You're good enough to play for me and you're good enough to win." —addressing his first defensive unit at Georgia in preseason practice of 1964

"There isn't anything meaner than a junkyard dog. They aren't good for nothing except for being mean and ornery. That's what we want our defense to be." —summer practice of 1975

"[The Junkyard Dogs] have to be in the proper frame of mind for this one. We call it intelligent fanaticism, with a little more emphasis on the fanaticism." —prior to the 1975 Florida game

"If we score, we may win. If they never score, we'll never lose."

"THERE AIN'T NOTHING LIKE BEING A BULLDOG ON A SATURDAY NIGHT—— AFTER WINNING A FOOTBALL GAME. I mean like whipping Tennessee's ass to start with, then 10 more and then another one." —in a July 7, 1980, letter addressed to "Gentlemen (and Linemen)"

"I looked down and there was a dime on the ground. I picked it up, put it in my left shoe.... We beat Clemson that day.... I taped the dime in my shoe so I wouldn't lose it, and made sure that I wore it throughout the season. We were 12–0 and won the national championship, and I'm sure the dime did it."

"At Georgia Southern, we don't cheat. That costs money and we don't have any."

"The best way to win a game is not to lose it."

Our favorite inspirational tactic of Russell's was his creation of the Junkyard Dogs defense of 1975. Georgia's defensive unit had lost nine of 11 starters from 1974, including two All-SEC performers, and was also switching to an unfamiliar split-60 formation. As fall practice began just three weeks prior to the season opener, seven of Georgia's starting defensive positions were unsettled.

Because of the defense's new faces and formation, Russell felt the unit needed a nickname. For what the defense lacked in experience and raw ability, it more than made up for it with intensity and an aggressive style of play demonstrated during fall drills. Plus, as Erk stated, "there isn't anything meaner than a junkyard dog," and a moniker was formed.

According to Russell, the 1975 defense "had three walk-ons, four [former] quarterbacks, and three running backs in our original Junkyard Dog starting cast, which averaged 208 pounds across the front." Regardless, by the end of a surprising 9–2 regular season for Georgia, its no-name defense had yielded just 15 points and 307 yards per game while proving that it's not always how quick the feet and size of the body that counts the most, but rather how quick the mind and size of the heart.

After Georgia won its national championship in 1980, Russell left the school and ventured to Statesboro, Georgia, for the challenge of restarting the Georgia Southern College football program, which had been dormant for 40 years. Remarkably, by the program's fourth season of 1985, head coach Russell had already won his first of what would eventually be three Division I-AA national titles.

After capturing his third national championship as head coach of the Eagles in 1989, Russell retired from coaching with an 83–22–1 overall record in eight seasons at Georgia Southern.

RAY GOFF

Oh, you can just hear the Gators now (if there just happens to be one reading this book), snickering that Ray Goff (or "Goof," as some prefer) is one of the selected coaches we cherish. Florida will point to Steve Spurrier's tremendous success against Goff-coached teams, when the Gators won by more than a 24-point margin over six seasons from 1990 through 1995, all the while the Ol' Ball Coach took verbal jabs at our beloved Bulldogs and Goff.

Notwithstanding, even a Gator must admit that Goff was probably a little in over his head when handed the head coaching position in 1989. He was a fine position coach and an effective recruiter, but not ready to coach big-time SEC football. For those Florida fans who can't quite understand, Goff's hire was the equivalent to when "the Zooker" took the reins of your football team beginning in 2002. Now, perhaps you get it...

Nevertheless, Goff did accomplish something in Jacksonville successors Jim Donnan and Mark Richt were not able to— defeat the Filthy Swamp Lizards on his first attempt. In 1989 Goff's unranked Bulldogs upset 20th-ranked Florida 17–10. The victory placed the first-year head coach in the Peach Bowl (while the Gators, might we add, would soon be placed on yet another probation).

More than for his coaching, the highly likable Goff remains appreciated by the Bulldog Nation because of his love for Georgia and his strong faith. In addition, while a player for the Bulldogs (1974–1976), Goff was one of the game's best veer quarterbacks during his era. Never were these attributes more evident than in Georgia's come-from-behind victory over Florida in 1976.

Goff, a senior who was on his way to a seventh-place finish in the Heisman Trophy voting, found himself trailing the Gators by two touchdowns at halftime. Running Georgia's veer formation to perfection, the senior quarterback rallied the Bulldogs to four second-half touchdowns in a 41–27 victory.

For the game, Goff rushed for 124 yards, completed all five of his passes, and was responsible for five of the team's six touchdowns in earning ABC-TV's Chevrolet Offensive Player of the Game.

As the contest's final seconds were ticking off, ABC sideline reporter Jim Lampley told Goff about his recognition. The quarterback thanked Lampley but thought a fallen teammate, who had died just prior to the start of the season from a rare blood infection, was more deserving.

"I'd like to give [the honor] to Hugh Hendrix and put it in his name," said Goff. "He inspired us all…. Praise the Lord."

WILL MUSCHAMP

We're sure you are fully aware of the heartfelt story: after attending high school in Georgia, Will Muschamp walked on and made the Bulldogs team; however, being from Gainesville,

Muschamp initially wanted to play for the Gators but no one bothered to show up for a scheduled meeting with him at Florida when he wanted to walk on there (just like the Gators to be unreliable and thoughtless). But, in being named Florida's head football coach in 2011, Muschamp eventually found his way back to the school he originally fell in love with.

Regardless, Muschamp was initially a Bulldog, and we love him for it. He was an energetic player who went from a walk-on in 1990 to an eventual starting strong safety, recording 84 tackles, five passes broken up, and two interceptions as a senior.

The reality that nearly all of Muschamp's playing time as a Bulldog came on two of the most lowly Georgia defenses in recent memory—1993 and 1994—is forgivable. The fact that he would later roam the sideline of the hated Gators is, well, only time will tell.

Although coaching the enemy, Muschamp earned some respect from us Bulldogs when he booted Janoris Jenkins off the Florida team following the cornerback's third arrest during the spring of the coach's first year. We could tell then there was a new sheriff in Gator Town totally unlike the one of the previous regime. The ex-Florida player put it best just over three months after getting run out of Gainesville by the new head coach:

"No doubt, if Coach [Urban] Meyer were still coaching, I'd still be playing for the Gators," said Jenkins. "Coach Meyer knows what it takes to win."

During the 2011 campaign, unlike his predecessor, Muschamp did indeed have a hard time winning as the Gators endured their first non-winning regular season in more than 30 years. In his first Georgia-Florida game as a Gator, the ex-Bulldog gave every bit the impression of an overmatched, first-year head coach. In Georgia's 24–20 victory, Muschamp became the only one of Florida's last five full-time head coaches since 1989 to lose to the Bulldogs in his first season at the school.

We confess, if Muschamp had instead defeated Georgia in 2011, it would have been difficult putting him in this section. However, as long as he keeps removing riff raff from the Florida team, and losing to his alma mater, here he'll remain.

MARK RICHT

Before he became an able assistant at Florida State under Bobby Bowden and later Georgia's celebrated head coach, Mark Richt had played second fiddle at the University of Miami (Fla.). As a quarterback for the Hurricanes, the Boca Raton native was known more as the backup to Pro Football Hall of Famer Jim Kelly than anything else.

However, Richt did have his one shining moment in the Florida sun, coming against the Gators in Miami's season opener of 1981. The Hurricanes trailed 17th-ranked Florida 20–11 in the fourth quarter when Kelly was sidelined with a calf injury. In stepped Richt, who had attempted all of 39 passes the previous three seasons combined. In the final minutes, the reserve quarterback passed for a 55-yard touchdown and later led Miami to a last-second field goal in a 21–20 comeback victory in what would be the junior signal-caller's lone appearance against the Gators.

As a volunteer assistant, the quarterbacks coach, and eventually offensive coordinator at Florida State from 1987 through 2000, Richt was part of Seminoles teams that lost just four of 15 games versus Florida. However, upon his arrival at Georgia in 2001, the head coach's past success against the Gators as a player and assistant did not promptly resume.

In 2002 and 2003 Coach Richt's Bulldogs captured the SEC East, winning the conference championship in '02; however, despite being favored over the Gators, and perhaps more telling, facing Ron Zook–coached teams, Georgia was upset by Florida on both occasions.

The Bulldogs entered the 2004 Georgia-Florida game having lost six straight to the Gators and 13 of their last 14 meetings. Regardless, Richt finally got the Gator off his back with a 31–24 victory in Jacksonville, and the normally passive head coach was elated.

"I'm so happy for the players and the coaches and anybody who's ever wanted to succeed at Georgia," said Richt. "A lot of [Georgia] people have been through a lot of pain and suffering [in the rivalry], and they finally get to enjoy it."

The following season, despite a loss to Florida, Richt's Bulldogs captured their second SEC championship in four years, and for only the second time in the program's rich history, Georgia finished ranked in the nation's top 10 for a fourth consecutive campaign.

After winning 11 games and finishing ranked second in the country in 2007, Richt's teams experienced a slow, steady decline over the next three seasons. In 2008 the Bulldogs were preseason ranked No. 1 in the nation but lost three games, including to Alabama after trailing 31–0 at halftime, to Georgia Tech for the first time in eight years, and to Florida by a 39-point margin. The following year, Georgia lost a staggering five games and unthinkably experienced its first losing season in 14 years in 2010.

Suddenly, the head coach, who once was regarded as one of the best in college football was now known more for being on the "hot seat" than anything else entering 2011. Richt certainly didn't help his case by beginning his 11th campaign with the Bulldogs by dropping the first two games.

Entering the Florida game, Georgia had won five games in a row, but Richt found himself in what many perceived as a must-win situation against the Gators. Because of their failures

GEORGIA

LARGEST DEFICIT OVERCOME TO WIN GEORGIA-FLORIDA

14 points: Georgia (41), Florida (27) in 1976
Georgia trailed 27–13 in third quarter
14 points: Georgia (26), Florida (21) in 1981
Georgia trailed 14–0 in second quarter
14 points: Georgia (24), Florida (20) in 2011
Georgia trailed 17–3 in second quarter
13 points: Florida (19), Georgia (13) in 1955
Florida trailed 13–0 in third quarter
13 points: Florida (31), Georgia (19) in 1986
Florida trailed 16–3 in second quarter

in this rivalry, head coaches—namely, the two at Georgia prior to Richt, Ray Goff and Jim Donnan—had ultimately lost their jobs. Facing the same possible fate, the Bulldogs' head coach rallied his team from a 14-point deficit to defeat Florida for the third time in eight years.

By the end of the season, Georgia had won 10 games, captured the SEC East division crown for the first time since 2005, and for the first time in 30 years, had defeated rivals Tennessee, Auburn, and the loathed Gators in the same season.

Above all, Richt was no longer on the "hot seat," and for most of the Georgia faithful, that was absolutely ideal.

For other Bulldogs fans entering 2012, Richt's 16 combined losses from 2009 to 2011 are way too many to bear. In addition, some of us say our head coach is simply too nice of a guy, too loyal, his decision-making—both during games and the hiring/not firing of his assistants—has been called into question more than we care for, and he recently hasn't won many "big games."

Some of us in the Bulldog Nation need reminding of Richt's .736 overall winning percentage since he was hired; the two Bulldogs head coaches before him combined for a .618 over 12 years, and even the great Vince Dooley had a lower career winning percentage at .715. From 2001 to 2011, nine of Richt's 11 teams finished ranked in the final AP Poll; the second-best mark prior to Richt's arrival for the same stretch of time is seven of 11 by Dooley during the 1970s and 1980s. And from 2002 through 2011, Richt's Bulldogs played in four of 10 SEC

Championship Games; Georgia did not appear in a single one of the first 10 conference title games.

Frankly, some of us in the Bulldog Nation yearn for a new head coach. However, we may need reminding of where our program was for nearly two decades prior to Richt's arrival, while the grass may often *appear* greener on the other side.

HONORABLE MENTION: DOUG DICKEY

Why would a Florida head coach with no ties to Georgia whatsoever be included as one we love? Simply, Doug Dickey—the Gators' head man from 1970 to 1978—was the gift to all Bulldogs that kept giving, and giving…

Prior to his head coaching tenure in Gainesville, Dickey was actually a thorn in Georgia's side. As the Gators' senior quarterback, he was primarily responsible for an upset victory over the Bulldogs in 1953. In a 21–7 win, Dickey passed for a touchdown, rushed for another, and made a touchdown-saving tackle on defense. In six seasons as Tennessee's head football coach from 1964 to 1969, he was undefeated against Georgia in two games.

However, upon his return to his alma mater, Dickey would suffer a reversal of fortune against the Bulldogs, much of which was his own doing.

In four of the five games against Georgia from 1972 through 1976, three of which Florida entered favored to win, a questionable call or two by Dickey would ultimately cost his team a much-needed victory in Jacksonville. Here's a rundown of Dickey's "dumb" decisions against the Dawgs:

- **1972:** Leading 7–0 in the fourth quarter, possessing the ball, and approaching Georgia territory, Dickey calls for halfback Nat Moore to throw a pass. Moore's pass is intercepted, leading to a Bulldogs touchdown. Georgia eventually wins 10–7 on a late field goal.

- **1974:** Trailing 7–0 in the second quarter and backed up against his own goal line, Dickey substitutes inexperienced sophomore Jimmy Fisher in place of fleet-footed and standout quarterback Don Gaffney for what Dickey described as a "change of pace." Fisher slips in his own end zone while dropping back to pass, costing the Gators a safety. The two points ultimately are the difference in a 17–16 Georgia win.

- **1975:** Trailing 10–7 with nearly two minutes remaining in the game, Florida has a first down on Georgia's 21-yard line. Dickey, who has one of the top rushing offenses in the nation and has gained almost 250 yards rushing for the game, calls for three straight passing plays—all incompletions thrown by Gaffney. Then, on fourth down, the coach inexplicably calls upon his field-goal unit because, as Dickey would later explain, he believed a tie with Georgia would still give Florida a good chance to eventually win the SEC title (although that meant counting on a conference loss from Alabama, which had won 18 SEC games in a row). The Gators players were so taken off-guard by their head coach's decision, the place-kicker and snapper had not even warmed up for a field-goal attempt. Florida's field goal and its attempt at a tie hardly got off the ground, and the Bulldogs escaped with a three-point victory.

• **1976:** Dickey's most infamous call—"Fourth and Dumb," according to a newspaper the following day. Leading 27–20 midway through the third quarter, Dickey tries for a first down instead of punting when faced with a fourth down and less than a yard to go from his own 29-yard line. The fourth-down play was a run by fullback Earl Carr, who would later admit, "When I was running the play, I was asking myself why in the world we were running this play." Carr was stopped for a loss, and Dickey's errant decision totally swung the game's momentum in the favor of Georgia, who would score three unanswered touchdowns in an eventual 41–27 win.

To Dickey's credit, he eventually was inducted into the College Football Hall of Fame—only the third Florida coach to be so honored. He would also have a reputable career as the University of Tennessee's athletics director from 1985 to 2002, earning the National Football Foundation's John Toner Award for his abilities as an administrator.

For Georgia fans, it's just too bad Dickey couldn't stick around Gainesville as the Gators' head coach for a little longer, like into the 1990s.

5
STORIES WE LOVE

A WINNING TRIO

Like Florida, the University of Georgia has also neglected to include past football results from the early 1900s in its records. However, whereas the Gators' oversight is undoubtedly intentional (see "Florida's Forgotten" in chapter 5, "Stories We Hate," on the flipside of this book), the Bulldogs' omission appears to be merely an error in record-keeping.

Officially, Georgia faced Georgia Tech on November 10, 1906, and Tennessee 11 days later on November 21. However, research has found that an omitted game was played in between the two opponents—a 53–2 victory over Dahlonega on November 17.

There should be no argument against including the Dahlonega game in 1906 as being an official game. Georgia played the "Mountain Team" on six other occasions in its history—all official results—including during the season before and after (1905 and 1907) the game in question.

Perhaps a small argument could be made regarding two other discovered games, both of which are currently not in Georgia's records, but most likely should be included.

The Red and Black did not officially begin its 1908 season until October 10 against, ironically, Dahlonega. However, a closer look reveals that a week before, on October 3, Georgia defeated "the Olympians of Atlanta"—a team from an Atlanta athletic club—at UGA's Herty Field by a score of 29–5. Not much was reported on the game besides the Olympians being captained by Dan Sage—interestingly, Georgia's team captain three seasons earlier in 1905.

A year later, the Red and Black officially began its season against The Citadel on October 9, although further research indicates Georgia actually opened its campaign a week earlier on October 2. What was initially scheduled to be a game against, again, Dahlonega, was instead a meeting with the Olympians for a second consecutive year.

Although the Red and Black defeated the Olympians 5–0 in 1909, where Georgia halfback John Cox scored the contest's lone points on a touchdown run up the middle (touchdowns counted for five points then), reportedly, the star of the game was actually a player from the losing side—quarterback Frank Dobson of the athletic club team. The bizarre thing about Dobson was that not only had he been an assistant coach at Georgia Tech the season before in 1908, but by the end of the 1909 season, he was Georgia's head coach!

This might be the only instance in college football history of an individual playing against and coaching for the same school in the very same season.

One could argue that perhaps Georgia's two games with the Olympians were not considered official since they may have been thought of as exhibitions, especially since the opponent seemed to be some sort of club team instead of being associated with a particular college. Also, it appears the Olympians were made up of former and not current college athletes.

Nevertheless, we feel these two games should be acknowledged in the football annals of the University of Georgia. For one, not once in game reports are the meetings against the Olympians referred to as exhibitions or practice contests. More so, like many other schools, Georgia played "official" games in its early history many times against athletic clubs, teams made up of college all-stars or former football players, and "preparatory" schools, including Savannah AC (Athletic Club), Augusta AC, Atlanta AC, Daniel Field, Locust Grove, and Gordon.

Toward the end of the 1909 season, in several of its editions, the *Atlanta Constitution* printed game results for selected southern football teams of interest, including Georgia. Routinely listed as the Red and Black's first result that season was—you guessed it—a 5–0 victory over the "Olympians."

Evidently, back in 1909, Georgia's game against the Olympians was considered an official result. More than a century later, it should be designated accordingly.

In the early days of college football, mistakes were often made in the record-keeping of game results, dates, sites, etc. The aforementioned contests against Dahlonega and twice against the Olympians are yet three more examples of such errors, where Georgia deserves a few more victories than what is currently regarded as being official.

GEORGIA

STATS WE LOVE

Officially, Georgia has won 747 games in its football history to Florida's 669.

The Bulldogs have captured 14 conference championships (12 in the SEC) to the Gators' eight (all eight in the SEC).

Georgia has made 47 bowl appearances, winning 26 of them; Florida has played in 39 bowls, losing nearly half of them.

The Bulldogs hold a 48–40–2 series advantage over the Gators.

There have been four football seasons in Florida history where the Gators were ineligible for the conference title because of NCAA rules violations; Georgia has never had to stoop so low.

We love a story revealing that our Bulldogs actually have three more wins than they officially get credit for. After all, that means there are three more victories that can be added to Georgia's already decided advantage over the Gators in the teams' all-time victory total.

HERE'S JOHNNY...AND THE MIRACLES

After an 11–1 and national title season of 1942, the personnel demand for World War II decimated the Bulldogs the following year, taking 82 players from the Rose Bowl championship roster. Returning for the following season was just a single letterman—starting fullback Pearce Barrett.

In the final week of fall practice, Barrett was lost to injury, and six other players who were enrolled in the university's advanced ROTC program were declared ineligible by the U.S. Army. Two days before the season opener against Presbyterian

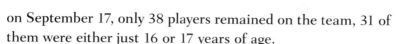

on September 17, only 38 players remained on the team, 31 of them were either just 16 or 17 years of age.

That season, eight of the 12 SEC teams decided to put football on hold for a season or so, including the daunted Florida Gators, and Georgia head coach Wally Butts believed his Bulldogs should follow suit. However, he wanted the team to decide for itself, and just one day before the first game, Butts asked the squad if they wanted to pay the price in defeats they'd have to take. The Bulldogs voted to stick it out and honor the games that had been scheduled. So began what the *Atlanta Constitution* declared "what looms as [Georgia's] most dismal gridiron campaign in history."

On a Friday night game in front of 6,000 spectators at Sanford Stadium, the Bulldogs faced a senior-laden and heavily favored Presbyterian squad. (Yes, you read correctly, Presbyterian was in fact favored to defeat Georgia.) Nevertheless, the Bulldogs won in a 25–7 upset and discovered in the process their next superstar player—Johnny Cook, all 17 years, 5'8" in height, and 152 pounds of him. For the game, the freshman tailback passed for 143 yards and a touchdown, rushed for a touchdown, returned four punts for 50 yards, punted eight times, and intercepted a would-be SEC-record four passes on defense.

A month into the season, the "dismal" Bulldogs were 3–1 and ranked 20th in the nation en route to an eventual 6–4 miraculous year. At season's end, Cook had earned first-team All-SEC honors in leading the nation in passing, was second on the team in rushing, and scored 12 touchdowns (nine rushing, two on punt returns, and one via a kickoff return). To date,

Cook remains the only Bulldog ever to lead the country in passing and, besides Heisman Trophy winner Frank Sinkwich, the only Georgia player to finish a season in the nation's top 10 in both passing and scoring.

Also at year's end, a preseason player's vote to go forth and play a season, which was believed to be absolutely senseless at the time, was instead described as "what will go down in history as the University's shining hour."

MOST INTERCEPTIONS IN A GAME

		No.	Vs.	Date
1.	Johnny Cook*	4	Presbyterian	Sept. 17, 1943
2t.	Joe Jackura	3	Alabama	Oct. 30, 1948
	Jeff Hipp	3	Georgia Tech	Nov. 24, 1979
	Terry Hoage	3	Vanderbilt	Oct. 16, 1982
	Tra Battle	3	Auburn	Nov. 11, 2006

*Unofficial record

SHINING IN THE RAIN

In regard to the 1968 Georgia-Florida game (see "Bulldog-Turned-Gator" in chapter 5 of *I Hate Florida*), if you were to side with the Gators, you might conclude that those particular Bulldogs were a band of ruthless villains and Coach Vince Dooley was the original "Evil Genius."

A popular Florida account of the Georgia "running-up-the-score" story was when the Bulldogs elected to attempt a field goal, with one of their linemen no less, as only seconds remained in the contest (when in actuality, a place-kicker kicked the field goal with more than five minutes left). Nevertheless, this is yet another example of disgruntled Florida fans exaggerating the truth…or perhaps they're just a little confused.

Silly Gators, Dooley didn't allow a lineman to attempt a field goal against y'all in '68, he let one play quarterback.

To give you an idea how out of hand the game was in 1968, Georgia led 35–0 at halftime in weather conditions described as "a monsoon." Florida fumbled on the opening possession of the second half when All-American Bill Stanfill bulldozed quarterback Larry Rentz into the quagmire-like Gator Bowl turf. Three plays later, the Bulldogs took a 41–0 advantage, and Dooley promptly decided to call off his dogs. Each first-stringer, if he hadn't already been benched, was ordered to the sideline.

Early in the third quarter, even place-kicker Jim McCullough was relieved of his duties. If the Bulldogs were to score again, which was almost guaranteed against a Florida squad that had started to show signs of giving up, a second Bulldogs player would attempt a place-kick—a rare feat which hadn't occurred in a single Georgia game in more than a decade!

"The coaches told the first-team defense that we were through for the day," said Stanfill. "So a bunch of us got our Gatorade cups and stood by the fence while the Georgia fans filled them up with liquor." For some Bulldogs players that day, the Cocktail Party evidently began early. For others, they would be given a chance of a lifetime.

Late in the ballgame, Georgia led 51–0 and possessed the ball one final time. Dooley had already used a backup place-kicker, Peter Rajecki, who made an extra point and the shot heard 'round the Georgia-Florida rivalry—the 22-yard field goal with 5:29 remaining.

At halftime, quarterback Mike Cavan had been replaced by Donnie Hampton, who had been sidelined for No. 3 quarterback Don Graham in the fourth quarter. After taking his first snaps ever as a member of the Georgia varsity, Graham had now been removed by Dooley. The Bulldogs were all out of quarterbacks! The team had traveled carrying only three signal-callers, and each of them had already been used. At that point, Dooley decided to try something similar to a maneuver

THE GEORGIA-FLORIDA "FIFTH DOWN" GAME

Most followers of college football are familiar with the legendary Colorado-Missouri game of 1990—the "Fifth Down" game—where officials erroneously permitted Colorado an extra snap following a fourth-down play, allowing the Buffaloes to defeat the Tigers. More than two decades before, Georgia was also victimized by an infamous fifth-down game of sorts, where officials might have ultimately cost the Bulldogs a victory in Jacksonville.

In 1969, a year after Georgia had defeated Florida in the most lopsided game in the series over the last 70 years, the Bulldogs found themselves trailing the Gators 7–0 late in the second quarter and with the opposition threatening to score again. Florida's Richard Franco was set to attempt a 37-yard field goal when the Gators decided to run a fake. A fourth-down pass fell incomplete and the ball was turned over on downs to the Bulldogs.

But hold the phone...

GEORGIA

he pulled two years before in the 1966 Cotton Bowl and play a lineman at quarterback.

Inserted under center was sophomore and third-string center Terry Henderson. Henderson had not played quarterback since high school and, in fact, mostly saw playing time on only special teams as Georgia's snapping specialist. For the Bulldogs' extra-point and field-goal attempts, Henderson did "all the hard work," according to McCullough.

As Henderson walked to the line of scrimmage and, instead of lining up at center, positioned himself *under* the center, a Florida defender instantly hollered, "I ain't believin' this. A center playing quarterback?"

Following the failed attempt, an official declared he had whistled the play dead before it started because he observed a photographer too close to the field of play. To add to the controversy, all photographers later claimed they weren't even close to the field. Also, it was reported the next day that the erratic whistle was actually because an errant football was spotted resting in the end zone.

Whether because of a supposed too-close-for-comfort photographer or an extra football, Florida was granted a "do over" by the officials. As Georgia fans booed mercilessly, the Gators attempted the field goal with their extra play, and made the kick to lead 10–0 at halftime.

The contest would eventually end knotted at 13–13 in only the second, and what would be final, tie game in the history of the series. Although, because of one of the most controversial plays in the Georgia-Florida series, the Gators were apparently fortunate to escape Jacksonville with the draw.

GEORGIA

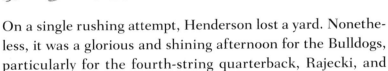

On a single rushing attempt, Henderson lost a yard. Nonetheless, it was a glorious and shining afternoon for the Bulldogs, particularly for the fourth-string quarterback, Rajecki, and the other seldom-used reserves, during a driving rainstorm at the Gator Bowl.

A week later, the Bulldogs defeated Auburn, clinching an SEC championship and a trip to the Sugar Bowl. Florida, who had been ranked fourth in the country only a month before, would finish its season with only six wins and stay home during the bowl season.

In 1991, after Florida had defeated Georgia to finally clinch its first conference championship in Gators football history, that same Bulldogs place-kicker—Jim McCullough, a little older and wiser—was eating with his family, and proudly dressed in red and black despite the loss, at Clark's Fish Camp in Jacksonville.

Some neighboring Gators fans had finished their meal and purposely walked by the McCullough family's table to rub the Bulldogs fans' noses in the Florida victory. One of the passing Gators threw some packets of sugar on the table and asserted, "I guess we're going to New Orleans and the Sugar Bowl."

Without hesitation, McCullough flashed his SEC championship ring from 1968 and said, "Help me remember what bowl y'all went to after we beat you 51–0, when I played."

According to McCullough, the fan responded by keeping his mouth shut and "leaving with that Gator tail tucked between his legs."

A BULLDOG FINALLY GETS THE GATORS' NUMBER

Like many Bulldog players of the mid-1950s through the early '60s, standout left end Jimmy Vickers had a difficult time defeating Florida. And hailing from Moultrie in South Georgia, perhaps there was no one Vickers would have preferred to beat more than the Gators.

In nine meetings from 1955 to 1963, three of which Vickers appeared in, the Gators won all but one Georgia-Florida game. What was the difference in the series then? Was it the same excuse that some of the Bulldogs faithful give today, indicating Jacksonville is not a true "neutral" site since Georgia must travel further, and thus the Bulldogs are at some sort of disadvantage?

"I don't believe that!" Vickers recently exclaimed. "When I played, because of all of the distractions—your family and friends—most of us would have rather played in Jacksonville than near home. On the road, we would get to the hotel, be isolated, and keep our minds on the game and the opponent."

Georgia's lone victory over the Gators during the aforementioned nine-season stretch was when Vickers was a senior and an alternate team captain in 1959. That year, the Bulldogs would go on to a surprising 10-win, SEC championship season, while Vickers was one of just two Georgia players recognized as a member of the All-SEC first team; the other was legendary Bulldog and NFL quarterback Fran Tarkenton.

Vickers returned to Athens in 1971 as the Bulldogs' offensive line coach, where his success on the gridiron translated to the

Georgia coach Wally Butts talks strategy with his team prior to the Orange Bowl in 1959. Butts is surrounded by, from left to right, Jimmy Vickers (82), Fran Tarkenton (10), Pat Dye (60), and Don Soberdash (37).

sideline. From 1971 to 1977, of Georgia's eight first-team All-Americans, remarkably, six of them—Royce Smith, Craig Hertwig, Randy Johnson, Mike "Moonpie" Wilson, Joel Parrish, and George Collins—were offensive lineman coached by Vickers.

"I coached a lot of good players while I was at Georgia," said Vickers. "And that is what it boils down to—who you got out on the field playing for you, and not where the game is played. That's why, whether as a player or a coach, I always felt that playing out of town was not that big of a disadvantage."

Vickers continued, "Besides, unlike when I played, when I coached at Georgia, I'm pretty sure we won more times in Jacksonville than Florida did."

In Vickers' six seasons as a Bulldogs assistant, Georgia won all but one game against the Gators. Of course, it took a miracle for one of those Bulldogs victories to transpire.

During the mid-1970s, Georgia ran the run-oriented veer offense directed by coordinator Bill Pace. Although the Bulldogs had a potent rushing attack, their passing game struggled from time to time, and it was often up to the Georgia assistants—namely, Pace and Vickers—to create innovative plays that could gain large chunks of yardage.

As Georgia prepared to face Vanderbilt midway through the 1975 season, Vickers noticed while watching game film that the Commodores defenders would often turn their backs while calling their signals. Because of Vanderbilt's apparent aloofness, he suggested the "shoestring" play to head coach Vince Dooley.

During the game, Georgia quarterback Ray Goff approached the football, which was spotted on the right hash mark. As Vanderbilt stood in its defensive huddle, Goff knelt in front of the ball pretending to tie his shoestrings while the other 10 Bulldog offensive players nonchalantly gathered at the left hash mark. Instantly, the quarterback, acting as the offense's center, flipped the ball directly to receiver Gene Washington, who raced untouched into the end zone for a 36-yard touchdown via the shoestring play.

To get a feel for the opponent and the contest at hand—"what was going on"—Vickers would begin every game in the press box before leaving for Georgia's sideline shortly after the start of the second quarter. Against Florida a few games after the win at Vanderbilt, Vickers was into his same routine. Although the Bulldogs were involved in a defensive standoff with the Gators, where Georgia was hardly able to muster much offense, Vickers did notice a flaw in Florida's defense.

When Vickers returned to the sideline just prior to halftime, Pace asked, "What do you think, Jimmy? What does it look like?"

"Looks like Florida is really sucking up on the run, Bill," replied Vickers. "Maybe we can get behind them."

With less than four minutes remaining in the game and Georgia trailing 7–3, a Gators' punt sailed into the Bulldogs' end zone for a touchback. The ball was brought out to the 20-yard line, where Georgia had possession. It was time for Vickers' innovation.

"Bill, let's run that fake counter trap up the middle and hit Gene [Washington] deep," Vickers hollered to Pace. "From our 20-yard line?!?" asked Pace. "Yeah, they're crowding us to death," replied Vickers. "We can get it out of there."

"And Bill," Vickers continued, "why don't we let ol' Richard [Appleby] throw the ball?"

During his career at Georgia, Gene Washington caught several long touchdowns—five to be exact, covering 74 yards or more, while tight end Richard Appleby ran plenty of end-arounds—six in 1975 alone. However, never before had Appleby run the end-around and then threw a pass to Washington. In fact, Appleby had thrown only two passes ever while playing organized football—the first came several years before while playing for Clarke Central High School in Athens while the other was just three weeks prior at Vanderbilt—and both attempts had been intercepted.

Regardless, Pace and Vickers had been working on the play for weeks in practice, and if they were ever going to run it, at that point was the perfect time.

The end result? That's probably best told by one who lived it:

> In this nightmare, I'm being blocked at the line. I know it's a reverse pass, and start screaming my lungs out. I get to Appleby just as he throws the ball. I have my hands up and he throws it just over my hand, so I know just about what the trajectory is—long and high. I figure he's thrown a high, slow-spiraling lob and somebody will surely intercept it. Then I hear the fans roaring. I can't believe it. Three minutes to go. Unbelievable. We play so well, then blow it all. [Florida's Darrell Carpenter, 1975 All-SEC Defensive Tackle]

THE PLAY

In the annals of Georgia football, it is simply known as "The Play"—the Bulldogs' 93-yard touchdown pass from quarterback Buck Belue to receiver Lindsay Scott that defeated

Florida in 1980 and saved a perfect season en route to a national championship. It's not only the most celebrated play ever in Georgia football but the greatest moment in the university's athletic history.

If you're old enough to remember it, you recall exactly where you were and what you were doing when the miracle took place. Such is the case for the former First Lady of Bulldogs football.

Barbara Dooley, wife of then–head coach Vince Dooley, had always been instructed by the nuns growing up in Catholic school that if your final thought right before you died was "Jesus, Have Mercy," you'd go straight to heaven. Barbara

BULLDOGS BOOKS WE LOVE

The Ghosts of Herty Field by John Stegeman

No Ifs, No Ands, a Lot of Butts by Ed Thilenius and Jim Koger

I've Seen 'Em All by Charles E. Martin

Touchdown: A Pictorial History of the Georgia Bulldogs by John Stegeman

Between the Hedges by Jesse Outlar

Leading a Bulldog's Life by Jack Troy

Dooley: My 40 Years at Georgia by Vince Dooley

From Herschel to a Hobnail Boot by Larry Munson and Tony Barnhart always remembered the nuns' advice, often repeating the three words over and over in her head.

On Homecoming Week in 1980, the Dooleys—Vince, Barbara, and 12-year-old (and later Louisiana Tech and Tennessee head football coach) Derek—rode into downtown Athens after a football game played by the youngest Dooley to see a face of an impressive bulldog that had been painted in the street for Homecoming. At the time, Vince drove a silver and black Lincoln Town Car with "Georgia red" upholstery, which Barbara appropriately dubbed the "Pimp Mobile."

Having stopped at a red light, the three Dooleys leaned toward the windshield to get a better look at the painted bulldog. Suddenly, they were slammed from behind by a drunk driver who was speeding from the police. Derek, dressed in full football uniform, flew from the back seat into the front. Vince's face went straight into the steering column; the Bulldogs' head man broke his nose and busted a lip. Barbara got the worst of it. She was thrown into the dashboard, shattering the windshield with her head. As she lay across the car's dashboard, Barbara thought that she might be taking her last breath at any moment, and now was probably the time to recall the phrase that would send her straight to Heaven. Just as she was about to go unconscious, Barbara said softly the words that came immediately to mind: "Oh, crap. They've hit Vince's Pimp Mobile."

Despite suffering 11 broken ribs and having her spleen removed, Barbara's goal was to make it to Jacksonville just three weeks following the accident; there was no way she was going to miss the Georgia-Florida game.

On the day of the game, Barbara barely made it through an entrance gate at the Gator Bowl. It was the Cocktail Party, so there was the usual crowded, festive-like atmosphere; however, this year there seemed to be more cramming and pushing than years past. Maybe it was because Georgia entered undefeated and ranked second in the nation while Florida, who hadn't won a single game the year before, was 6–1 and recently nationally ranked for the first time in three seasons.

Barbara's ribs couldn't endure the chaos; there would be no way she would be able reach her seat. However, she had been told earlier by the Georgia Bulldog Club of Jacksonville that a trailer would be parked in the stadium parking lot, and if she wanted to watch the game there, the club could accommodate. So, she made her way over to the trailer.

Barbara finally reached her destination, promptly flipped on a television inside the trailer, and much to her delight, observed that the Bulldogs had a 14–3 lead early in the second quarter. Nonetheless, over the next couple of hours, Barbara's happiness would turn into anxiety as the Gators slowly but surely made it a ballgame.

Halfway through the final quarter, Brian Clark's field goal gave the Gators their first lead over the Bulldogs since the first quarter of their meeting from two years before in 1978. Worse, the way Georgia's offense was sputtering, the Florida lead appeared to be an advantage the Gators would not relinquish.

Trailing 21–20, just as the Bulldogs forced a Florida punt, the trailer door abruptly swung open and there stood Vince

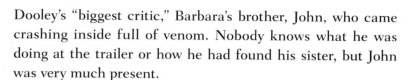

Dooley's "biggest critic," Barbara's brother, John, who came crashing inside full of venom. Nobody knows what he was doing at the trailer or how he had found his sister, but John was very much present.

"What's Vince doing, Barbara?!?" John wondered very aloud. "What's been going on with the play calling? It's been awful! Now we have to pass, and we haven't been able to throw the football all day!"

John was right. Georgia had the ball on its own 8-yard line with just 1:35 to play and it had no choice but to pass. For most of the game, it had been Herschel left, Herschel right, and Herschel up the middle, but tailback Herschel Walker was of little use now. And the Bulldogs had struggled in the passing game, completing just six passes for 52 yards while throwing two interceptions.

On first down, Belue was forced to scramble and lost a yard. On second down, a sideline pass by the quarterback for Charles Junior fell incomplete.

"It's over, Barbara!" hollered John. "And it's all because of the recent play calling! Vince should be ashamed of it! I give up!"

Trailing with only 1:20 left and facing third down and 11 from the 7-yard line, admittedly, most of us had given up. From the legendary Larry Munson—"I gave up, you did, too"—to the esteemed Lewis Grizzard—"I gave up at Jacksonville.... I left the stadium. I was in the street"—to Barbara Dooley's brother...on second thought, forget "most of us"—nearly *all* of us had given up.

Buck Belue's 93-yard touchdown pass to Lindsay Scott to defeat Florida in 1980 is recognized as one of college football's greatest plays, and those of us old enough to remember it, will never, ever forget "The Play." Photo courtesy of Wingate Downs

While the Bulldog Nation was dejected, Florida was celebrating like it had already won. From a number of Gators players dancing on the field to the Florida fans rejoicing outside the stadium after leaving their seats early to beat traffic, one would have thought the game was already over.

Just as Barbara noticed one particular Florida fan outside the trailer with a transistor radio in one hand and the index finger of his other hand raised high in the air, declaring the Gators were "No. 1," she said to her brother, "It's far from over, John. It's only third down and we have over a minute remaining." And just then, it happened.

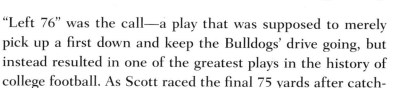

"Left 76" was the call—a play that was supposed to merely pick up a first down and keep the Bulldogs' drive going, but instead resulted in one of the greatest plays in the history of college football. As Scott raced the final 75 yards after catching Belue's pass on a simple curl route, the Bulldog Club's trailer nearly uprooted and rolled out of the Gator Bowl parking lot. Like most Georgia fans, John had gone absolutely berserk.

"Damn, genius!" screamed John. "I tell you, Barbara, that play call was absolutely genius! We've won this thing! I just knew the Dogs would come back!

"Jesus, Have Mercy!" John exclaimed.

They say God doesn't root for a particular football team—not even Notre Dame—but on that day of November 8, 1980, for that one play, some of us believe God was indeed a Bulldog (or He at least had something to do with Tim Groves slipping to the Gator Bowl turf, allowing Scott to streak by the Florida safety and down the sideline into the end zone).

Just after the touchdown, Barbara made it a point to quickly look out the trailer door at the parking lot crowd. In the disarray, the Florida fan who was holding the radio in one hand, promptly chucked the device across the parking lot in disgust. And his other hand, which once declared the Gators "No. 1," was dangling by his side.

When the rankings were released two days later, ranked No. 1 were the Georgia Bulldogs, where they would remain through the end of the season.

6

WE LOVE UGA, ATHENS, AND OUR BULLDOG BRETHREN

UNIVERSITY of GEORGIA

Chartered in 1785, the University of Georgia is the oldest public university in the United States—the "birthplace of the American system of higher education." A couple other institutions claim to have the same distinction; however, we don't see what all the fuss is about.

Your school was either established before 1785, or it wasn't, enough said. Even a Gator could figure that out.

Situated on a beautiful and historic 600-acre campus located in arguably the greatest college town in the country, the university currently has an enrollment of approximately 35,000 students. It was once said that if one was to ride through the town of Athens with a window rolled down, UGA would throw a diploma in the car. The late, great Lewis Grizzard further clarified this old rumor. "It ain't true," declared Grizzard. "You have to stop first."

Times have certainly changed as the university's academic reputation has risen significantly over the last 20 years. Recognized as a "Top 10 Public Ivy League School," UGA has been transformed into a university *first*, with a football program *second* (unlike that school in Gainesville that has these priorities mixed up), leaving some of us older alumni extremely relieved that we got accepted into the school when we did.

We'd be remiss if we failed to mention perhaps the campus' most distinguished landmark—the Arch. Patterned after the state seal of Georgia, the UGA Arch has faced downtown Athens ever since it was erected more than 150 years ago. For most of the duration, a tradition has held that students may not pass beneath it until they have received a diploma from UGA. Legends persist if a student was to prematurely walk under the Arch, including the myth of never graduating, and even tales of freshmen becoming sterile by walking through the historical structure.

Many UGA alumni have found these superstitions regarding the Arch to be absolutely false. For others attending the school, we weren't quite daring enough to tempt fate.

ATHENS

Soon after the establishment of the University of Georgia, Athens officially became a town in 1806. As cotton mills fueled the town's growth during its early years, Athens became known as the "Manchester of the South" after the city in England recognized for its mills.

In time, because of its historical attractions, traditional heritage, and neoclassical architecture, the moniker would change as Athens developed into the "Classic City."

NOTABLE UGA ATTENDEES

Kim Basinger: An Athens native, Basinger attended UGA for two years in the early 1970s before pursuing an acting and modeling career. She has been the recipient of a Golden Globe Award, an Academy Award, and a Screen Actors Guild Award.

Robert Benham: In 1970 Benham became just the second African American to ever graduate from UGA's School of Law. He later was the first African American appointed to the Georgia Supreme Court and the first to serve as chief justice of the Supreme Court.

D.W. Brooks: After obtaining both his B.S. and M.S. in agriculture at UGA during the 1920s, Brooks founded Gold Kist Inc., and was an advisor to seven U.S. presidents.

Alton Brown: A drama degree graduate, Brown is a well-known TV personality on the Food Network and author of several books on cookery.

Teresa Edwards: A two-time All-American in women's basketball, Edwards led the Lady Dogs to the 1983 and 1985 Final Four and was a member of the 1984, 1988, 1992, 1996, and 2000 U.S. Olympic teams, becoming the first American basketball player to participate in five Olympic Games.

Henry Grady: The namesake for Grady Memorial Hospital in Atlanta, Grady served as the managing editor of the *Atlanta Constitution* during the 1880s and was known as the "Spokesman of the New South."

Lewis Grizzard: Grizzard, one of the biggest Bulldogs of them all, became the sports editor of the *Atlanta Journal* at only 23 years of age. Until his death in 1994, he was a distinguished writer, humorist, and speaker known for his southern demeanor and commentary.

Wayne Knight: Hello, Newman. As an honor student just one credit shy of graduating, Knight left UGA during the mid-1970s to eventually land on Broadway. Over the years, he has appeared in a number of movies and TV series, including as annoying neighbor Newman on the sitcom *Seinfeld*.

Crawford Long: A member of the Demosthenian Literary Society while a student at UGA, Long became a medical doctor best known as the first to administer ether anesthesia for surgery.

Julie Moran: A 1984 graduate of UGA, Moran was a host and reporter for ABC Sports and a correspondent for the TV show *Entertainment Tonight* from 1994 to 2001. She once indicated her primary reason for attending the school was her fondness of her grandfather—longtime Georgia football assistant Sterling Dupree.

Deborah Norville: The broadcast journalist has hosted *Today*, anchored both the *CBS Evening News* and *NBC Nightly News*, and has been the host for the program *Inside Edition* for more than 15 years. Norville was once engaged to former Gators offensive back Harmon Wages (who also dated Kim Basinger) during the 1980s, but we forgive her for it.

Billy Payne: As a sophomore and junior on Georgia's football team, Payne was a standout offensive end, who switched sides as a senior in 1968 and became an All-SEC defensive end. He is best known for heading up the Atlanta Committee for the 1996 Olympic Games and has been the chairman of the Augusta National Golf Club since 2006.

R.E.M.: All four members of the world-renowned rock band—Michael Stipe, Peter Buck, Mike Mills, and Bill Berry—attended the university in the early 1980s.

Deborah Roberts: A 1982 UGA graduate, Roberts has been an esteemed national journalist for both NBC and ABC television for more than 20 years.

Ryan Seacrest: Prior to hosting the hit television show *American Idol*, Seacrest attended UGA during the 1993–1994 academic year, taking 10 credit hours while working at radio station Star 94-FM in Atlanta and hosting ESPN's *Radical Outdoor Challenge*.

Dominique Wilkins: After an All-America basketball career as a Bulldog, "the Human Highlight Film" was a nine-time NBA All-Star in 15 seasons before his retirement in 1999.

GEORGIA

R.E.M.—former UGA students Michael Stipe, Peter Buck, Bill Berry, and Mike Mills—pose in Athens in 1985. Photo courtesy of Getty Images

Athens consists of more than a dozen neighborhoods on the National Register of Historic Places, includes more than 20 significant African American heritage sites, and is a notable stop on Georgia's Antebellum Trail. Still, while the city is rich in history and architecture, there is likely no other college town that possesses the energy of Athens, stemming from a vibrant music and nightlife scene.

Playing at world-famous Athens venues like the 40 Watt Club and the Georgia Theatre, the B-52's, R.E.M., and Widespread Panic got their start in the city during the 1970s and 1980s prior to becoming nationally acclaimed rock bands. The city is currently the home of more than 100 restaurants, bars, and night spots in the heart of its downtown area alone. You can probably see why former UGA football coach Erk Russell would often say, "There ain't nothing like being a Bulldog on a Saturday night."

In short, many students annually come to Athens to spend their college years at UGA. For those that eventually get a degree, and for those who aren't as fortunate, there's good reason why a significant portion of them have a difficult time leaving the Classic City upon finishing school, if they ever leave at all.

SANFORD STADIUM

In 1929 the Georgia Bulldog football team moved from what had been its home venue since 1911—Sanford Field—to nearby, newly constructed Sanford Stadium. The stadium was built in a natural valley with a small creek running through it, cost $360,000 to construct, had an initial capacity of just over 30,000 spectators, and was uniquely surrounded by privet hedges.

The Bulldogs celebrated the stadium's grand opening on October 12 that season by upsetting Yale 15–0, capturing the first memorable victory of many more to come for Georgia on the hallowed grounds.

In 1940 the Bulldogs hosted their first night game at Sanford Stadium—a 7–7 tie with Kentucky. Four decades later, the stadium's east end zone was enclosed, increasing the capacity from roughly 60,000 to 80,000. However, with the expansion came an end to a longstanding stadium tradition—the "Track People."

The Track People watched the games from the railroad tracks that run directly across the street from the stadium. From their free seats, the rowdy crowd would often be seemingly celebrating no matter the happenings on the field, while becoming as much a part of Sanford Stadium's lore as its surrounding hedges. Once the end zone was enclosed in 1981, the view of the Track People was no longer of the beloved Bulldogs but an enormous side of concrete instead.

In 1982 Georgia defeated Clemson on Labor Day night under Sanford Stadium's "new" lights; the old ones had been removed in the mid-1960s. In 1991 the stadium's seating capacity increased to 85,434. Several years later it was the site of the men's and women's soccer medal competition for the 1996 Olympic Games.

Today Sanford Stadium seats 92,746 spectators and is the seventh-largest on-campus stadium in all of college football. It has been increasingly more difficult to obtain tickets for games at the historic stadium. From the beginning of the 2001 football season to 2011, the Bulldogs sold out 64 consecutive home games. Also, prior to the 2008 season, for any new donor wanting to acquire two season tickets at Sanford Stadium, he or she would have needed to "donate" nearly $11,000 for merely the right to buy tickets!

Understandably, there's a price to pay for success. The Bulldogs have been quite successful on their home turf, winning approximately 75 percent of their games in more than 80 years at Sanford Stadium, including better than 81 percent during the current Coach Mark Richt era (2001–2011).

THE BULLDOG NATION

It's not unusual for other fan bases to allege that the Bulldog Nation, on the whole, is too "obsessed" with its team, or Georgia fans excessively "live in the past" in regard to their football program. However, we tend to characterize ourselves as "passionate" more than anything else, while simply appreciating our team's rich football tradition.

Unlike the University of Florida's, our Bulldogs' fine football tradition is rather historic, beginning long before the 1990s.

Most Georgia fans are located in the heart of SEC country surrounded on all sides by a number of detested rivals—too many for us to even think about. Regardless, the competition only increases our enthusiasm for the Bulldogs, while making us one of the most passionate fan bases in all of college football.

Of course, we appreciate everyone who has ever rooted for the Bulldogs, but there are a few fans, from the past and present, who stand out among the red and black–clad crowd:

If you don't know who "Big Dawg" Mike Woods is, we guarantee you have at least seen him on television. He's the big guy that wears black overalls to the games, a red shirt, and has a bulldog face painted on his bald head. Woods' father first painted a bulldog on his head for the 1981 Sugar Bowl and continued doing so for games until his death in 1987. The son made it a family tradition beginning in 1990, and has been the Big Dawg ever since.

Notably, Woods has missed just one Georgia-Florida game in the last 42 years through the 2011 season. In 1988 he had to undergo back surgery just prior to the game, and the doctor would not let the Big Dawg out of the hospital.

In addition, better known as "Mr. Bulldog"—the name he was listed as in the phonebook—Herschel Scott did not miss a single Georgia football game from 1962 until his death in 2003—a span of 471 consecutive attended games. The Georgia House of Representatives declared Scott was "widely recognized as Georgia's biggest fan." Prepared years before his death, Mr. Bulldog's tombstone reads: "Bulldog Born, Bulldog Bred, Here I Lie, A Bulldog, Dead."

Finally, for those of us who remember Georgia football from the 1950s through the 1970s, there's no forgetting Howard Marshall Moss—arguably the biggest and most "involved" Bulldogs fan in history.

Residing in Louisville, Kentucky, of all places, Moss often led large groups in cheers at Sanford Stadium, particularly the raucous "Track People" from the railroad tracks just outside the stadium. In the late 1950s, Moss literally attempted to walk on the Georgia team at the age of 54. In addition, a number of Bulldogs players admitted to often keeping an eye out for him during games to see what he was up to or, more likely, what he had gotten into. And there were several occasions when Moss was chased by police from the football field during games—both home and away—including against Georgia

Tech in the early 1950s after he stomped a remote-controlled yellow jacket into pieces during Tech's halftime show.

"Every week I get three or four plays [sent to me] from Moss," said head coach Vince Dooley in the mid-1970s. "The plays are drawn up in the I formation. I haven't told him we run the veer, yet."

From the slightly modest to the most fanatical of Georgia fans, like the aforementioned, for many, their passion is never more evident than at the annual Cocktail Party in Jacksonville. There, even the meekest of Bulldogs fans become raging fanatics for one day.

Speaking of the Cocktail Party and fanatics, the day before the Georgia-Florida game in 1976, the Bulldogs were going through their customary walk-through at the Gator Bowl when suddenly, but not all that surprisingly, Moss had joined the team on the field. Running back Rayfield Williams recalled, "He was running around the field straight-arming imaginary would-be tacklers."

Well, maybe some of us are indeed obsessed with the Georgia Bulldogs, if not down right crazy for them!

7

WE LOVE THE WORLD'S LARGEST OUTDOOR COCKTAIL PARTY

You know this game has always been called the World's Greatest Cocktail Party, do you know what is gonna happen here tonight, and up in St. Simons and Jekyll Island, and all those places where all those Dawg people have got these condominiums for four days? Man, is there going to be some property destroyed tonight!

—Larry Munson (After Georgia's
miraculous victory at the 1980 Cocktail Party)

HOW DO WE BULLDOGS describe the World's Largest Outdoor Cocktail Party, or the annual Georgia-Florida football game in Jacksonville and its surrounding days of partying? The easiest way to describe it is for you to simply go experience it for yourself. It's something every football enthusiast should go do at least once in their lives, and if you do indeed have the experience, it likely won't be your last trip to Jacksonville in late October.

Perhaps the best way to describe Georgia-Florida weekend where the "weekend" is as long as four or five days for a good portion of Bulldogs followers is by the time Saturday finally arrives, many of us have nearly forgotten that there is actually a football game to be played.

Thus, the Bulldogs and Gators battling it out on the gridiron is only a small part of the Cocktail Party, which actually is a series of parties. The partying lasts for days and stretches for roughly 125 miles from St. Simon's Island in Georgia to the north to Florida's St. Augustine to the south, while leaving the fans of the losing team exclaiming an outcry that can be traced back in the rivalry for nearly 40 years: "We might have lost the game, but we'll win the party!"

WHY JACKSONVILLE?

Outsiders to the Georgia-Florida rivalry often wonder why the game is played at an off-campus site and why particularly in Jacksonville, especially considering the "neutral" city is approximately 250 miles further from Athens than Gainesville.

In the beginning, it's evident that no one could determine the permanent site of the game, as four different cities hosted the series' first four meetings. In the rivalry's first 13 games over 30 seasons, from 1904 to 1933, not once was it held at the same site in consecutive years.

Played in 1904, the game's first site was Central City Park in the city of Macon, Georgia. Like the game of football, the location of Georgia-Florida would soon change drastically and repeatedly, yet it's interesting to note that the foundation of the Cocktail Party was already being built. Leading up to the initial meeting of the schools, Macon's *Telegraph* stated, "The social side of the game will be a feature. Football has ever been the favorite of the ladies and doubtless will continue to be."

In 1933 Jacksonville's Fairfield Stadium hosted the Georgia-Florida game, and like the three previous meetings in the city, the contest was a complete sellout. It was decided then that because of the large crowd and since the two teams and their fans could easily reach Jacksonville by train, the following year's game would be held at Fairfield Stadium, as well.

In the early era of the sport, several rivalries, particularly in the South, usually met at a neutral site since the teams' on-campus stadiums could not accommodate a large crowd. In fact, for a quarter-century, Georgia would face rival Auburn annually in neutral Columbus, Georgia, only a week or two after playing Florida in Jacksonville. However, by the late 1950s, Columbus' Memorial Stadium could no longer hold the number of spectators the Georgia-Auburn game was attracting, and the yearly meeting was moved to the home stadiums of the two schools.

Since 1933, except for a two-year period during the mid-1990s, when the Gator Bowl was being renovated, Georgia-Florida has remained in neutral Jacksonville. Currently, it is one of only two annual games in college football played at the same neutral site every year. The other is the Oklahoma-Texas rivalry—the "Red River Shootout," or "Red River Rivalry" if you prefer to be politically correct—which takes place during the State Fair of Texas.

So how do the last two remaining neutral-sited rivalries in college football compare to one another? For most Georgia fans, we haven't the slightest idea. The weekend of Oklahoma-Texas, we're usually in Athens or a place like Knoxville, watching our Bulldogs play. It's hard to comprehend a football game at a State Fair, which prides itself on serving unusually deep-fried items. For most of us, a good party and a cocktail seem much more enticing than a huge Ferris wheel and a deep-fried Twinkie.

THE PARTY HAS JUST BEGUN

Even before the start of World War II, the Georgia-Florida meeting in Jacksonville had already become an annual tradition. Just as anticipated as the game itself, if not more so, was the social aspect of the weekend, especially considering the performances by most of the Gators' teams back then.

Economically, the weekend was acknowledged as the biggest of the year for the city of Jacksonville, where the Bulldogs and Gators played a game on Saturday after the "spectators play one all night long," according to sportswriter Jack Troy in 1939.

"[The fans are] still up by the dawn's early light," said Troy. "There is no thought of sleep…if there is time, they go gaily to municipal stadium and see if they had figured things out."

In the late 1950s, the annual event first came to be known by its distinguished title—the World's Largest Outdoor Cocktail Party. Bill Kastelz, the editor of the *Florida Times-Union*, created the moniker but would use it just once in a column. Regardless, the nickname was soon picked up by other writers and the title stuck.

"All the other sportswriters in the press box asked me why I wrote that, and I said because it was true," said Kastelz in 2000. "There was drinking all over the place in those days. People would use their binocular cases to put a flask in there and drink very openly, and there was no crackdown."

Prior to the 1960s, Florida Gators football was mostly about the parties rather than the team's performances. The World's Largest Outdoor Cocktail Party was brought to the attention of a national audience by writer John Underwood of *Sports Illustrated*, indicating that even "all the fun of the [Georgia-Florida] weekends could not make Florida fans happy with their lot." Over the next decade or so, while Gators football started to slowly improve, the Cocktail Party was steadily growing even more in popularity.

HEYDAY OF THE COCKTAIL PARTY

By the 1970s, Georgia-Florida was viewed nationally as more of a spectacle lasting for days rather than a single football game. While the host city of Jacksonville had begun to devote months of planning for the weekend, some surrounding areas would prep for nearly an entire year for the pre- and postgame partying.

The rivalry was "the 100 proof bowl. The 2:00 PM happy hour," said writer Ron Hudspeth just prior to the 1972 meeting. "The game with the extra touch of spirit and spirits. Hic."

However, during this time, the weeklong spectacle was evolving into something the city and its Gator Bowl had not originally planned for: the Cocktail Party was now fully

A view of Jacksonville Municipal Stadium as Georgia prepares to take on Florida. The stadium is divided, with Bulldogs fans in red and black on one side and Gators fans in blue and orange on the other. Photo courtesy of Getty Images

overflowing into the stadium itself, while the crowd—split down the middle of the stadium according to rooting interest—had never been so raucous and inebriated, perhaps a little too much so. More and more Bulldogs and Gators fans were stuffing liquor bottles into every little nook and cranny of clothing prior to entering the Gator Bowl, and often in plain view of law enforcement without hesitation.

After Georgia's memorable comeback victory over Florida in 1976, elated Bulldogs fans spilled into the stadium's end zones and tore down both goal posts in what was thought to be the first time the Jacksonville stadium's posts had ever been dismantled. A high school football game immediately followed

Georgia's win and the teams were forced to use a single make-shift structure as a goal post. The celebratory act by Bulldogs fans would eventually cost the Gator Bowl $2,695 for a set of new goal posts.

During the game in 1978, reports of gate-crashing by frustrated fans unable to get tickets surfaced. Groups of as many as 50 individuals rushed past ticket-takers or climbed fences to enter the stadium and join the party in the stands. When Georgia defeated Florida by a mere two points, some UGA students attempted to do exactly what they had done the last time the Bulldogs had defeated the Gators and tear down the goal posts. This time, however, they were met by a ring of police, preventing any fans from getting into the end zone. For any student who happened to reach the field, he or she was soon tackled or beaten back away from the Gator Bowl's newly installed goal posts.

EVIDENTLY, THE MAYOR WAS A GATOR

For six straight years from 1978 to 1983, Georgia defeated Florida, and for each of the six occasions, Bulldogs fans attempted to rush onto the Gator Bowl turf, but to no avail. For some of those who tried to reach the field, they were met by Jacksonville's finest, who would often make arrests and on occasion physically throw students over a dividing fence.

In 1984 Florida defeated Georgia soundly by a score of 27–0 for what seemed like the Gators' first victory in the series in an eternity. Florida fans stormed the field, unearthed a newly sodded playing surface, tore down and dismantled both goal posts, carried them around, and eventually left the Gator

Bowl with the goal posts in tow. Like previous years, police had been posted around the field to prevent fans from entering. However, during the mêlée, officers merely watched as the destruction took place and did not make a single arrest. Police restraint was exercised, according to a spokesman for the Jacksonville Sheriff's office, "because the surge of fans was too great."

Jacksonville's mayor at the time and an apparent Florida fan, Jake Godbold, inexplicably stated that the city "would be tickled to death to pay for [any damages to the field]. If [the Gators] beat 'em like that next year, they can tear it down then, too."

Much to the mayor's presumed dismay, there would be no victory for the Gators in 1985, but instead a 24–3 Georgia upset win over a top-ranked Florida team. As the Gators had done the year before, Bulldogs fans attempted to rush the field following the victory by climbing over a fence; however, this time, the jubilant crowd was held back by police. Nonetheless, spectators would eventually open a gate and soon there was a red and black throng covering the field.

Jacksonville police did not exercise restraint that particular year as law enforcement took to the Georgia crowd wielding nightsticks. Numerous arrests were made while 15 fans were treated on the field alone for injuries suffered during the police-engaged chaos.

Entering the 1986 matchup, a "war on alcohol" was more or less declared in and around the stadium, and security was greatly increased. This included the addition of police dogs, mounted police, undercover law enforcement, reinforced fences, and, if necessary, even helicopters and marine patrol boats could be used. Apparently, lessons had been learned from previous years, and drastic steps were taken by both teams and the city of Jacksonville to keep the Cocktail Party out of the confines of the Gator Bowl.

WHY NOT JACKSONVILLE?

The notion of moving the Georgia-Florida game out of Jacksonville periodically or entirely, and converting the rivalry to an on-campus series or one which includes an additional neutral site, like Atlanta, is nothing new. The idea was suggested as far back as the 1970s when the city of Jacksonville and the stadium's handling of the game was first widely criticized. Specifically, price gouging by hotels, poor supervision of parking by police officers, and gate-crashing at the Gator Bowl, which had reportedly increased attendance by as many as 3,000 spectators above capacity, were all cited as primary reasons why the game possibly needed a new home.

The idea of moving the game was again suggested off and on throughout the 1990s and 2000s. However, instead of the host city's management of the game being challenged as before, the actual "neutrality" of Jacksonville was questioned by Georgia supporters. As indicated, "The Bold New City of the South," as Jacksonville is called, is a heck of a lot further south toward Gainesville than Athens.

Admittedly, for the Bulldogs backers who want to take the game out of Jacksonville, the primary reason for this sentiment—and if we're being totally honest—is simply because of

Georgia's struggles in the series the last couple of decades. However, that's not the city of Jacksonville's fault or its stadium, rather players and coaches should be held accountable. Few Bulldogs wanted to take the game out of town when we defeated the Gators 13 of 16 times from 1974 to 1989.

Most Georgia fans want to keep this game right where it is. Besides the rivalry's tradition and party-like atmosphere, both universities currently make more revenue from the game at its current location on a yearly basis than if the site rotated between the schools' respective home stadiums. In addition, the week of the game is extremely lucrative for the city of Jacksonville, which stands to lose millions of dollars each year of not hosting the rivalry. As mentioned, the weekend is the biggest of the year for the city and has been since the 1930s.

Former Jacksonville mayor Hans Tanzler might have put it best when the possibility of moving the game out of his city was introduced to him in 1978: "Talking about moving, it doesn't make any sense. It ain't going to be moved. No. 1, it's too valuable."

The mayor would be correct in his assessment, at least for the next nearly 40 years. In 2009 UGA's athletics board unanimously agreed to a multiyear contract, keeping the game in Jacksonville through 2016.

WHAT'S IN A NAME?

Soon after the city cracked down on excessive drinking at the game during the mid-1980s, Jacksonville dropped its use of the "World's Largest Outdoor Cocktail Party" title. In 2006

SITE HISTORY of *GEORGIA-FLORIDA*

City	Games	UGA Wins	UF Wins	Ties	UGA Points	UF Points
Macon	1	1	0	0	52	0
Savannah	2	0	1	1	6	26
Athens	5	4	1	0	159	73
Tampa	1	1	0	0	16	0
Gainesville	2	1	1	0	47	58
Jacksonville	79	41	37	1	1,508	1,326
Total	90	48	40	2	1,788	1,483

UGA President Michael Adams led a campaign to do away with the phrase altogether. CBS Sports, who televises the game annually, and two other networks were approached and asked to drop the phrase due to concerns regarding alcohol abuse by attendees. Reportedly, preferred titles were the "Georgia-Florida Football Classic" or the "Florida-Georgia Football Classic," depending on which school was considered the home team.

During the president's campaign, his spokesman stated to the Associated Press: "We don't like phrase. We don't use the phrase. We would prefer that nobody use the phrase."

The fact that Adams, or anyone for that matter, doesn't use the "World's Largest Outdoor Cocktail Party" is absolutely fine, but to suggest that nobody should use the title may be going too far. Many Bulldogs familiar with the rivalry have used the phrase since they can remember and will continue to do so.

In reality, when CBS Sports was initially contacted about the issue, the network indicated that it rarely used the phrase to begin with, if at all. "[The phrase is] not part of the focus of CBS coverage," said Leslie Anne Wade, vice president of communications for CBS Sports. "CBS coverage is about the rivalry and the competitive matchup of these two schools."

The fact of the matter is that Georgia-Florida could be labeled the "World's Largest Outdoor Ring-around-the-Rosie Party," and drinking—some of it binge, most of it controlled—would undoubtedly still occur outside the stadium. For most Georgia fans, the campaign to drop a phrase that had been around since most anyone could remember was believed to be yet another example of people in power attacking everything but the actual problem itself.

In closing, you can have your "Georgia-Florida Football Classic," or whatever ho-hum label you choose. For Georgia and Florida fans alike, most undoubtedly *prefer* to use the "World's Largest Outdoor Cocktail Party."

ACKNOWLEDGMENTS

IT WASN'T EASY JUGGLING a family, a full-time job, and a five-month deadline to write this book. There were many times during the writing process my family heard from me something on the order of, "I can't right now. I'm working on my book." First and foremost, I am deeply appreciative for the understanding and support from my foundation— my children, Trip and Rebecca, and wife, Elizabeth, who often gave me the same response of "That book better be good!" For you three, I hope this book is not too much of a disappointment, and at least slightly worth any inconveniences I created.

I would like to especially recognize my publisher, Triumph Books, particularly Tom Bast and Adam Motin. I have written five books on University of Georgia football and three of them have been published by Triumph. I cannot imagine why they keep asking me to write for them, but for whatever the reason, I am extremely indebted.

I want to acknowledge my wonderful parents—Al and Carol Garbin. My mother, who will inform just about anyone she encounters about her son's books on Bulldogs football, has been my chief sales representative beginning with the publishing of my first book in 2007. My father, who has always been my writing's foremost proofreader, editor, and harshest critic, turned me on to UGA football more than 30 years ago. I will forever cherish the moment when my dad took me to my first Bulldogs game against Tennessee in 1981. However, the fact that he couldn't have done so a year before, when the Bulldogs won their first and only undisputed national championship, is rather regrettable.

During my research for this book, I had the privilege to interview several former Bulldogs players, coaches, and coaches' wives, who shared stories related to the Georgia-Florida series. Warranting being individually recognized are Barbara Dooley, wife of coach Vince Dooley, Jimmy Vickers, former All-SEC football player and coach, and All-America tailback Tim Worley. Tim was kind enough to write the foreword to the book, for which I am most appreciative. In addition, I want to thank the dozens of readers of my blog who sent me anecdotes and jokes regarding the rivalry, several of which I implemented within these pages. (By the way, you can visit my About Them Dawgs! Blawg at www.patrick garbin.blogspot.com; my advertisers and I would be very grateful for it!)

The fall of 2012 marks the 40ᵗʰ anniversary of when Horace King, Chuck Kinnebrew, and Larry West became the first three African Americans to appear in a varsity football game for the University of Georgia. Two years before in 1970, halfback Leonard George and wide receiver Willie Jackson had broken the color barrier for the Gators' varsity team. I wish to extend special recognition to these players for their pioneering efforts in integrating the Georgia and Florida varsity football teams. In so doing, they had to endure a number of adversarial situations, but in the process, their commendable action opened the doors for many African Americans to play football at both universities.

Last and certainly least, I want to acknowledge the Florida Gators— their fans, university, city of Gainesville, and football program in its entirety. Without you, there would be one less rival for the Bulldog Nation to love to hate and one less team for our Bulldogs to savor in victory. For this author, most importantly, without the Gators and their despised Gator Nation, there would have been no book.

ABOUT THE AUTHOR

PATRICK GARBIN IS A freelance writer and researcher who has written five books on Georgia Bulldogs football. A graduate of the University of Georgia in 1998, Garbin has earned the reputation as an authority and historian of college football, especially Bulldogs football, and is always open to a trivia challenge on the subject with anyone who dares.

Patrick maintains the About Them Dawgs! Blawg—the only blog on the Internet primarily dedicated to the rich history and tradition of Georgia's football program. For more information on Patrick and his work, or in case you're just really bored and have nothing better to do, please visit his website at www.patrickgarbin.com and blog at www.patrickgarbin.blogspot.com.

Garbin and his wife, Elizabeth, have one son, Trip, one daughter, Rebecca, and one chocolate lab, appropriately named "Herschel" for the greatest college football player in the history of mankind.

I
HATE
FLORIDA

PATRICK GARBIN

TRIUMPH
BOOKS

CONTENTS

1

GAMES WE HATE

EVERY SINGLE LOSS TO THE Gators has been difficult to endure. Even with Georgia's lack of success in the series the last couple of decades, there's no getting used to any victory by our jean shorts–wearing neighbors to the south. What makes any loss to Florida more difficult to withstand is realizing that it will be approximately 365 days until the Bulldogs will get their next shot at the Gators. This becomes even harder to tolerate for those of us suffering from a Cocktail Party Sunday hangover while making the long journey back home from Jacksonville.

Here is a countdown of the 10 most hated games of all time in the Georgia-Florida rivalry. The listing of losses is somewhat shorter than that of the victories in the "Games We Love" chapter. This is the case because the Bulldogs have a solid advantage in the series and, in addition, rehashing these defeats became way too much for us to stand once we reached No. 10.

No. 10: 1977

| FLORIDA | 0 | 10 | 6 | 6 | 22 |
| GEORGIA | 7 | 10 | 0 | 0 | 17 |

Florida's victory over Georgia in 1977 was significant for several reasons. For one, it would be the lone Gators win against

the Bulldogs over a span of 10 seasons (1974–1983). In addition, the Georgia loss would ultimately lead to a 5–6 campaign for the Bulldogs—Coach Vince Dooley's only losing year
in 25 seasons at UGA (1964–1988). And, finally, for the first
time in four years, a decision made by Florida head coach
Doug Dickey didn't cost his team the game.

For Dickey, the victory likely saved his job, that is, for a year, until
he was run out of Gainesville immediately after the 1978 season.

After winning the SEC title in 1976, misfortune seemed to
follow the Bulldogs the very next year. First, Georgia lost to
Clemson in Athens for the first time since 1914. Next, the
Bulldogs were blown out on Homecoming by Kentucky 33–0
in front of Prince Charles. The entire season, the team could
not hold onto the football, losing 35 fumbles—a school record
that will never be broken (well, we hope not).

With a 7–0 lead early in the second quarter against the Gators,
starting quarterback Jeff Pyburn was lost for the rest of the
season with an injury. By the way, at the end of the year, just
three weeks later, Georgia would be forced to play a quarterback against Georgia Tech who had appeared in the junior
varsity game just days before and was listed as the varsity's
sixth-stringer when summer practices began.

That's the kind of season it was for the Bulldogs in 1977.

Pyburn's replacement against Florida, Jacksonville native
Danny Rogers, lost fumbles on the first two snaps he received
from center. In all, Georgia fumbled eight times on the day,
losing five, including one following an interception by a

Bulldogs linebacker, who tried to pitch the ball to a teammate on the return.

Georgia's Willie McClendon did rush for 153 yards in the first half, including a 74-yard touchdown, but carried just once for 10 yards after halftime. In fact, the Bulldogs offense was held to six total yards the entire second half after gaining 258 in the first.

The Gators were led by All-America receiver Wes Chandler, who scored all three of Florida's touchdowns—the first was on a one-handed reception in the end zone and the final two were on rushes while lined up at halfback.

One of the few Georgia highlights was the "Godfather of Soul" James Brown performing "Dooley's Junkyard Dogs" at halftime with UGA's Redcoat Band.

"It really was a good ballgame," said Brown. "It's just lousy that Georgia lost." (*One time, uh, good God, ha!*)

No. 9: 1928

FLORIDA	6	7	7	6	**26**
GEORGIA	0	6	0	0	**6**

It was bound to happen eventually, even after losing the first seven games of the series by an average score of 35–1 (yes, that is a "1"—nine combined points by Florida in seven games averages to just over one measly point per game). Twenty-four years after their initial meeting on a gridiron, the Gators finally defeated the Bulldogs in 1928.

For the first time in eight games, Georgia-Florida was played in Savannah, and the city was in chaos during the weekend. Ben Cothran of the *Atlanta Constitution* reported: "The Florida [visitors] have hit the whoopee trail, the liquor runs freely, and this entire staid old city, one of the last strong-holds of famed southern aristocracy, is in a turmoil."

Averaging more than 37 points per game, the Gators would eventually finish the season as the highest scoring team in the nation. Plus, they were on the verge of a conference championship and possible Rose Bowl bid. However, like a handful of Gators teams of several decades later, they would eventually suffer a crucial loss, costing them a conference title and major bowl appearance.

Nevertheless, as mentioned, Florida did get the best of Georgia on this day. The Bulldogs answered an opposing touchdown with a score of their own on a 28-yard pass from H.F. Johnson to Frank Dudley in the second quarter.

The Gators added three more touchdowns, including a 36-yard reception by legendary end Dale Van Sickel.

Not making any excuses, but it was reported the Bulldogs battled a stiff wind for much of the game that blew right at them. Georgia's punting average was only 29 yards per punt—and that does not include two kicks Florida blocked.

The Gators' high-scoring offense gained a grand total of 120 yards for the entire game, or 30 yards less than the Bulldogs.

No. 8: 1995

FLORIDA	21	7	10	14	**52**
GEORGIA	0	3	0	14	**17**

Few Georgia fans truly believed their Bulldogs—depleted with injuries and fortunate to have won five of eight games—could defeat the high-powered, third-ranked, and more than three-touchdown-favored Florida at Sanford Stadium in 1995.

We prayed that maybe, just maybe, the ghosts of ole Sanford would rise up and come to the aid of our crippled canines, saving Coach Ray Goff's job, while upsetting the Gators and their "Evil Genius" of a head coach.

It was not to be, not even close.

Facing Florida in Athens for the first time in 63 years, Georgia stumbled out of the gate and then was stomped upon in its own backyard. The Bulldogs fumbled on their first possession and couldn't handle a snap while punting on their second. Each miscue turned into Florida touchdowns, and just over three minutes into the second quarter, the Gators had already built a 28–0 lead. It was over that quickly.

Quarterback Hines Ward saved some face for Georgia by throwing for 226 yards and a touchdown on 20-of-33 passing, while rushing for 65 yards on eight carries. Florida quarterback Danny Wuerffel and reserve Eric Kresser passed for five and two touchdowns, respectively. With under two minutes left in the game, Coach Steve Spurrier decided it was necessary to run a flea-flicker play with a 45–17 lead.

"A lot of our coaches had mentioned to me that no [opponent] had scored 50 in [Sanford Stadium] before," said Spurrier following the game. "So we wanted to do that."

Although rather far-fetched, what possibly could have been a memorable day for the Bulldogs at their old stadium instead resulted in what Georgia fans would like to forget. Rather, most Bulldogs backers prefer to remember this day as the one on which the Braves clinched the city of Atlanta's first major league baseball championship.

No. 7: 2010 (OT)

| FLORIDA | 0 | 21 | 0 | 10 | 3 | **34** |
| GEORGIA | 0 | 7 | 3 | 21 | 0 | **31** |

For the first time in 31 years, both teams entered the rivalry game unranked in the AP Poll, yet the 4–4 Bulldogs and 4–3 Gators were both still very much in contention for the SEC Eastern Division title. Early on, it appeared Georgia would easily be knocked out of the divisional race, until scoring 21 points in the final quarter. However, in the end, the Bulldogs would ultimately be defeated by the unlikeliest of Florida heroes.

Trailing by two touchdowns at halftime and 21–10 entering the final quarter, Bulldogs freshman quarterback Aaron Murray began picking apart the Gators' secondary. His 29-yard touchdown pass to tight end Orson Charles and two-point conversion run tied the game at 24–24 with 9:01 to play.

Murray and Charles—both Florida natives from Tampa's Plant High School—had game-highs of 313 passing yards and

108 receiving yards on six catches, respectively. All-purpose Gators back Trey Burton, who rushed for 110 yards, made five receptions, and completed a pair of passes for 26 yards, gave Florida the lead back on a 51-yard scoring run. However, a third Murray touchdown pass with 4:36 remaining in regulation tied the game again.

In the first-ever overtime game in series history, Murray was intercepted on the first possession of the extra frame—his third interception of the contest after throwing just three errant passes the first eight games of the season. It was also Georgia's 12th turnover in its last three games of the rivalry, compared to Florida's mere one.

PLAYERS *FROM* FLORIDA *ON THE* 2011 GEORGIA FOOTBALL ROSTER

	Year	Pos.	Hometown (H.S.)
Orson Charles*	Jr.	TE	Tampa (Plant)
Marc Deas	Fr.	SS	Kissimmee (Osceola)
Zach DeBell	Fr.	OL	Tarpon Springs (Tarpon Springs)
Michael Erdman	Fr.	WR	Merritt Island (Central Catholic)
Aaron Murray	So.	QB	Tampa (Plant)
Nathan Theus	Fr.	OL	Jacksonville (The Bolles School)
Carlton Thomas	Jr.	TB	Frostproof (Frostproof)
Kosta Vavlas	Fr.	ILB	Tarpon Springs (Tarpon Springs)
Blair Walsh	Sr.	PK	Boca Raton (Cardinal Gibbons)
Ramik Wilson	Fr.	LB	Tampa (Jefferson)
Rantavious Wooten	Jr.	FLK	Belle Glade (Glades Central)

* *On a recruiting trip to Florida in 2008, Charles knocked over the 2006 BCS National Championship Trophy just outside of coach Urban Meyer's office, where it shattered to the ground. Although purely an accident, Charles proved even before signing with Georgia, he was already a Gator hater.*

FLORIDA

Florida place-kicker Chas Henry celebrates after booting the game-winning field goal in overtime of the Gators' 34–31 victory over Georgia in 2010.

The Gators' overtime possession would result in a 37-yard, game-winning field-goal attempt by Chas Henry. Senior reserve Henry was filling in for an injured Caleb Sturgis and, just four weeks beforehand, had attempted his first field goal since his senior year of high school in 2006.

Before Henry attempted his kick, Georgia defensive coordinator Todd Grantham infamously grabbed his neck, signaling to the kicker the "choke" sign. To that point, Henry had indeed choked in his place-kicking role for Florida, missing a combined three critical field goals in close losses in the two previous games against LSU and Mississippi State. Unfortunately

for Georgia, on this particular attempt, Henry's kick split the uprights, seizing the Gators' 18th win in the last 21 meetings of the series.

In one of the Bulldogs' most difficult losses in recent memory, the normally erratic place-kicker celebrated with teammates by buzzing and posturing around the field while the Georgia faithful looked on in disgust and heartache.

No. 6: 1958

| FLORIDA | 0 | 0 | 0 | 7 | **7** |
| GEORGIA | 0 | 0 | 6 | 0 | **6** |

Georgia's 1958 squad has been called the "best losing team ever," considering the Bulldogs always looked impressive on the field but hardly on the scoreboard. The team entered the Florida game with a losing 2–4 record and would exit Jacksonville having lived up to its moniker.

The Bulldogs' effort against the Gators was considered perhaps their best all year. For the game, Georgia had an overwhelming 18–3 advantage in first downs, 84–28 in total plays, and 360–121 in total yardage. The problem for the Bulldogs was that 76 of Florida's total yards came on a single scoring play.

After threatening the entire game, Georgia finally scored in the third quarter when sophomore Fran Tarkenton passed to Fred Brown for a 20-yard touchdown. Halfback/place-kicker Carl Manning missed what would turn out to be a critical extra-point attempt.

Early in the final quarter, Gators quarterback Jimmy Dunn ran what was intended to be a simple keeper from his 24-yard line, but turned into a 76-yard scoring jaunt. Florida's kicker, Billy Booker, was true on his extra-point attempt, and the Gators hung on to a one-point lead.

Tarkenton led the Bulldogs back down the field, battling not only the seventh-best defense in the nation, but also a Gator Bowl scoreboard clock that was no longer functioning. Upon reaching the Gators' 16-yard line, Tarkenton thought there was more time remaining than the few seconds that were actually left. The quarterback felt he could run one more play, and after that, if need be, the Bulldogs could try a game-winning field-goal attempt.

Tarkenton's final play was a pass attempt intercepted by Jack Westbrook, marking the fifth time Georgia penetrated the Florida 20-yard line but came away without points.

When the two head coaches met at midfield afterward, Bob Woodruff indicated how lucky his Gators had been against Wally Butts' Bulldogs. "Yes, sir, you were [lucky]," said Butts. "It looks like everybody is lucky against us."

No. 5: 1984

FLORIDA	7	7	3	10	**27**
GEORGIA	0	0	0	0	**0**

In a highly anticipated meeting between top 10 teams, fighting for the top spot in the SEC, Georgia suffered its first shutout in five years and first loss to the Gators since 1977.

After scoring only 16 combined points against the Bulldogs in the previous 10 quarters of play, Florida tallied 14 before halftime, while Georgia was held scoreless and gained just 46 yards of total offense.

Trailing 17–0 late in the third quarter, the Bulldogs finally mounted a drive, reaching the Gators' 2-yard line with a first-and-goal. Four rushing plays netted only a yard, and the ball was turned over on downs. Three plays later on third down from his own 4-yard line, freshman walk-on Kerwin Bell passed to Ricky Nattiel for the longest pass play in the series' history, a 96-yard touchdown.

Adding insult to injury after the Bulldogs' loss, Florida fans, acting like they had not been there before—at least, not in seven years—stormed the field and succeeded to, as described, "destroy the stadium." Reportedly, Jacksonville police simply sat and allowed the destruction to happen while the city's mayor would say he was "tickled to death" by the damage.

The loss to the Gators would be the first of four consecutive Georgia losses to end the season. Whereas Florida, which was considered at the time the best team in school history, finished ranked third in the nation while capturing its first-ever conference title.

The Gators were finally SEC football champions…until roughly five months later when they were rightfully stripped of the title because of previous NCAA violations.

No. 4a: 1990

FLORIDA	14	10	14	0	38
GEORGIA	7	0	0	0	7

No. 4b: 1991

FLORIDA	7	21	3	14	45
GEORGIA	3	3	7	0	13

After dominating the series during the 1970s and 1980s, Georgia received a rude awakening with back-to-back blowout losses to Florida in 1990 and 1991. Each defeat was by nearly the same margin and equally painful for Dawgs fans. But each represented much more than a typical thrashing.

Significantly, the beatings announced the return of Steve Spurrier to the Gators—a new winning era filled with championships for Florida after decades of being a second-rate team—and the coach's willingness to do whatever it took to ridicule and embarrass Georgia.

"In the past, Georgia has always said Florida always gives up," Gators defensive end Mark Murray said in 1990. "This is a new Florida team, a new attitude."

Besides determination and a new attitude, Spurrier brought to Florida his then-innovative "fun 'n' gun" offense, which would have tremendous success against Georgia, and nearly every other opponent, during the decade of the 1990s.

Consider that in the three Georgia-Florida games prior to Spurrier from 1987 to 1989—all Bulldogs victories—the

Gators averaged less than eight points per game, 185 passing yards, and threw for a combined two touchdowns and seven interceptions.

In 1990 and 1991 against Georgia, Spurrier's "fun 'n' gun" averaged nearly 42 points per game, 343 passing yards, and threw for a combined eight touchdowns and no interceptions.

With the arrival of Spurrier, the Bulldogs also had to become acquainted with a tactic rather uncommon in the sport—running up the score. Possessing comfortable, late leads against Georgia in both 1990 and 1991, the coach attempted to attain a scoring margin as large as possible, and would do so a few more times against the Bulldogs before the decade would end.

TOP 5 FLORIDA PASSING GAMES vs. GEORGIA

1. **Kerwin Bell** | 408 yards | 1985
   33-for–49 | 24–3 (UGA)

2. **Rex Grossman** | 407 yards | 2001
   27-for–35, 2 TDs | 24–10 (UF)

3. **Shane Matthews** | 344 yards | 1990
   26-for–39, 3 TDs | 38–7 (UF)

4. **Rex Grossman** | 339 yards | 2002
   36-for–46, 2 TDs | 20–13 (UF)

5. **Shane Matthews** | 303 yards | 1991
   22-for–32, 4 TDs | 45–13 (UF)

FLORIDA

In an interview following the 1991 game, Spurrier made a derogatory comment regarding Georgia's development of its players. When this was brought to the attention of Ray Goff, the Bulldogs' head coach's only comment was that he "had a little more class than [Spurrier]." Avoiding a possible war of words, the much classier Goff then walked off, biting his lip.

No. 3: 1967

FLORIDA	0	7	0	10	**17**
GEORGIA	6	3	7	0	**16**

It was expected to be a relatively easy victory for Georgia in Jacksonville. The Bulldogs had been ranked fifth in the country only a week before and had the best pass defense in the nation, allowing just 70 yards per game. What's more, Heisman winner Steve Spurrier, now struggling in the NFL, was gone and replaced by a converted wide receiver, Larry Rentz.

Georgia entered as a seven-point favorite, but popular opinion was the Bulldogs would leave the Gator Bowl as victors by a much wider margin.

Things were going as expected early on when Ronnie Jenkins' one-yard touchdown run gave Georgia a 6–0 lead. However, on the extra-point attempt, Florida's Jim Hadley was knocked upside down on the play, but somehow managed to block the kick, literally with his foot.

Following a field goal by Georgia's Jim McCullough, Rentz, who had not played quarterback prior to 1967 since being a member of Florida's freshman squad, got the Gators on the

GEORGIA-FLORIDA ALL-TIME YARDSTICK
(1904–2011)

	UGA	UF
Points	1,788 (19.9)	1,483 (16.5)
First Downs	1,353 (15.6)	1,291 (14.8)
Rush Yards	15,687 (180.3)	12,003 (138.0)
Pass Yards	10,673 (122.7)	13,011 (149.6)
Total Yards	26,360 (303.0)	25,014 (287.5)

Total Attendance for all 90 games: 4,520,177 (50,224 average)

Note: First downs and rush/pass/total yards are unavailable for the first three meetings in the series—1904, 1915, and 1916.

FLORIDA

scoreboard with a 33-yard touchdown pass to Mike McCann late in the second quarter.

Early in the second half, legendary Jake Scott intercepted Rentz and returned the errant throw 32 yards for a Bulldogs touchdown. Rentz would soon leave the game with an injury; however, when reserve Harmon Wages was ineffective, the soon-to-be savior was inserted back into the game.

With just over six minutes to play and leading 16–7, Georgia appeared to have its anticipated victory wrapped up. However, a Rentz-to–Richard Trapp 52-yard touchdown pass pulled the Gators within two points.

After forcing a Bulldogs punt, Rentz and company began from their own 32-yard line, driving 55 yards in 14 plays to

the Georgia 13. With 29 seconds remaining, Gators kicker Wayne Barfield, a native of Albany, Georgia, broke the Bull-dogs' hearts with a game-winning, 31-yard field goal.

For the game, Georgia's No. 1–ranked pass defense allowed a season-high 235 passing yards with Trapp on the receiving end of 171 of them.

Two days prior to the game, the school's beloved retired mas-cot, Uga I, had passed away, making the Bulldogs' one-point upset loss particularly difficult for Georgia fans to stomach.

No. 2: 1993

FLORIDA	13	10	7	3	**33**
GEORGIA	3	17	0	6	**26**

One of the most hated Georgia-Florida games of all time was played in likely the worst weather conditions ever in the his-tory of the series. Battling in a sea of mud, steady rain, and swirling winds, the Bulldogs looked for revenge in Jacksonville after the Gators had stolen the SEC East divisional title from them the year before.

Late in the first half, an upset was in the making as Geor-gia held a 20–13 advantage. Nevertheless, Florida scored 10 points in the final 1:35 of the second quarter and another touchdown in the third to take a 30–20 lead.

Behind the arm of Eric Zeier, who attempted a school-record 65 passes, and a group of talented receivers, includ-ing tight end Shannon Mitchell, who made a school-record

15 receptions, the Bulldogs pulled within a touchdown in the final minutes.

With 1:36 remaining and trailing 33–26, Zeier drove Georgia from its 36-yard line to Florida's 12, where the Bulldogs appeared to have one chance for victory with five seconds remaining.

On the next play, Zeier completed a 12-yard touchdown to Jerry Jerman, and the score, for a brief moment, was 33–32 on the Gator Bowl scoreboard, until the touchdown was waved off by an official.

It will forever be known as "The Timeout"—the game where a supposed Florida timeout caused the officials to negate a possible game-winning touchdown for Georgia. Time was called by Gators defensive back Anthone Lott after noticing that his sideline was screaming for a timeout. An official responded by waving off the play just as Jerman made the scoring reception.

The Bulldogs had two additional shots to reclaim the touchdown that was taken from them, but to no avail, as both of Zeier's passes fell incomplete.

Following the game, Lott insisted to the media that his controversial timeout and the official's whistle blowing the play dead both came *prior* to the center's snap to Zeier. On the contrary, Lott was one mistaken Gator.

Although the timeout was clearly asked for by Lott before the snap of the ball, the official did not wave off the play nor was his whistle heard until *after* the snap was made.

"[Florida] didn't get the timeout called in time," declared ESPN's Craig James after watching a slow-motion replay. "[The officials] blew the call."

No. 1: 2002

FLORIDA	0	12	0	8	**20**
GEORGIA	7	6	0	0	**13**

For Georgia fans, there is little worse than losing to the Gators, especially if a loss ultimately costs our Bulldogs a chance to play for a national championship.

If ever a case could be made that Georgia has been jinxed in this series since the start of 1990s, such a curse was evident for the 2002 meeting with Florida. After roughly a decade or so, the Bulldogs finally entered the annual game with unquestionably the better team. Georgia was a perfect 8–0 and ranked fifth in the nation while unranked Florida had already suffered an un-Gator-like three losses on the season.

Steve Spurrier was gone and replaced with first-year coach Ron Zook, who was just two years away from being fired from his post. Whereas Georgia was guided by its best head coach since the 1980s, and the 2002 Bulldogs were the program's best team in two decades.

Early on, it appeared any curse might have been lifted as Georgia struck for the game's initial touchdown in the first quarter following an interception that had deflected off the hands of a Florida receiver. However, to some of us Dawgs fans, it was soon evident that the "Jacksonville Jinx" was alive

Florida quarterback Rex Grossman celebrates his team's 20–13 win over Georgia on November 2, 2002, which spoiled the Bulldogs' chances of playing for the national championship in an otherwise unblemished 13-win season.

and thriving. For the game, in Georgia's three other possessions which started in Gators territory following the first, the Bulldogs scored a combined three points. In addition, Georgia

committed an unusually high three turnovers, including an interception that was returned for a 47-yard touchdown.

After entering with one of the best third-down conversion rates in the entire country—46.3 percent—the Bulldogs were 0-for-13 on third downs against the Gators. Standout place-kicker Billy Bennett missed two field goals while sure-handed receiver Terrence Edwards dropped a critical, long pass late in the game that might have resulted in a touchdown.

"We missed opportunities, didn't execute, and didn't play Georgia football out there, and we lost," said All-America offensive lineman Jon Stinchcomb following the 20–13 defeat.

By the end of the season, Georgia had won a school-record 13 games, was SEC and Sugar Bowl champions, and finished ranked third in the nation just behind the two teams that had played in the national championship game.

Notwithstanding, it was the Bulldogs' loss to the Gators that kept them from playing for that national title. Furthermore, the setback was yet another example of a team expected to win the annual game, and failing to do so.

2
PLAYERS WE HATE

WITH SOME RELUCTANCE, Georgia fans will admit Florida has had some outstanding players in its football history (but that certainly doesn't mean we have to like them). In fact, through 2011, three Gators had taken home the coveted Heisman Trophy (albeit the Bulldogs whipped two of these three recipients the year they captured the award).

Although we despise all Florida players, the following is a chronological listing of the notable Gators we hate with a little more passion than all the others.

DALE VAN SICKEL

End Dale Van Sickel became Florida's initial first-team football All-American in 1928, or 15 years after the first Bulldog earned the same recognition. Although he was born in Eatonton, Georgia, which is about 50 miles from Athens, Van Sickel grew up in Gainesville, Florida, where he is still regarded as one of the greatest high school players ever from the area.

On the Gators' high-scoring team of '28, Van Sickel was a primary reason for Florida's 8–1 campaign and near-capturing of the conference title and a bowl berth. In the Gators'

26–6 win over Georgia—Florida's first-ever victory over the Bulldogs—Van Sickel made a 36-yard touchdown reception in the third quarter.

In Florida's meeting with Georgia the following season, senior Van Sickel, suffering through an injury, blocked a Bulldogs third-quarter punt. On the ensuring drive and facing fourth down, the star end caught an eight-yard touchdown pass from Clyde Crabtree.

Van Sickel's two career touchdowns against Georgia would not be bettered in the series by a Gator for another 20 years, while Florida's back-to-back victories over the Bulldogs in 1928 and 1929 would not be duplicated for nearly another quarter-century.

After coaching at Florida as an assistant in 1930 and 1931, Van Sickel moved to Hollywood, where for the next four decades, he either performed on-screen stunts or made appearances in more than 400 films and television episodes. During this time, he also became the first president of the Motion Picture Stuntman's Association.

CHARLES HUNSINGER

Charles "Chuck" Hunsinger introduced himself to the Bull-dogs as a mere freshman in a 33–14 loss in 1946. In the Gators' setback, he totaled 136 all-purpose yards on just nine touches, including a 57-yard reception. Two years later in Jacksonville, in what was expected to be a runaway victory for Georgia, Hunsinger returned a punt for a 64-yard touchdown in a close 20–12 Florida loss.

For the 1948 season, Hunsinger was recognized as a first-team All-SEC member, rushing for 842 yards—the eighth-most in the nation—while averaging 7.3 yards per carry—the fifth highest.

A week after rushing for 199 yards against Furman in 1949— at the time, the second-most rushing yards in school history for a single game—Hunsinger spearheaded Florida's first victory over Georgia in nine years. In being recognized as the SEC's Back of the Week, he rushed for 174 yards and three touchdowns on 18 rushes in the Gators' historic 28–7 win.

Hunsinger became the first Gator to rush for 2,000 yards in a career, gaining 2,017 from 1946 to 1949, which would be a

HE'S A "HUM-" WHAT?!?

Whereas Georgia fans sang the catchy "You Gotta Give Herschel Walker the Ball" in the early 1980s, the Gators were stuck with "The Hunsinger Song" a few decades before. Chuck Hunsinger was so popular with the University of Florida student body, a song was written about him. However, he did not deserve this intolerable tune, which without a doubt must rank among the worst theme songs in the history of college football:

> *Hunsinger's a Humdinger not ever will he linger*
> *in ramming a ball thru the enemy's wall.*
> *No player is torrider than this lad from Florida,*
> *Hunsinger the Humdinger you ought to see him go!*
> *I may be a bumsinger but he's the goods is Hunsinger,*
> *no campus flirt but an end he can skirt.*
> *No player is torrider than this lad from Florida,*
> *Hunsinger the Humdinger you ought to see him go!*

FLORIDA

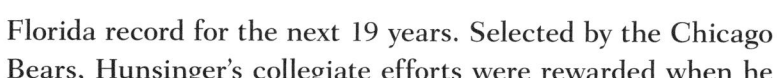
Florida record for the next 19 years. Selected by the Chicago Bears, Hunsinger's collegiate efforts were rewarded when he was the third overall pick of the 1950 NFL Draft.

LARRY DUPREE

Although our hatred for Florida runs deep, Georgia fans are compassionate people and receptive to an inspiring story, even if it might be at the expense of our Bulldogs.

From just over the southern Georgia border in Macclenny, Florida, fullback Larry Dupree decided to attend his state school after an all-out recruiting battle between the Gators and Bulldogs. In 1962 Dupree reminded Georgia of what it was missing by rushing for 111 yards against the Bulldogs, including touchdown runs of 41 and 11 yards, in a 23–15 Florida victory. That season as just a sophomore, Dupree would lead the SEC with 604 rushing yards.

Two days before the Georgia-Florida game a year later, Dupree took his wife, Denise, to a Gainesville hospital for the birth of their first child. However, four hours later, the Duprees were dealt an unthinkable tragedy when the baby, a son, was born dead.

While Coach Ray Graves left it up to Dupree to decide whether he would travel with the team to Jacksonville, Denise urged her husband to play in the game against the Bulldogs. Dupree complied and arrived at the Gator Bowl just prior to kickoff.

"I had practically no sleep the past two nights," Dupree said right before the start of the game. "My legs are tired."

If Dupree's legs were tired, no one would have ever known, particularly the Bulldogs. Rushing for 74 yards and a touchdown on 19 carries and catching a 34-yard pass, the junior fullback was the "vital force in our victory," according to Graves, and the inspiration in a 21–14 Florida win—the Gators' fourth consecutive victory over Georgia.

In 1963 Dupree bettered his conference-leading efforts from the year before by gaining 745 yards. A year later, he scored Florida's lone touchdown in its 14–7 loss to Georgia. For his final season, Dupree was recognized as first-team All-America by the American Football Coaches Association while becoming only the third back in league history to earn first-team All-SEC three consecutive years.

STEVE SPURRIER

He could pass, run, punt, kick, and even caught three passes while at Florida, and before he was the Gators' hated head coach, Stephen Orr Spurrier was their loathed, but legendary, quarterback from 1964 to 1966.

As a sophomore, Spurrier supplanted senior Tom Shannon as Florida's starting signal caller and finished the year passing for nearly 1,000 yards, while executing two of the longest punts in school history with 63-yarders against both Miami (Fla.) and LSU.

In 1965 Spurrier passed for 1,893 yards, rushed for another 230, was selected as first-team All-America by the Football Writers Association of America, and finished ninth in the Heisman Trophy voting. A year later as a senior, he would

HEISMAN WINNERS IN THE
GEORGIA-FLORIDA RIVALRY

Of the three Gators recipients of the Heisman Trophy through 2011, only one defeated the Bulldogs the season he captured the award. In comparison, both of Georgia's Heisman recipients were on teams that easily beat Florida.

Year	Heisman Recipient	UGA-UF Result
1942	**Frank Sinkwich** (UGA)	Georgia, 75–0
	10 rushes, 71 yards, 2 TDs, 5-for-9 passing, 112 yards, 2 TDs, 2 punts, 41.5-yard avg.	
1966	**Steve Spurrier** (UF)	Georgia, 27–10
	16-for-29 passing, 133 yards, 3 INT, 9 rushes, −21 yards, 6 punts, 39-yard avg.	
1982	**Herschel Walker** (UGA)	Georgia, 44–0
	35 rushes, 219 yards, 3 TDs	
1996	**Danny Wuerffel** (UF)	Florida, 47–7
	16-for-23 passing, 279 yards, 4 TDs, 1 INT, 3 rushes, −21 yards	
2007	**Tim Tebow** (UF)	Georgia, 42–30
	14-for-22 passing, 236 yards, 1 TD, 13 rushes, −15 yards, 2 TDs	

win the distinguished trophy after completing 61.5 percent of his passes for 2,012 yards, punting for a 41-yard average, and kicking three field goals, including a game-winning 40-yarder to defeat Auburn.

Even so, what many Bulldogs fans recall from Spurrier's Heisman-winning campaign was his miserable second-half performance against Georgia, dealing the Gators an upset loss

in 1966 while ruining their chances for an undefeated season and SEC title. For the Bulldogs, it was their second unexpected victory over a Spurrier-led team in three years. In 1964 a late Georgia touchdown on a botched field-goal try and an interception thrown by Spurrier secured the first upset win.

Spurrier's one shining moment against the Bulldogs was as a junior in 1965. Trailing 10–7 with just more than four minutes to play, he completed two consecutive passes for a total of 78 yards; the second was a 32-yard, game-winning touchdown to Jack Harper.

For his Gators playing career, Spurrier passed for 4,848 yards, rushed for 442, was responsible for 30 touchdowns, and had a 40.3 punting average. In three games against Georgia, he completed only 51.5 percent of his passes for 414 yards, passed for just one touchdown, and threw five interceptions.

Most importantly, Spurrier was 2-for-3 when it came to being on the losing end against the Bulldogs.

JACK YOUNGBLOOD

Although Jack Youngblood's toughness and endurance is respected and admired, the fumble he "stole" from the Bulldogs in 1970 is a play we would like to forget.

Well into the fourth quarter of that season's Georgia-Florida game, the Bulldogs looked to build upon their 17–10 lead as they had possession on the Gators' 1-yard line, facing second-and-goal. Subsequently, quarterback Paul Gilbert made a bad pitch, and a mass of players piled up on the loose ball. Coming

Florida defensive end Jack Youngblood (74), in action against the Georgia Bulldogs at the Gator Bowl in Jacksonville, made one of the most controversial fumble "recoveries" in the rivalry's history in 1970. Photo courtesy of Getty Images

out of the pile with the fumble recovery was senior Youngblood. The Gators would soon tie the game with 5:13 remaining and then take a 24–17 lead they would not relinquish with 1:39 to play.

After Florida's comeback win, Youngblood admitted to the press that he originally didn't recover the decisive fumble; he stole it from a Georgia player in the pile-up. "They had [the ball] in their hands, and I just snatched it away from him," said Youngblood.

Youngblood, who is still regarded as the school's greatest defensive end of all time, capped his Gators career by being recognized as first-team All-America. Youngblood's 29 career sacks, including 10 in 1970, were an unofficial school record until the early 2000s.

Notably, Youngblood is likely the only player in the modern era of college football to be recognized as a conference's most valuable defensive lineman (1970) only two years after serving as his team's primary place-kicker (14 PATs and seven field goals in 1968).

Youngblood had a stellar career with the NFL's Los Angeles Rams from 1971 to 1984, remarkably missing just one of the 203 games his teams played. In 2001 he became the first Gator inducted into the Pro Football Hall of Fame.

CARLOS ALVAREZ

First and foremost, we'd like to point out that Carlos Alvarez managed a remarkable feat not pulled off by any other Gator

FLORIDA

GATORS *AND* BULLDOGS *IN THE* COLLEGE FOOTBALL HALL *OF* FAME

Florida Players (6)	Pos.	Years	Inducted
Dale Van Sickel	E	1927–1929	1975
Steve Spurrier	QB	1964–1966	1986
Jack Youngblood	DE	1968–1970	1992
Emmitt Smith	RB	1987–1989	2006
Wilber Marshall	LB	1980–1983	2008
Carlos Alvarez	WR	1969–1971	2011

Florida Coaches (3)		Years	Inducted
Charles Bachman		1928–1932	1978
Ray Graves		1960–1969	1990
Doug Dickey		1970–1978	2003

Georgia Players (12)	Pos.	Years	Inducted
Bob McWhorter	HB	1910–1913	1954
Frank Sinkwich	HB	1940–1942	1954
Charley Trippi	HB	1942, 1945–1946	1959
Vernon Smith	E	1929–1931	1979
Bill Hartman	FB	1935–1937	1984
Fran Tarkenton	QB	1958–1960	1987
Bill Stanfill	DT	1966–1968	1998
Herschel Walker	TB	1980–1982	1999
Terry Hoage	DB	1980–1983	2000
Kevin Butler	PK	1981–1984	2001
John Rauch	QB	1945–1948	2003
Jake Scott	DB	1967–1968	2011

Georgia Coaches (4)	Years	Inducted
Glenn "Pop" Warner	1895–1896	1951
Vince Dooley	1964–1988	1994
Wally Butts	1939–1960	1997
Jim Donnan	1996–2000	2009

or Bulldog in history: he was recognized as a consensus All-American in his first season on the varsity team, but then inexplicably was not even a first-team all-conference honoree in any of his subsequent seasons.

In 1969 the "Cuban Comet" made 88 receptions for 1,329 yards and 12 touchdowns. For the 1970 and 1971 seasons, Alvarez's totals *combined* did not equal his performance as a sophomore. Nevertheless, his best performance against the Bulldogs was as a junior in 1970, when Alvarez made five catches for 135 yards, gained 22 yards on an end-around, and scored the tying and winning touchdowns to upset Georgia 24–17.

Besides his blazing speed, Alvarez was one smart Gator. The three-time Academic All-American became the first Florida player inducted into the Verizon Academic All-America Hall of Fame in 1989. After earning his law degree, Alvarez has spent the last quarter-century as a lawyer, likely representing his fair share of the many arrested Gators during the Coach Urban Meyer era.

In 2011 Alvarez accomplished another rarity by having played at Florida—he was inducted into the College Football Hall of Fame.

JOHN REAVES

As a sophomore in 1969, quarterback John Reaves passed for 24 touchdowns and nearly 3,000 yards, while leading the Gators to a 9–1–1 record. However, Reaves' output in 1970 and 1971, along with the entire team's, regressed, and the Gators finished with a 4–7 record his final season.

After being limited to 2,104 passing yards and 17 touchdowns while throwing 21 interceptions as a senior in 1971, Reaves still was somehow selected as *Time* magazine's first-team All-America quarterback. He also was the recipient of the Sammy Baugh Trophy as the nation's best college passer. Auburn quarterback Pat Sullivan, who won the Heisman Trophy that season, apparently wasn't quite as good as Reaves to be on the receiving end of those two honors.

With approximately two minutes remaining against Miami (Fla.) in his final game at Florida, Reaves trailed the great Jim Plunkett of Stanford by 13 yards as the NCAA's all-time leading passer. In an attempt to get its offense back on the field, Florida purposely allowed a Miami (Fla.) touchdown by falling to the ground in mid-play.

In what was called by Hurricanes head coach Fran Curci as the worst exhibition of football he'd ever seen, the Gators got the ball back on offense, and Reaves fittingly broke the all-time record with a completion to his primary target for three seasons, Carlos Alvarez.

Not until 1987 were Reaves' school records of 7,549 career passing yards and 54 touchdowns broken. His 59 career

interceptions remain a Florida record by 13 more than any other Gator.

Despite completing just 41 percent of his 83 career passes in three games against Georgia, Reaves was intercepted just one time and managed to lose only once to the Bulldogs.

WES CHANDLER

It is hard to imagine Florida, or nearly any team nowadays, for that matter, running out of the wishbone formation. Nonetheless, the Gators did indeed run some form of the run-oriented offense from 1974 to 1977. It was during these four seasons that Wes Chandler—ironically, a wide receiver—emerged as one of the greatest Gators to ever grace a gridiron, including the Gator Bowl's.

As a junior in 1976, Chandler made 44 receptions, including 10 for touchdowns, for nearly 1,000 yards, and was recognized as first-team All-America. Against Georgia, he caught two touchdown passes in the first half as the confident Gators, who had been quite boastful the week of the game, led the Bulldogs 27–13 at halftime. However, in the second half, Florida's wishbone sputtered while Georgia's veer formation flourished, and the Bulldogs scored 28 unanswered points en route to a victory.

In 1977 Coach Doug Dickey thought it would be beneficial to have his All-America receiver run the ball, as well. Chandler, who had rushed for only three yards in his first three seasons combined, would lineup at a halfback position when the Gators were in their wishbone but move to receiver when the offense converted to an I formation.

In a 22–17 win over Georgia, Chandler had three receptions for 50 yards, including a one-handed touchdown grab, and gained 52 rushing yards and two touchdowns on 15 carries. His five career touchdowns in the Georgia-Florida rivalry was a stand-alone series record for a Gator until matched by Chris Doering in 1995, and recently surpassed by Tim Tebow.

In 1977 Chandler earned All-America honors for a second time and finished 10th in the Heisman Trophy voting. His 353 rushing yards as a senior were a school record by a receiver which stood for almost 30 years.

On a side note, after quarterback Ray Goff led Georgia to its memorable comeback victory over Florida in 1976, he was asked how he felt about all the pregame boasting by the Gators. "I remember reading in a Florida paper that Wes Chandler said that only God can stop him and that he could *still* probably get a first down," said Goff. "It really bothered me that he didn't have anymore respect for the Lord than that."

Particularly in 1976 and 1977, Chandler was truly a nemesis of the Bulldogs; he was perhaps the most versatile player to ever appear in this series—a fact of which he was evidently fully cognizant.

CRIS COLLINSWORTH

Cris Collinsworth came to the University of Florida as not only a highly touted quarterback prospect, but was also a state high-school champion in the 100-yard dash. In his first game as a Gator in the 1977 season opener against Rice, he completed a 99-yard touchdown pass to Derrick Gaffney.

Completing just two of nine passes with two interceptions the rest of his freshman year, the NCAA-record pass completion would be Collinsworth's lone bright moment as a collegiate quarterback. Head coach Doug Dickey moved the signal-caller to wide receiver, where Collinsworth would earn first-team All-SEC honors for the next three seasons.

In 1978 Collinsworth caught 39 passes for 745 yards and nine touchdowns and returned a kickoff 97 yards for a score versus LSU. Against Georgia, he caught a 33-yard touchdown pass from John Brantley in the second quarter. Late in the game, he caught a lateral, and reminiscent of his days as a quarterback, passed for a 36-yard touchdown to Ron Enclade.

As a senior in 1980—a season he led the SEC in receiving—Collinsworth was relatively held in check by the Bulldogs. In Georgia's 26–21 victory, the All-American caught just three passes for 29 yards.

Collinsworth played eight years in the NFL with the Cincinnati Bengals, including the first three (1981 to 1983) as a Pro Bowler. (Interestingly, against the Pittsburgh Steelers in 1985, the only professional pass he ever attempted was intercepted.)

Although there are some who say his style of journalism can be viewed as one who is somewhat bitter and arrogant, Collinsworth has enjoyed a flourishing television broadcasting career for more than 20 years.

For what it's worth, following Georgia's win over Florida in 1980, Collinsworth was quoted as saying that the Buck Belue–to–Lindsay Scott miracle touchdown was merely a "fluke" and

the Gators deserved to win. He would later add, "Take away the 72-yard run by [Herschel] Walker and [Lindsay] Scott's 93-yard touchdown run, and we would have beaten the [Bull-dogs] in a rout."

Cris Collinsworth—bitter and arrogant? Never!

KERWIN BELL

A week prior to Florida's season opener of 1984, the Gator Nation was astonished when head coach Charley Pell announced his resignation effective at the end of the year, the result of an NCAA 20-month probe into possible violations. (Pell would ultimately last just three games before his firing.)

A few days later, Pell dropped another bombshell by declaring walk-on and redshirt freshman Kerwin Bell, who at one time was eighth on the Gators' depth chart, the starting quarterback against the defending national champion Miami Hurricanes.

Bell and the Gators were defeated by the Hurricanes in that opening game, but it would be Florida's only setback of the season as it finished with an improbable 9–1–1 record and an SEC title. (Like Pell, the championship wouldn't last long at Florida, either.)

Bell, who sported the greatest mustache in the history of the Georgia-Florida rivalry, had possibly the best season ever by a walk-on quarterback. In being named the SEC Player of the Year by the league coaches, Bell was the fourth-highest-rated passer in the nation. He was especially efficient in a 27–0 win

over the Bulldogs, passing for 178 yards, two touchdowns, and no interceptions.

A year later, quarterbacking the No. 1–ranked Gators, Bell set single-game school records with 408 passing yards on 33 completions against Georgia, but his team still lost by a score of 24–3. Regardless, the former walk-on would end his sophomore season with the second-highest passing-efficiency rating in the country and the Gators once again finished with a record of 9–1–1.

In 1986 and 1987, as Florida struggled to achieve a combined 12–11 record, Bell's passing prowess slipped, as well. He managed to end his career as the SEC's all-time career leader with 7,585 passing yards and 56 passing touchdowns. In four career games against the Bulldogs, Bell completed 64 percent of his passes for 1,020 yards, six touchdowns, five interceptions, and was a winner in two of four games.

Not bad for a former walk-on who wasn't even pictured in the Gators' 1984 media guide.

EMMITT SMITH

Clemson football fans love to rehash how our legendary Herschel Walker never scored a touchdown against their Tigers. However, conveniently not brought up is how Herschel twice rushed for more than 100 yards in the three meetings and, most importantly, the Bulldogs won two of the three games.

But perhaps that's a *Love/Hate* book for another time…

Rarely will you hear Bulldogs fans recount how Florida's Emmitt Smith never scored in three games against Georgia. In addition, Smith rushed for more than 100 yards just once in three tries, and above all, Georgia won all three meetings.

At any rate, Smith's lack of production against Georgia is hardly a big deal to the Bulldogs (although maybe we can touch upon it solely for the purpose of this book). In 1987 Smith broke the NCAA freshman record by reaching the 1,000-yard rushing mark in just his seventh game. Two weeks later, Georgia would be facing Florida's freshman sensation— the best first-year running back in college football since the Bulldogs' own Herschel Walker seven years before.

"I'm really looking forward to playing in my first Florida-Georgia game," said Smith. "They have a strong defense, particularly against the run. We'll need a good week of preparation to play in this one."

Come to find out, Smith and his fellow Gators would have needed much more than a week to prepare as Georgia cruised to a relatively easy victory. In the 23–10 Florida loss, Smith was held to 46 yards on 13 carries.

In 1988 it was more of the same as Smith was limited to 68 yards on 19 rushes in a 26–3 Bulldogs victory. A year later, in his final season at Florida, Smith totaled 106 yards in Jacksonville but yet again, he couldn't find the end zone, and the Gators were defeated 17–10 by Georgia.

In three games against the Bulldogs, Smith averaged just 73 rushing yards per contest, gained 4.1 yards per carry, and did

not score a touchdown. Compare those figures to Smith's 132-yard average, 5.7 yards per carry, and total of 36 touchdowns in his 28 games against other regular season opponents.

Prior to a brilliant NFL career, there's no denying Emmitt Smith had an outstanding three-season run at Florida. His accolades included being a three-time first-team All-SEC pick, a two-time top-10 finisher in the Heisman Trophy voting, the 1987 SEC Freshman of the Year, and the 1989 SEC Player of the Year.

Be that as it may, Smith certainly had his troubles against—as he himself identified—the Bulldogs' "strong defense, particularly against the run."

HUEY RICHARDSON

For the Georgia Bulldogs, linebacker Huey Richardson is an example of homegrown talent who was lost to the enemy. Recruited heavily from Atlanta's Lakeside High School, Richardson decided to become a Gator and uphold Florida's rich tradition of producing first-rate linebackers. In 1987 he was off to a good start when he was named to the SEC's All-Freshman Team.

Shortly after the end of his sophomore season, Richardson was involved in an altercation with a clerk at a Gainesville liquor store. The dispute began when the clerk would not sell beer to the of-age Florida player because, as Richardson stated, "he didn't like my ID"—a valid state of Georgia driver's license.

To any top-notch Georgia high-school recruit: see what can happen if you decide to leave the state for Florida?

FLORIDA

TRAITORS TO GEORGIA

Prior to each football season beginning in 1985, the *Atlanta Journal-Constitution* has selected its 11 most highly regarded senior football players from the state of Georgia—the AJC Super11. In 27 years, from 1985 to 2011, of the 282 of these Super11 players signing with FBS schools, an overwhelming 115 signed with the University of Georgia.

A number of Georgia's best-of-the-best high schoolers decided to venture out of state, including 25 signing with Auburn, 18 with Tennessee, 16 with Florida State, 11 with Alabama, 11 with Clemson, and eight with the hated Gators:

	Florida Signee	Pos.	High School
1985	Huey Richardson	DL/TE	Lakeside (Atlanta)
1993	Nafis Karim	WR	Pope
1997	Robert Cromartie	RB/DB	Douglass (Atlanta)
1998	Jeff Womble	DL	Dunwoody
1999	Kelvin Kight	WR	Lithonia
2005	Justin Williams	WR	Charlton County
2007	Omar Hunter*	DT	Buford
2009	Mack Brown*	RB	M.L. King

*Hunter, Brown, and freshman linebacker Michael Taylor of Atlanta's Westlake High School were the only players/traitors on the Gators' 2011 roster hailing from the state of Georgia.

Approximately two months later, Richardson was stabbed under his collarbone in a parking lot after coming to the aid of a friend involved in a fight. Despite suffering a collapsed lung, the junior linebacker recorded 12½ sacks during the 1989 season, 10 other tackles for loss, was a first-team All-SEC selection, and was named the Gators' MVP in their Freedom Bowl appearance.

A year later, Richardson helped reinforce the fact that UGA's football recruiting had dropped off during the mid- to late 1980s. Four of the 25 first-team players on the Associated Press' 1990 All-America team, including Richardson, were from the state of Georgia, however, none played for the Bulldogs.

Also that year Richardson became only the fourth Florida football player ever to receive the NCAA Post-Graduate Scholarship Award and was the first in school history to be named to the SEC Academic Honor Roll for four consecutive years.

It figures that an intelligent Gator was not actually from the state of Florida.

SHANE MATTHEWS

Although quarterback Shane Matthews, sporting a mullet-style haircut, obviously fit in immediately with the student body at the University of Florida, it appeared early on that the Pascagoula, Mississippi, native would not fit in with the Gators' out-of-date offense.

After redshirting as a true freshman, Matthews found himself way down the depth chart in 1989. "I just stood there [during

practice], shooting the bull with everybody," said Matthews of his redshirt freshman season. "The trainers even used to bring me packs of gum to chew, because I was so bored."

Based on an anonymous letter sent to Florida's athletics director Bill Arnsparger midway through the 1989 football season, four Gators players, including Matthews, were temporarily kicked off the team for betting on college and NFL games. The bets were placed by phoning a friend in Athens, Georgia.

For the sake of the four players, we hope they weren't betting on the Gators over the Bulldogs during the latter part of the 1980s.

By the time Steve Spurrier arrived in Gainesville in 1990, the players had been reinstated to the team. At the time, Matthews was listed as a fifth-stringer; however, like so many other things that changed after Spurrier's arrival, so did the fate of the sophomore quarterback.

Matthews quickly climbed up the depth chart and entered the 1990 season as the Gators' starting quarterback, beating out Kyle Morris, who had been Florida's starting signal-caller in 1988 and 1989 before being one of the four Gators booted for gambling.

(Surely it didn't help Morris' case to be the starter of the Gators when, come to find out, he had wagered on Clemson over the Spurrier-coached Duke Blue Devils the year before.)

Against Oklahoma State in the 1990 season opener, Matthews proved to be the perfect fit for Spurrier's new system, completing 20 of 29 passes for 332 yards in a 50–7 Florida victory.

By season's end, the improbable record-breaking quarterback had been named the SEC Player of the Year while leading the Gators to a 9–2 record.

As a junior, Matthews repeated as the conference's best player and finished fifth in the Heisman Trophy balloting, while Florida captured its first conference championship (and it was about time). In his final season of 1992, Matthews was the recipient of the Unitas Golden Arm Award and was a first-team All-SEC quarterback for the third consecutive year.

And did Matthews also have tremendous success when facing the Georgia Bulldogs? You can bet on it. In three games—all Florida victories by an average of nearly 22 points—he completed 76 of 116 passes (66 percent) for 948 yards, nine touchdowns, and remarkably was not intercepted.

ERRICT RHETT

What could be so frustrating for opposing defenses of Coach Steve Spurrier's "fun 'n' gun" offense of the early 1990s? Just when it appeared a defense was beginning to contain the Gators' passing game, Errict Rhett—arguably Florida's most dangerous weapon at the time—would seemingly run wild. For four games in the early 1990s, this was certainly the case for Georgia's defense, particularly in 1993.

In a rainy quagmire called the Gator Bowl that year, the Bulldogs actually led heavily favored Florida by a touchdown late in the second quarter. Georgia's dismal defense had somehow stopped the Gators' aerial attack and forced the benching of Freshman All-America quarterback Danny Wuerffel.

So what does the pass-oriented Spurrier do? He turns to Rhett, turning and handing him the ball on what seemed like every play. In the end, the senior running back had a school-record 41 carries for 183 yards and two touchdowns as the Gators outlasted the Bulldogs in the mud 33–26.

Rhett was no stranger to Georgia, or most any other opposing defense, for that matter. After gaining 845 yards as a freshman, he led the SEC in rushing the following season in 1991. Entering the Georgia-Florida game that year, the Bulldogs resembled a team with a legitimate shot against the Gators after a 31-point loss the year before. Georgia was armed with Eric Zeier's passing, Garrison Hearst's rushing, and the school's best defense in years. Still, Rhett was not phased the least bit.

"I don't care if [the Bulldogs] had Lawrence Taylor, we're not going to be intimidated by anyone," Rhett said the week of the game. "We're still going to run it straight at them." And run it Rhett did, gaining 124 rushing yards and a touchdown on 25 carries. Add in a near-perfect day passing for Shane Matthews and the result was a second straight easy victory by Florida over Georgia, 45–13.

Rhett's 4,163 career rushing yards remains a school record and is the fifth most in SEC history. Notably, he was the first player in NCAA Division I-A history to rush for over 4,100 yards and make more than 140 receptions. To date, Rhett is the only Gator to lead his team in rushing for four straight seasons.

CHRIS DOERING

The son of a University of Florida pharmacy professor, Chris Doering grew up in Gainesville, attending Florida football games and idolizing Cris Collinsworth—a sad, but true set of unfortunate circumstances that shouldn't be bestowed upon anyone. Nevertheless, few would have guessed the slow, skinny kid would actually play for the Gators, while no one predicted he'd eventually break his idol's records.

When it became clear no Division I school was going to offer Doering a scholarship after high school, he decided to walk on at the school that had shown him some interest in the recruiting process—Florida State.

While attending a baseball game, hearing the Seminole chant countless times and watching the tomahawk chop ad nauseam, Doering finally turned to his father and said there was no way he could attend Florida State.

Doering walked on at Florida in the summer of 1993 and was eventually offered a scholarship, but only after a Gators recruit was declared ineligible. "When [Coach Spurrier] offered it to me, I ran upstairs and signed it right quick, before they could take it away from me," Doering said.

In the season opener of 1993, Doering made three receptions in his first game as a scholarship player. A week later against Kentucky, he became a household name in the Gator Nation when his 28-yard touchdown reception from Danny Wuerffel—or "The Catch"—defeated the Wildcats.

Doering, a first-team All-SEC selection and a second-team All-American as a senior in 1995, caught 149 career passes for 2,107 yards in just three seasons. His 31 touchdown receptions, including 17 in 1995, were an SEC record that stood for seven years until broken by Georgia's Terrence Edwards. Five of Doering's career touchdown catches—two in 1994 and three in 1995—were against the Bulldogs, while all five were scored within the first 19 minutes of their respective games.

Florida football prides itself on its walk-on program, which has produced the likes of quarterback Kerwin Bell, Thorpe Award finalist Louis Oliver, and the Gators' all-time leading scorer Jeff Chandler. A case can be made that the best of the bunch is Chris Doering, who walked on to become one of the greatest receivers in Florida history and a true Bulldogs adversary.

DANNY WUERFFEL

Gator haters often take pleasure in the fact that nearly all Florida quarterbacks excelling at the collegiate level have struggled upon taking the next step to the pros. A prime example is Danny Wuerffel, who had a forgettable NFL career after being perhaps the most decorated Gators football player of all time.

Wuerffel entered his redshirt season of 1993 battling with Terry Dean for the Gators' starting quarterback position. Whereas Wuerffel was described as a "choirboy," Dean had already predicted that he could lead Florida to a national championship. This, after the cocky junior had completed just 19 combined passes as a backup the previous two years.

In the second game of the season, starter Dean was benched against Kentucky, and Wuerffel promptly led the team to a comeback victory over the Wildcats. Thus began Coach Steve Spurrier's infamous tendency to play "musical quarterbacks" with his Gators signal-callers. Wuerffel would start the following week and lead Florida to a victory over fifth-ranked Tennessee, but he too would eventually be sidelined by Spurrier.

For the entire 1993 and 1994 seasons, Wuerffel and Dean split time under center for Florida, each attempting more than 400 combined passes.

With Dean having departed, Wuerffel was absolutely extraordinary in 1995, completing approximately 65 percent of his passes for 3,266 yards and 35 touchdowns. He finished third in the Heisman Trophy voting and guided the Gators to a perfect 12–0 regular season record.

In his senior season, Wuerffel even bettered his staggering numbers of the year before, passing for 3,625 yards and 39 touchdowns. In 1996 he took home the school's second Heisman Trophy, and roughly a month later the choirboy was the quarterback leading Florida to a national championship with a 52–20 win over Florida State in the Sugar Bowl.

And Dawgs fans were quite glad when this Gator no longer played in Gainesville (and Jacksonville). In four games against Georgia, Wuerffel completed 63 percent of his passes for 767 yards, 11 touchdowns, and five interceptions. Notably, he is the only Florida starting quarterback with a perfect 4–0 record in the series.

FLORIDA

MISSING THOSE COLLEGE DAYS

Of the 10 Gators who have started at quarterback in at least one regular season NFL game through 2011, only two had winning professional records as a starter. In order of their NFL career passer rating, each Florida quarterback is listed with their career record as a starter, passing yards, TDs, and interceptions. Keep in mind the average passer rating in the NFL for the 2011 season was 82.5, proving, at least for Gators quarterbacks, college certainly is the best time of your life.

	Record	Pass Yds	TDs	INT	Rating
Tim Tebow	8–6	2,383	17	9	75.1
Shane Matthews	11–11	4,756	31	24	75.0
Rex Grossman	25–22	10,232	56	60	71.4
Doug Johnson	2–9	2,600	13	18	69.4
Steve Spurrier	13–24–1	6,878	40	60	60.1
Jesse Palmer	0–3	562	3	4	59.8
Danny Wuerffel	4–6	2,123	12	22	56.4
John Reaves	4–13	3,617	17	34	51.4
Kay Stephenson	0–3	481	6	9	36.3
Carl Brumbaugh	1–1	656	9	14	34.9

Although his NFL career floundered, Wuerffel is a prime example of a Gator gone good. Since his professional playing days, he has led a non-profit Christian organization, engaging in charitable work in a number of states.

"THE BACHELOR"

Although Gainesville is more than 1,300 miles from Nepean, Ontario, Canada, Jesse Palmer did not hesitate to travel far from home after high school to join fellow cheeseballs at the University of Florida.

Palmer found himself backing up Doug Johnson at quarterback from 1997 to 1999 and a reserve to Rex Grossman as a senior. Although he was a member of Florida teams that were 3–1 against Georgia, Palmer hardly contributed against the Bulldogs, appearing in just two games and gaining 84 yards of total offense in 27 plays—a whopping average of 3.1 yards per play.

Despite never leading the Gators in annual passing, Palmer was a fourth-round selection in the 2001 NFL Draft. With the New York Giants, he started the last three games of the 2003 season, losing all three contests, in what would be Palmer's final appearances in the league.

In the spring of 2004, Palmer began a budding television career by becoming ABC-TV's *The Bachelor*. On the reality show, Palmer hassled women, handed out roses, and annoyed most everyone—characteristics of your typical Gator—in front of millions of viewers. Not that we were watching, but in the end, Jesse picked Jessica; however, like the former's NFL career, the relationship between the two was short-lived.

In 2011 ESPNU began airing *The Palmer and Pollack Show* cohosted by Palmer and former Bulldogs great David

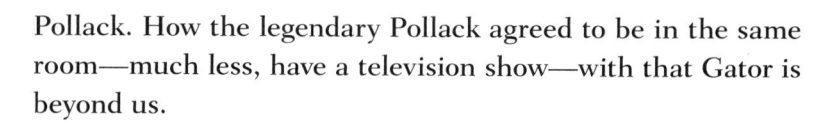

Pollack. How the legendary Pollack agreed to be in the same room—much less, have a television show—with that Gator is beyond us.

REX GROSSMAN

Despite having lost starter Doug Johnson, the Gators opened their summer practices in 2000 apparently in good shape at the quarterback position. Senior returnee Jesse Palmer had been a solid backup for three years, true freshman Brock Berlin was considered the No. 1 prospect coming out of high school, and then there was the other guy—Rex Grossman.

Grossman, a redshirt freshman with an unconventional delivery, was merely hoping to get a fair shot at the starting position. By the start of the season, Palmer was declared the starter while Grossman was the Gators' No. 2 quarterback. During Florida's fifth game—a 47–35 embarrassing loss at Mississippi State—Palmer was benched, and the quarterback who seemingly was overlooked only a month or so before finally got his shot.

Like others before him under Steve Spurrier, Grossman's talents were not extraordinary; however, he was a perfect fit for the coach's offensive system. Beginning with a 41–9 win over LSU in 2000, Grossman would start each of his last 30 regular season games as a Gator.

As a sophomore in 2001, Grossman passed for nearly 4,000 yards, completed 66 percent of his passes, and threw 34 touchdowns. Against Georgia, he picked apart a skilled secondary, completing 27 of 35 passes for 407 yards—the fifth-most individual passing yards ever against the Bulldogs.

It's a wonder we lost that game in 2001 to Rex and the Gators by only a 24–10 score.

Grossman finished runner-up for the Heisman Trophy voting that season to Nebraska quarterback Eric Crouch, losing by a scant 62 points. Although we hate to admit it, Grossman should have received the coveted award that year, and probably would have if the voting had rightfully occurred following the bowl games.

Entering the Georgia-Florida game of 2002, Coach Ron Zook had replaced a departed Spurrier, and the Gators were struggling, including their All-America quarterback. Regardless, Grossman dinked and dunked Florida to a 20–13 upset win over the Bulldogs, passing for 339 yards on a school-record 36 completions. In his career against Georgia, Grossman passed for just four touchdowns and threw seven interceptions, but yet was 3–0 against the Bulldogs.

Even when the chips were stacked against Grossman, like when he became Florida's starting quarterback as a freshman, he still seemed to somehow always deliver. Unfortunately, for us Dawgs fans, this was particularly the case in Jacksonville.

BRANDON SPIKES

Undeniably, Brandon Spikes is one of the greatest defenders ever to play football for the University of Florida. As only a sophomore in 2007, he led the Gators in tackles and repeated the feat a year later as a junior. From his linebacker position, Spikes remarkably returned a school-record four interceptions for touchdowns during his career.

Spikes was a three-time first-team All-SEC selection from 2007 to 2009 and a first-team All-American in 2008 and 2009. He was also the first Gator ever to be selected as both a Lombardi Award and Butkus Award finalist in two different seasons.

That's all well and good—accolades even us Georgia fans can appreciate (just a little). We even acknowledge Spikes' thunderous hit on Knowshon Moreno on the second play of the 2008 Georgia-Florida game, knocking back the Bulldogs' star player a few yards and setting the tone for a 49–10 Gators rout.

FLORIDA

GATORS ACTIVE *IN THE 2011 NFL SEASON*

Player	Pos.	2011 Team	Since
Ahmad Black	DB	Tampa Bay Buccaneers	2011
Andre Caldwell	WR	Cincinnati Bengals	2008
Cooper Carlisle	OG	Oakland Raiders	2000
Riley Cooper	WR	Philadelphia Eagles	2010
Jermaine Cunningham	LB	New England Patriots	2010
Andra Davis	LB	Buffalo Bills	2002
Carlos Dunlap	DE	Cincinnati Bengals	2010
Jabar Gaffney	WR	Washington Redskins	2002
Marcus Gilbert	OT	Pittsburgh Steelers	2011
Earnest Graham	RB	Tampa Bay Buccaneers	2004
Rex Grossman	QB	Washington Redskins	2003
Joe Haden	CB	Cleveland Browns	2010
Derrick Harvey	DE	Denver Broncos	2008
Percy Harvin	WR	Minnesota Vikings	2009
Chas Henry	P	Philadelphia Eagles	2011
Aaron Hernandez	TE	New England Patriots	2010
Maurice Hurt	OG	Washington Redskins	2011

What cannot be respected nor tolerated, however, was Spikes' infamous eye gouge of Georgia's Washaun Ealey in 2009, when the senior linebacker was caught by cameras literally jamming his fingers into the eye socket of the Bulldogs' freshman back. Adding insult to injury, one of Spikes' four career returns for touchdowns capped the game's scoring, when the eye-gouging Gator grabbed a Joe Cox pass and returned it five yards for a score.

Just after the 41–17 Florida victory in 2009, some of us in the Bulldog Nation were told to calm down and stop complaining about Spikes and the eye incident. Apparently, we were blowing

Player	Pos.	2011 Team	Since
Ray McDonald	DE	San Francisco 49ers	2007
Jeremy Mincey	DE	Jacksonville Jaguars	2006
Jarvis Moss	DE	Oakland Raiders	2007
Louis Murphy	WR	Oakland Raiders	2009
David Nelson	WR	Buffalo Bills	2010
Reggie Nelson	S	Cincinnati Bengals	2007
Mike Peterson	LB	Atlanta Falcons	1999
Maurkice Pouncey	C	Pittsburgh Steelers	2010
Mike Pouncey	C	Miami Dolphins	2011
Lito Sheppard	CB	Oakland Raiders	2002
Brandon Siler	LB	Kansas City Chiefs	2007
Brandon Spikes	LB	New England Patriots	2010
Max Starks	OT	Pittsburgh Steelers	2004
Tim Tebow	QB	Denver Broncos	2010
Marcus Thomas	DT	Denver Broncos	2007
Justin Trattou	DE	New York Giants	2011
Gerard Warren	DT	New England Patriots	2001
Major Wright	S	Chicago Bears	2010

FLORIDA

things out of proportion, and—our favorite—if we had ever played football, we'd know that a lot worse than eye-gouging went on at the bottom of a pile of players. To Whom It May Concern: a lot of us did play football, thank you very much, and some of us might have even pulled a dirty deed or two at the bottom of a pile. We just weren't ignorant enough to do it out in the open for all to see.

TIM TEBOW

Besides the fact he was a Gator, what was there to hate about Tim Tebow while he was at Florida? In addition to being a one-of-a-kind talent on the football field, he was a young man of character, integrity, and an inspiration to many.

Sure, Georgia fans may point to the Florida quarterback's actions the year after he and his Gators were upset by the Bulldogs in 2007. Basking in the moment of a 49–10 blow-out victory, Coach Urban Meyer called two timeouts in the final 44 seconds of the game. During the first timeout, Tebow motioned the "Gator Chomp" as he ran down a sideline to fans and then waved his towel at the other side of the stadium. On the next timeout, Tebow ran to the other end of the stadium to see the Florida band.

At the time, it seemed like unusual behavior by the normally humble and good-natured Tebow; however, if anyone was to blame for the Gators rubbing in Georgia's loss, it was the vindictive Meyer.

From 2006 through 2009 at Florida, Tebow passed for 9,285 yards, rushed for 2,947, was responsible for 145 touchdowns,

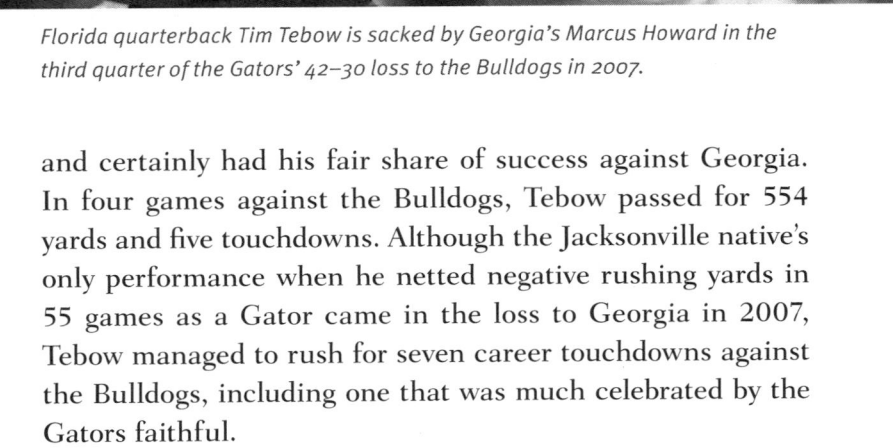

Florida quarterback Tim Tebow is sacked by Georgia's Marcus Howard in the third quarter of the Gators' 42–30 loss to the Bulldogs in 2007.

and certainly had his fair share of success against Georgia. In four games against the Bulldogs, Tebow passed for 554 yards and five touchdowns. Although the Jacksonville native's only performance when he netted negative rushing yards in 55 games as a Gator came in the loss to Georgia in 2007, Tebow managed to rush for seven career touchdowns against the Bulldogs, including one that was much celebrated by the Gators faithful.

Toward the end of the first half of the 2009 Georgia-Florida game, Tebow scored on a 23-yard rush, breaking Herschel Walker's SEC record of 49 career rushing touchdowns. A big deal was made of the record since it was broken against the school Walker had played for in the city where Tebow grew up.

"It's breathtaking," Tebow said on breaking the record. "It's Herschel Walker. How am I going to be in the same air as Herschel Walker?"

Tim, to answer your question, you're really not in the same air. It took you 49 games to total what Herschel achieved in 33. Still, Tebow was without a doubt one of the greatest players in the history of college football. After becoming the first

FLORIDA

TOP 10 ALL-TIME INDIVIDUAL SERIES SCORERS

	Pts	TD	XP	FG
Charley Trippi (UGA, 1942, 1945–1946)	48	8	0	0
Herschel Walker (UGA, 1980–1982)	48	8	0	0
Tim Tebow (FLA, 2007–2009)	42	7	0	0
Cy Grant (UGA, 1932–1933)	33	5	3	0
Wes Chandler (FLA, 1976–1977)	30	5	0	0
Chris Doering (FLA, 1994–1995)	30	5	0	0
Bart Edmiston (FLA, 1992, 1995–1996)	29	0	14	5
Rex Robinson (UGA, 1977–1980)	28	0	10	6
Jeff Chandler (FLA, 1998–2001)	28	0	13	5
Frank Sinkwich (UGA, 1941–1942)	27	6	0	1

sophomore ever to win the Heisman Trophy in 2007, he followed it up by finishing third in the trophy's voting as a junior and fifth in 2009.

To illustrate how valuable Tebow was to the Gators and Meyer, Florida lost just five combined regular season games and won two national championships in the quarterback's four seasons. In Meyer's other two years as the Gators' head coach—the season before (2005) and after (2010) Tebow's tenure—Florida lost a combined eight regular season games.

You can understand why Meyer was so quick to leave the Gators after just six seasons; he realized no more Tim Tebows existed. Or maybe it was having to live in Gainesville, Florida—tough one to call.

3

TRADITIONS WE HATE

ACCORDING TO THE SCHOOL, football had been played at the University of Florida for 105 seasons as of the end of the 2011 campaign. Over this extended period, Georgia fans acknowledge the Gators have undeniably established a reputable football tradition. However, we also recognize that if it hadn't been for the last 20 or so years, or just a small portion of the entire program's history, Florida's winning and championship tradition would instead be one of mostly mediocrity.

The Gator Nation should forever praise the 1990 arrival of Coach Steve Spurrier. Without the coming of the Ol' Ball Coach, Florida football might still be annually taking a backseat to the SEC's elite.

And the Georgia-Florida game, as it primarily stood until the 1990s, wouldn't be much of a football rivalry at all.

WE ARE THE BOYS FROM OLD FLORIDA

Prior to the start of the fourth quarter of games, Gators fans stand up, lock arms with their neighbors, and sway back and forth while singing in unison the celebrated tune of "We Are the Boys from Old Florida." It has been claimed that two of

ALL-TIME VICTORIES AND BOWL WINS FOR SEC SCHOOLS ENTERING 2012

	All-Time Victories			Bowl Wins	
1.	Alabama	814	1.	Alabama	34
2.	Tennessee	794	2.	**GEORGIA**	26
3.	**GEORGIA**	747	3.	Tennessee	25
4.	LSU	733	4t.	LSU	22
5.	Auburn	711	4t.	Auburn	22
6.	Texas A&M	681	6.	Ole Miss	21
7.	Arkansas	680	7.	**FLORIDA**	20
8.	**FLORIDA**	669	8.	Texas A&M	14
9.	Missouri	625	9t.	Missouri	13
10.	Ole Miss	621	9t.	Arkansas	13
11.	Kentucky	578	11.	Mississippi St.	9
12.	Vanderbilt	564	12.	Kentucky	8
13.	S. Carolina	555	13.	S. Carolina	5
14.	Mississippi St.	506	14.	Vanderbilt	2

FLORIDA

Florida's very own students wrote the song nearly 100 years ago, and the ritual has been popular with Gators fans since at least the 1930s.

Frankly, if you're not a Gator, you might find this tradition to be quite boring, far from thrilling, and possibly the cause of severe motion sickness. While former Florida player and coach Steve Spurrier said it sent "chill bumps all over me," a number of opposing players have claimed that observing the ritual at the Swamp made them literally sick to their stomach.

Notably, also observed has been the Gators' ineptness in the fourth quarter of football games over the last two seasons.

Consider that in the first three quarters combined in the 2010 and 2011 campaigns, Florida outscored its opposition by an average of 6.7 points per game. On the contrary, in the fourth quarter of games during the two years, the Gators allowed as many points as they scored (158). Therefore, our only suggestion to the Gators is if they must perform this dull and nauseating tradition, at least during these apparent times of inadequate play by the team, they should do so prior to a different quarter, and not the final and most important one.

GATOR CHOMP

While the Pride of the Sunshine band plays the familiar shark motif from the movie *Jaws*, the Florida faithful perform the "Gator Chomp" by extending their arms and moving them back and forth to symbolize an alligator's mouth. The two-note arrangement from *Jaws* was first played by the school's band in 1981, and soon the arm movement was added to evolve into the Gator Chomp as we all know it today.

Although it is not quite understood what a movie about a shark has to do with a chomping alligator, the Gator Chomp has become quite prominent over the years. Recently, famous chomps included one from Michelle Obama during a visit to Gainesville in 2008. Less than three months later, quarterback Tim Tebow performed an acclaimed chomp directed toward Oklahoma in the final minutes of Florida's victory in the BCS National Championship Game.

Unlike most of the chomps from Gators fans in the stands or the one from Mrs. Obama, a Gator Chomp on the gridiron from a player—like Tebow—can be a symbol of disrespect

and ridicule. However, the mocking gesture works both ways; Florida's Gator Chomp is a tradition that can be enjoyed by not only Gators, but by Gators haters, as well.

An opposing chomp of note occurred following Georgia's first touchdown against Florida in 2007. After the Bulldogs team rushed into the end zone to celebrate the game's initial score, many of the Georgia players mimicked the gesture to spectators behind the end zone.

Another well-known Gator Chomp that Florida won't soon forget came less than a year after Tebow's in the national title game. In the closing moments of Alabama's 32–13 resounding victory over the Gators in the 2009 SEC Championship Game, the Crimson Tide's Mark Ingram, who would soon capture the Heisman Trophy and his team a national title, chomped it up on one sideline.

During Ingram's act, another Heisman winner and player on a national championship team put on quite a performance on the other sideline. But instead of chomping, Tim Tebow was infamously crying.

MR. TWO BITS

We all know the legacy of Florida's Mr. Two Bits, and some of us are even aware of the story behind it. We just don't quite understand why it would be a long-standing tradition for nearly 60 years.

So, let's get this straight. During Florida's 1949 season opener against The Citadel at Florida Field, a man in his late twenties

George Edmondson Jr., of Tampa—aka "Mr. Two Bits"—leads a cheer on the field before the first half of Florida's 21–7 loss to Florida State on November 26, 2011, in "the Swamp."

who attended The Citadel—George Edmondson Jr.—decided to try to boost the morale of a booing Gators crowd. He promptly led them in a cheer about "bits," or currency that hasn't been made in this country for more than 200 years.

The Gators would go on to defeat The Citadel, as one would hope, the Florida fans were encouraged, and Edmondson—or Mr. Two-Bits—dressed in the same yellow shirt, orange and blue tie, and pair of white-and-blue-striped seersucker pants, has been leading the Gators in the "Two Bits" cheer ever since (that is, until his retirement in 1998, a quick return to the field, a second retirement in 2008, and then another return for an appearance at the 2011 Florida State game).

First off, the fact that fair-weathered Florida fans were booing their own team isn't surprising; little has changed in more than 60 years. Also, why would anyone openly cheer, while encouraging others to do so, against his very own alma mater? So much for Edmondson's military education and training at The Citadel, where cadets are supposed to value honor and integrity.

To his credit, Mr. Two Bits was never given a dime, or even a bit, for his cheering troubles and once turned down a lucrative offer from the Tampa Bay Buccaneers to do the same sort of thing. However, and with all due respect to college football's most well-known cheerleader, why tens of thousands of fans would cheer on a little old man flailing his arms in the middle of a football field is beyond us.

WALK-ONS

Every true college football enthusiast admires the walk-on player—a full-time student who pays his own way while trying to make a football team. For the average walk-on, there is little hope of eventually receiving financial aid or getting playing time, but a chance to practice with scholarship players and essentially get his brains beat out.

At Georgia, some of the football program's best of all time initially walked on the team. Former walk-on linebacker Nate Taylor ended his Bulldogs career in 1982 as the school's second all-time leading tackler. After walking on in the mid-1960s, "Sputnik" Spike Jones became an outstanding Georgia punter and would play eight seasons in the NFL. Also, place-kicker Billy Bennett would become the first Bulldog to score 400 points in a career after walking on in 2000.

Likely the best Bulldogs walk-on in history is Biarritz, France's Richard Tardits, who did not even know the rules of American football when he arrived at UGA in 1985. Nevertheless, the "Biarritz Blitz" or "Le Sack" walked on, made the squad as a pass-rushing specialist, and eventually set the Georgia record in 1988 for career sacks.

Hence, Bulldog Nation is certainly accustomed to a formidable walk-on program.

Perhaps no one in the country prides itself more on its walk-on tradition than Georgia's chief rival to the south, where, according to Florida in 2011, 45 former Gators walk-ons had eventually earned football scholarships over the previous 20 years. Florida's walk-on program is a cherished part of the Gators' football heritage, which, according to the university, "has provided an opportunity for countless young men to prove that the evaluation and recruiting process is far from faultless."

Among other things, the Gators boast that their memorable team of 1985 had 18 prominent players originally join the program as walk-ons. In addition, as of 2011, 14 former Gators walk-ons had gone on to play pro football.

If you're going to brag about your cherished tradition, you might as well be totally upfront, so we're going to assist the Gators and reveal some additional facts. Depending on how one defines "play" and "pro football," there have indeed been 14 former Gators walk-ons to play football at the next level; however, only three of those—Hagood Clarke, James Harrell, and Louis Oliver—started in more than three career games in the NFL at a non–special teams position.

Additionally, at one time during the 1980s, the Gators did have the nation's second-largest walk-on program, only behind Nebraska's. And as indicated, a number of walk-ons played prominent roles on some reputable Florida teams of the mid- to late 1980s, including linebacker Pat Moorer—Florida's leading tackler in 1988 and 1989—and the aforementioned Oliver—a two-time All-America defensive back. However, while Nebraska's walk-on program was excessive mainly because the school was the only Division I university in the state, Florida's developed primarily because of the football program being placed on NCAA probation.

You don't hear the school boasting about or even mentioning that particular piece of information.

Because of its probation during the 1980s, Florida football was reduced 20 scholarships within a two-year period. "There has been an increase in walk-ons because of the NCAA sanctions," said Bo Bayer, the Gators' head of recruiting and the walk-on program, in 1985. "I think the kids see more of an opportunity here at Florida."

Thus, the walk-on program might very well be a valued aspect of Gators football history; however, facts reveal that the tradition apparently evolved from Florida's cheating and a necessity to fill its roster with players.

GATORS WEAR JEAN SHORTS
(AND OTHER ABSURD ATTIRE)

While most conventional southeastern college football fans are primarily dressed in presentable common attire, many in

Gator Nation are known to dress themselves simply a little differently. Your typical Florida fan might very well be wearing a tank top, sporting a mullet, and usually, to complete the look, wearing jean shorts, or "jorts" for short.

And for many Gators, the shorter, the older, the more tattered, the uglier the jorts are, the better.

Although the Florida faithful have been wearing jorts for an awful, and we mean *awful*, long time, the expression "Gators wear jean shorts" did not originate until apparently 1997, when it was first blurted by a Bulldogs fan, no less.

The story is that UGA student Kevin Davis and some friends were being heckled by a Gator-chomping, tank-top-and-jean-shorts-wearing Florida fan on the way to the game that year. After another tiresome "Gator bait!" insult from the heckler, Davis answered the cry with his original phrase that would soon sweep the Southland: "Gators wear jean shorts!" During the game, Davis and his Bulldogs buddies would have much of the Georgia student section chanting the words.

By the way, the Gators were routed that day for a rare series victory at the time for Georgia. Although Davis' phrase may have become widespread regardless of the 1997 game's result, there likely would have been far fewer shouts of "Gators wear jean shorts" from the stands had the Bulldogs suffered their typical 1990s Gator Bowl beatdown by Florida.

Over the years, online message boards, YouTube, and other websites have ingrained Davis' distinguished catchphrase into the minds of many Florida rivals who desire to insult Gators fans.

In 2005 the Jacksonville Bulldog Club offered a promotion where the member taking the most pictures of Gators donned in their finest jean shorts at the Cocktail Party would receive an annual membership the following year for free. One particular member—a highly regarded family practitioner from North Georgia—was up for the contest but refused to go out of his way to take photos of Gators fans. However, if the opportunity presented itself and a Gator wearing jean shorts just happened to walk by the doctor's tailgate, he snapped a quick photo with his old digital camera.

Although he did not seek out a single Gator for a photo and his camera's battery died three full hours prior to kickoff, the doctor managed to capture 63 separate Florida fans wearing jean shorts just outside the stadium.

"Sometimes there is truth in stereotypes," said the doctor. "I managed to win the contest, but I still felt like I let everyone down.... I was well on my way to hitting triple digits."

The fashion faux pas and running joke among the Bulldogs and the rest of the Southeast is curiously a proud tradition for many Florida fans. Countless Gators have oddly taken the "Gators wear jean shorts" insult in stride, wearing their jorts with no hesitation and much pride.

4
COACHES WE HATE

WHERE TO BEGIN? Whether shown the door for not capturing a championship, getting the Gators placed on probation, or simply unable to bear the city of Gainesville, a multitude of men have come and gone as head football coach at the University of Florida. From 1940 through 2011, the school had 13 different head coaches, only one of whom reached the 100-win mark. In comparison, just six head coaches roamed the Georgia sideline during the same time period, three of whom won 100-plus games.

With more than its share of head coaches in Florida's football history, especially during the modern era, it's rather difficult to decide which ones we hate more than others. Perhaps worthy of mention are the first five at Florida, who should probably be more deplored by Georgia fans than hated.

Dr. James Farr, a professor of history at Florida Agricultural College in Lake City, was the head football coach for the program's first two seasons of 1901 and 1902. Considered "the University of Florida" by 1903, the team had two head coaches in its third year—the first with the last name of "Fleming" followed by A.B. Humphreys. Notably, Fleming couldn't wait to leave the program, quitting after two games to reportedly

return "to Jacksonville to resume his law practice." Two more coaches—M.O. Bridges and C.A. Holton—headed up the football squad in its final two seasons before the university's move to Gainesville in 1906.

The changing of the school's location from Lake City to Gainesville is the rationale given for why the 1901 through 1905 seasons are not acknowledged by the Gators, and thus is the reasoning Farr, Fleming, Humphreys, Bridges, and Holton are not considered football coaches from the school's past. It's problematic for one to actually "hate" a Gators football coach, or five of them, who apparently were not Florida coaches to begin with. Seemingly, the aforementioned five men were discredited of having any relationship whatsoever with University of Florida football.

As detailed in the next chapter, along with these five "coaches," their combined 3–10–1 record over the five seasons has been erased from the memory of the Gators, as well.

It took some time, but Florida finally landed a head football coach deserving of recognition when Charles Bachman left Kansas State for Gainesville in 1928. Bachman's Gators lost just six combined games in the coach's first three seasons, but followed it up with six-loss campaigns in both his fourth and fifth year.

Despite the Gators' decline in 1931 and 1932, university president John Tigert urged Bachman to continue at Florida past his original five-year contract. Instead, the head football coach promptly left for Michigan State, receiving the exact annual salary he was making with the Gators ($7,500), because he

believed "the material would be better up there." Bachman was correct in his determination as he suffered just one losing season in 13 with the Spartans (1933–1946) and would eventually be inducted into the College Football Hall of Fame.

From 1935 to 1949, four Gators head coaches combined for 13 non-winning seasons in 14 years and a 3–11 mark against the Bulldogs. In 1950 Florida took a gamble by hiring 34-year-old Bob Woodruff for an unthinkable $17,000 annual salary for seven years. According to the first-year Gators coach, who was ironically born in Athens, he was given just one order from the Florida administration: "They told me I had to beat Georgia."

After 10 years, Woodruff was forced to resign from Florida in 1959 despite suffering just two losing seasons, guiding the Gators to their first two bowl appearances in school history, and winning six of 10 games against the Bulldogs. After years of dismal play, Woodruff had built a program into one that was routinely competitive. Moreover, he laid the groundwork for the achievements (and even more despised coaches) that would soon follow.

RAY GRAVES

Like Bob Woodruff, Ray Graves had played football at the University of Tennessee under General Robert Neyland, and he was also an assistant at Georgia Tech under Bobby Dodd just prior to becoming Florida's head coach. In addition, like Woodruff, Graves won six of 10 games against Georgia. However, unlike his predecessor, Graves needed no time to build the Gators program, achieving immediate success in his first year.

In 1960 Florida set a school record with nine overall victories, including an 18–17 upset over Graves' previous team—10th-ranked Georgia Tech. After a 4–5–1 mark the following year, Graves recorded eight consecutive winning seasons to end his head coaching career in 1969. Prior to the arrival of Steve Spurrier—the coach's starting quarterback during the mid-1960s—Graves was the most accomplished head man in Gators football history, winning 70 games, coaching in five bowls, and achieving an overall winning percentage of nearly 70 percent.

Following his 10-season tenure, Graves declared that his greatest regret while the head coach of the Gators was "not winning the SEC title." He was close on several occasions, coming within a game of winning the conference three different years—1960, 1966, and 1969. Nevertheless, you know what they say are the only times "close" actually counts…

The Gators' success during the Graves era is especially impressive considering the university had high in-state entrance requirements at the time. Admirably, Graves upheld these high standards and avoided conflict with the school's "academic family"; 93 percent of the head coach's players graduated from the university with their undergraduate degrees. Considered one of the sport's true gentlemen, Coach Graves was able to win at Florida and do so the "right way." But, as indicative of the head coach's era, the times would be a-changin'…as would the Gators' standards.

CHARLEY PELL

After disappointing 6–4–1 and 4–7 seasons for Florida in 1977 and 1978, respectively, Doug Dickey was forced out as

the team's head coach. The Gators sought out a hard-nosed replacement who could recruit the best of talent and, no matter the cost, quickly resurrect a program to prominence.

As head coach at Clemson for two seasons, Charley Pell achieved an outstanding record of 18–4–1 after the team had won just five of 22 games in 1975 and 1976. A player and one-time assistant under Paul "Bear" Bryant, Pell was lured away from the Tigers in 1979 and named Florida's new head coach. Within weeks of his arrival at the school, "Give 'em Hell, Pell!" bumper stickers could be seen all over campus and the surrounding area. There was a new head coach in town, bringing a new attitude to the team, and the Gators faithful were delighted for it.

FLORIDA

THE WINLESS CAMPAIGN

Despite the schools having winning traditions in football, Georgia and Florida have both suffered the occasional losing campaign in their long histories. However, the Bulldogs have never quite experienced what the Gators went through not too terribly long ago, when first-year head coach Charley Pell and his team went winless in 11 tries. In fact, Georgia has never even come close to having a year like Florida's miserable 0–10–1 season of 1979. Over the last century since Georgia began playing at least eight games per season, the worst record that ever resulted for the Bulldogs was a 3–8 year in 1953.

In 1979 the Gators entered four of their 11 games—against Georgia Tech, Mississippi State, Tulsa, and Kentucky—actually favored to win. One of Florida's biggest defeats was a 23-point setback by a Georgia team, who had been routed 31–0 the week before on its Homecoming by Virginia. For the Gators, their biggest of many downfalls was a

Any joy in Gainesville was put on hold for a season as Florida slumped to an all-time low in Pell's first year—a winless 0–10–1 campaign. However, in recording one of the biggest one-year turnarounds in the history of college football, the Gators recovered in 1980 by winning eight games, including the team's first bowl victory in more than a decade.

From 1980 to 1983, Pell averaged eight wins per season and appeared in a bowl game each year. Although he lost all five games against Georgia in his five full seasons at Florida, Pell defeated the school's chief rival, Florida State, three consecutive times—twice by 32 points or more—and ended 1983 ranked sixth in the country—the Gators' then-highest final ranking in their history.

dismal offense, which scored only 10 touchdowns all season and averaged a staggeringly low 250 total yards per game.

Date	Opponent	Result	Score
Sept. 15	@ Houston	LOSS	10–14
Sept. 22	Georgia Tech	TIE	7–7
Sept. 29	@ Mississippi State	LOSS	10–24
Oct. 6	@ Louisiana State	LOSS	3–20
Oct. 13	Alabama	LOSS	0–40
Oct. 27	Tulsa	LOSS	10–20
Nov. 3	@ Auburn	LOSS	13–19
Nov. 10	Georgia (Jacksonville)	LOSS	10–33
Nov. 17	Kentucky	LOSS	3–31
Nov. 24	Florida State	LOSS	16–27
Dec. 1	@ Miami (Fla.)	LOSS	24–30

FLORIDA

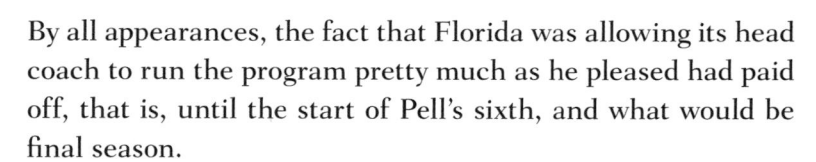

By all appearances, the fact that Florida was allowing its head coach to run the program pretty much as he pleased had paid off, that is, until the start of Pell's sixth, and what would be final season.

In 1982 there had been a sign of possible troubles on the horizon for Florida when Clemson, while under Pell's watch several years before, was cited for NCAA violations. Regardless, one month after the Tigers were placed on probation, Pell was given a contract extension and a raise by the Gators. However, just prior to the start of the 1984 season, the NCAA revealed that Florida had also broken some rules while coached by Pell. The Gators' head coach offered his resignation less than a week before the season opener, but asked to remain in his position through the end of the season.

Suddenly, instead of "giving 'em hell," the Florida head football coach had earned a new motto: "If your program smells, it's gotta be Pell's."

In mid-September of 1984, five days after the NCAA notified Florida of more than 100 alleged violations, Pell was relieved of his coaching duties at the school only three games into the season and despite the coach's request to finish out the year. The incident would ultimately keep Pell, who was only 43 years of age at the time, from ever coaching again in college football while scarring him for life until his passing in 2001.

GALEN HALL

Only a few games into the 1984 season, first-year offensive coordinator Galen Hall was left to pick up the program's

pieces following Charley Pell's dismissal as head football coach amidst NCAA violations. Hall had been a long-time assistant under Barry Switzer at Oklahoma from 1973 to 1983 and had accepted his new role at Florida after the Gators' old offensive coordinator—Mike Shanahan—had departed for the NFL. Hall had never been a head football coach, but was finally getting his chance, albeit on an interim basis and under unusual circumstances.

After starting the 1984 season with a 1–1–1 record under Pell, the Gators reeled off eight consecutive wins with Hall at the helm. At the end of the year, the interim head coach was honored as the Associated Press Coach of the Year and was soon promoted to permanent head coach. Hall's Gators were declared national champions by a number of NCAA-recognized polls and ratings, while the program had finally captured its first conference championship. Hall's championship season was short lived, however, as the SEC title was soon taken away from the Gators, along with the possibility of them winning a championship in the next two years because of the rule violations committed by Pell.

In his first full season as head coach in 1985, Hall guided Florida to the same 9–1–1 record as the year before. In early November, the Gators were ranked as the No. 1 team in the nation for the first time in school history, but sat atop the AP rankings for just one week before being upset by Georgia.

The next three seasons for Hall weren't nearly as successful as his first two at Florida. After losing just one of his first 19 games as head coach, Hall slumped to three consecutive 6–5 regular season campaigns from 1986 to 1988. A portion of Gator Nation

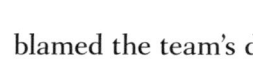

blamed the team's descent on the results of Pell's wrongdoings finally taking their toll on the program. However, it would soon be revealed that Hall himself had misbehaved, as well.

Just after the start of the 1989 season, a pretrial motion was filed, alleging Hall and some of his assistants had paid a number of their players. Soon afterward, amid charges that he paid a football player and supplemented the incomes of his coaching assistants without the knowledge of the university, Hall resigned as the Gators' head coach. Just like his predecessor five years before, Hall abruptly left Florida a few games into the football season, leaving the team with an interim in charge, while ultimately placing the Gators on probation because of his misconduct.

Since leaving Florida more than 20 years ago, Hall has yet to return as a head coach on the college level. Beginning in 2004, he was the offensive coordinator at Penn State under Joe Paterno, until another scandal—one far more inconceivable than NCAA violations—resulted in a head coaching change and sent Hall packing again.

STEVE SPURRIER

Whether referred to as the "Head Ball Coach," "Ol' Ball Coach," the "Evil Genius," or something much more derogatory by Georgia fans, Steve Spurrier has a long, hate-filled history with the Bulldogs.

After winning the Heisman Trophy as a Gators quarterback in 1966 and a far-from spectacular 10-year NFL career, Spurrier entered the football coaching profession in 1978. His first

*Florida coach Steve Spurrier pats quarterback Doug Johnson (12) on the back
after he threw the first of three first-half interceptions against Georgia in the
Bulldogs' 37–17 victory on November 1, 1997.*

position was back at his alma mater as the Gators' offensive
backfield coach under head coach Doug Dickey. Just a year
later, Dickey was fired, and Spurrier was not retained by
new coach Charley Pell. For this, the Florida football legend
reportedly always resented Pell, and as the Bulldogs would
eventually find out, you don't necessarily want Steve Spurrier
holding a grudge against you (see "Bulldog-turned-Gator" in
the next chapter, "Stories We Hate").

Spurrier had first been a candidate for the Florida head-coaching position in 1984. He was the people's choice when Galen Hall was elevated to the post following the forced exit of Pell after the third game of the season. Hall won his eight remaining games and was retained by the Gators, while Spurrier remained in the United States Football League as the head coach of the Tampa Bay Bandits.

Spurrier's first college head-coaching job was at Duke from 1987 to 1989, guiding the Blue Devils to back-to-back winning seasons in his second and third years and an ACC championship in his final season. Notably, in the 22 seasons since Spurrier's departure from the school, Duke has achieved only one winning campaign through 2011.

When the head position for the Gators became available again following the 1989 season, Spurrier seemed the logical candidate. He had remained a popular figure in the state, plus, the belief was that if a coach could win at Duke, he obviously could be successful at Florida.

On December 31, 1989, when Spurrier returned to the school for a second time, he walked into a program that had lost five or more games for four consecutive seasons and would soon be placed on probation for the second time in five years.

"Our school doesn't just need an outstanding coach," said Gene Peek, a teammate of Spurrier's at Florida. "We're looking for a Messiah."

While the Gators felt they might have found their savior, Spurrier reportedly found something disturbing for an old signal-

caller upon his arrival: Florida's quarterbacks hardly knew how to call an audible at the line of scrimmage. Nevertheless, the new head coach instantly issued a playbook that was much thicker than most of those in the NFL, while instilling a revolutionary offensive system like nothing college defensive coordinators had seen before.

In 12 seasons at Florida from 1990 to 2001, Spurrier became one of the greatest coaches in the sport's history. He registered an exemplary 122–27–1 overall record, captured six SEC championships—the school's first six conference titles in football—and won a national championship in 1996. In addition, Spurrier was a near-perfect 11–1 against Georgia while at Florida, turning a series from one where the Bulldogs usually had the upper hand to one totally dominated by the Gators.

Florida's Spurrier is remembered by the Georgia faithful as a hated Gators player who eventually turned into a visor-tossing and tantrum-throwing head coach, who often made snide remarks about our team while running the score up on the Bulldogs whenever given the chance.

We are firm believers that if you don't want to yield any additional points to your opponent, simply stop it from scoring. However, when given the opportunity against Georgia, Coach Spurrier repeatedly took the act of running up the score to a whole new level. The lowlights:

- **1990:** With Florida leading by 31 points late in the game, Spurrier sent his first-team defense back onto the field to prevent the Georgia offense from merely picking up a first down.

STEVE SPURRIER QUOTES WE HATE

"The biggest thing they got going for them is tradition."
—when asked what, if any, strengths Georgia possessed
entering the 1990 game

"How is it when [Georgia] signs people, they get the 'best'
players. But when we play, we've got the best players?
Georgia has signed a lot of good players. Something just
happens to them at Georgia, I guess." —on the Bulldogs'
nationally ranked recruiting classes of the early 1990s after
Florida's 45–13 victory over Georgia in 1991

"We need to let the world know what's happening to us. At
some point we've got to get an even break from the officials."
—complaining about SEC officiating, after receiving a huge
break from refs in the "Timeout" victory over Georgia in 1993

"I don't know how they got 84,000 people in here. I know
that they weren't here for very long." —after Florida's 47–7
win over Georgia in the renovated Gator Bowl in 1996

"That other coach [Ray Goff] they [Georgia] had used to say
bad things about me all the time. Maybe we ought to get
coach [Jim] Donnan to say a few bad things about me." (1998)

"Oh, we just ran a quick play with our seventh or eighth
receiver on the team. But I don't ever care what the other
coach thinks." —responding to Coach Jim Donnan's criticism
of Florida's running an end-around late in the 1998 game

- **1991:** With a 38–13 lead, standout quarterback Shane Matthews wasn't replaced until Florida's next-to-last offensive series. Even when the starter was finally sidelined, backup Brian Fox passed for a 24-yard touchdown with less than two minutes to play.

- **1995:** In his quest to have his Gators be the first team to score 50 points against Georgia in Sanford Stadium, Spurrier ordered eight passes and a flea-flicker on Florida's final possession with a 45–17 lead. With only 1:10 remaining, the drive concluded with a touchdown pass. (Ducking to avoid thrown drinks and tobacco-laced spit from angry Bulldog fans, Spurrier was forced to summon several bodyguards to help him leave the field.)

- **1996:** After kicking a late field goal to take a 40–7 lead, Florida forced a Georgia turnover. On the very next play from the Bulldogs' 14-yard line with just over two minutes remaining, Spurrier ordered a pass, resulting in a Gators' touchdown.

- **1998:** Leading 24–7 midway through the final quarter, Florida scored a touchdown on a flanker-reverse pass to starting quarterback Doug Johnson. Later, with the ball on Georgia's 8-yard line with only 38 seconds remaining, Spurrier ran another trick play—a wide receiver end-around run—for a touchdown.

RON ZOOK

When Steve Spurrier left Florida following the 2001 season after 12 long years, and plenty of headaches for Georgia, many Bulldogs fans were as anxious as Gator Nation to see who

would be replacing the "Evil Genius." When it was announced that Ron Zook was Florida's new head coach, it appeared to be good news for the Dawgs, while sending many a Gator into despair.

Zook had been Florida's defensive coordinator from 1991 to 1993, but was then reassigned, or *demoted*, if you will, as the Gators' special teams coordinator for 1994 and 1995. The following season, Zook was off to the NFL, where he was an assistant with three teams over the next six years through 2001.

In its hiring process, Florida had first sought Oklahoma head coach Bob Stoops, who had captured a national championship the year before. Next in line was Mike Shanahan of the Denver Broncos, who had won back-to-back Super Bowls in 1997 and 1998. After both high-profile coaches turned the job down, athletics director Jeremy Foley, based on "instincts," as he described it, turned to the very low-profile Zook.

Even many of the Florida faithful turned on their newly hired head man before Zook coached his first game. Gaining national media attention, one Gators fan went as far as creating the website FireRonZook.com within a day of the head coach's hiring.

In his three years at Florida before he was eventually fired in 2004 (so much for Foley's "instincts"), Zook did demonstrate that he was an excellent recruiter and a good communicator with his players and the followers of the program; however, his decision-making during games and on-field management was at times downright dreadful.

During his entire tenure at Florida, Spurrier never won less than nine games in any of his dozen seasons. In comparison, Zook never won more than eight. Thus, we come to the primary reason why many Georgia fans still cannot stand Zook.

In Zook's first two games against Georgia, the Bulldogs were superior to the Gators and certainly had the better coach, yet somehow, some way we were inexplicably beaten both times by Florida and the far-from-"Genius" Zook. In 2004 Georgia saved a little dignity by defeating the Gators and their recently fired head coach. Regardless, even to this day, we still can not get over, nor comprehend, those two consecutive losses in 2002 and 2003 that came at the hands of "the Zooker."

URBAN MEYER

After 15 seasons as a college assistant coach with four different schools, Urban Meyer was hired at Bowling Green in 2001, beginning an extraordinary—yet rather unstable—head-coaching career leading to Gainesville and beyond.

At Bowling Green, Meyer guided the Falcons to a 17–6 combined record in two seasons after the Falcons had won only two games in 2000. The head coach left for greener pastures in 2003 for the University of Utah, where he achieved a 22–2 combined record in 2003 and 2004 after the Utes had gone just 5–6 the year before his arrival.

In December 2004 Meyer was on the move again, becoming the head coach at Florida after turning down the same position at Notre Dame, where he had been an assistant from 1996 to 2000. After the disappointing Ron Zook era, the Gators

welcomed the "Urban Legend" and his unorthodox spread-out offense with open claws, while filled with anticipation that Meyer would turn around their program just like he had at his two previous coaching stops. As an added benefit, after three different head-coaching jobs in a period of only four years, the Gators' new head man indicated his stay at Florida would be for quite some time.

"[Going from Bowling Green to Utah to Florida] happened fast," said Meyer on the day he was hired by the Gators. "But I'm not a guy looking for moves, not a guy on the phone all the time."

Soon after becoming a Gator, Meyer made Florida fans all but forget Coach Steve Spurrier. By his second season in 2006, he had already won a national championship (albeit with the benefit of Zook's recruits). Just two years later in 2008, Meyer added a second national title (albeit with the benefit of a once-in-a-lifetime player, Tim Tebow). From 2005 to 2009, the coach won a remarkable 85 percent of his games, including 13 victories in each of the 2006, 2008, and 2009 seasons.

Granted, Meyer's motives were often called into question. Approximately 30 Gators players were arrested during the coach's tenure. Yet, Meyer was as good at turning a blind eye as he was at winning ballgames, and often his players would go unpunished by missing little, if any, game time.

Nevertheless, based on some of the individuals who ran the program (and the probations) in the past, Gator Nation was already accustomed to a "whatever it takes to win" approach from its head coach.

Citing health concerns, Meyer surprisingly announced his resignation—the first one—from Florida on the day after Christmas 2009, effective following the Gators' bowl appearance. However, just a day later, he announced that he was instead taking a leave of absence until Florida's spring practice began in March 2010.

Minus quarterback Tebow, but apparently managing the "esophageal spasms" which caused his one-day resignation, Meyer slumped to an 8–5 season in 2010. Following the regular season, the head coach resigned—for a second time—from Florida, citing his desire to spend more time with his family.

After bailing on the Gators, Meyer immediately began work as a college football analyst for ESPN. In November 2011, or less than one year after leaving Florida, he became the head football coach at Ohio State University—his fourth head-coaching job in a period of only nine years.

So much for Meyer's concerns over his health and family...

In conclusion, we hate a coach who, despite his accomplishments, abandons a program when it's seemingly on the decline, conveniently using his "health" and "family" as excuses, only to reemerge and start over soon afterward at another school. This is something both the Bulldogs and the Gators should agree on.

In the not-too-distant future, we wouldn't be surprised if the Buckeyes faithful share our sentiments, as well.

5
STORIES WE HATE

FLORIDA'S FORGOTTEN

The Gators claim their football history didn't begin until 1906, or until the school moved from Lake City to Gainesville. Research indicates, however, that the University of Florida fielded a football squad each year from 1901 to 1905. But all five of the pre-Gainesville teams are disregarded by the university.

After going winless in its first four games of its football history, the Florida State Agricultural College (FAC), as it was known then, defeated the Florida State College of Tallahassee by a 6–0 score on December 20, 1902, for the program's first victory. By the following season, FAC had begun referring to itself as the "University of Florida," as did newspaper reporting of the school's football games. In 1903 Florida won just its season finale—a 6–5 victory over East Florida Seminary on November 26. Notably, a man by the name of A.B. Humphreys not only coached Florida to a victory that day, but according to a game report, he was also generous enough to referee the contest. (Florida football had wasted little time to begin its cheating ways.)

In 1904 Florida recorded likely one of the worst campaigns in the history of southern football, losing all five of its contests by

a combined 225–0 score. To illustrate how inferior the team must have been, Florida was defeated 52–0 by Georgia in the series' first game and the Red and Black's season opener. That Georgia team would play five more games the rest of its season, and lose them *all* by a combined score of 68–16.

The pre-Gainesville football era concluded in 1905 when Florida quit at halftime of a 6–0 victory over "Julian Landon," whomever he, she, or they may have been. After relocating to Gainesville the following year, the Gators finally started to acknowledge their football history, and thus what Georgia claims is the rivalry's second game—a 37–0 rout over Florida in 1915—is what the Gators declare is the first.

Leading up to the 1906–1907 academic year, the assets and academic programs of four separate institutions in the state of Florida, including the University of Florida in Lake City (formerly FAC), were consolidated to form what we know today as the University of Florida in Gainesville. Yet, the university claims it was established in 1853, when the first of the predecessor institutions was opened.

If the university claims it was established prior to the consolidation of the four institutions, shouldn't the school's football teams prior to 1906 also be recognized? And, as mentioned, by 1903 the FAC football team was already widely known as the "University of Florida." Heck, the school in Lake City even had its own "Fightin' Florida" marching band by 1905.

We might be somewhat biased, but we'll side with UGA sports historian and coaching icon Dan Magill who, in acknowledging Georgia's win over Florida 1904, has said, "That's where

Florida was back then. We can't help it if they got run out of [Lake City]."

In 1941 Jacksonville's *Florida Times-Union* identified the 1904 Georgia-Florida game, and not the 1915 contest, as "the No. 1 game in the famous series." In addition, and for what it's worth, both Alabama and Georgia Tech, like Georgia, recognize their 1904 games against Florida in their records, while the University of Florida (at Gainesville) stubbornly does not.

Dr. William Rowlett, who was a respected physician and governmental leader in Tampa, was interviewed during the 1970s at the age of 91 prior to his death. Rowlett, who was captain of the 1904 University of Florida (Lake City) team, recalled, "We played in Alabama...Georgia and we played Georgia Tech. I remember we were the first University of Florida team to play those schools, to travel so far."

We have a suspicion that if the University of Florida football team, whether located in Lake City, Gainesville, or any other place, for that matter, had achieved, let's say a 7–2 mark instead of its actual 2–7 record from 1903 to 1905, the results might be counted by the school, including the 1904 Georgia game. However, since it's somewhat of a gray area and those early Florida teams were dreadfully awful, the Gators have picked and chosen what to recognize, beginning in 1906 when Florida began a streak of 10 consecutive winning campaigns.

Furthermore, although the Florida players and coaches from the pre-Gainesville teams have long passed away, like Dr. Rowlett, we're rather certain they would want their efforts (or lack thereof in their case) recognized.

FLORIDA

FLORIDA FOOTBALL'S EXCLUDED ERA
(1901–1905 RESULTS)

1901	Coach: James M. Farr	Result	Score	Site
11/21	Stetson	LOSS	0–6	Jacksonville

1902	Coach: James M. Farr			
N/A	Stetson	TIE	0–0	N/A
N/A	Stetson	LOSS	5–22	N/A
12/12	Florida State College	LOSS	0–6	Tallahassee
12/20	Florida State College	WIN	6–0	Lake City

1903	Coach: Fleming & Humphreys			
N/A	Stetson	LOSS	5–6	N/A
11/13	Florida State College	LOSS	0–12	Tallahassee
11/26	E. Florida Seminary	WIN	6–5	Lake City

1904	Coach: M.O. Bridges			
10/3	Alabama	LOSS	0–29	Tuscaloosa
10/4	Auburn	LOSS	0–44	Auburn
10/15	Georgia	LOSS	0–51	Macon
10/17	Georgia Tech	LOSS	0–77	Atlanta
10/22	Florida State College	LOSS	0–23	Lake City

1905	Coach: C.A. Holton			
10/23	Julian Landon	WIN	6–0	Lake City

"Oh, I remember some of the players [from the 1904 team]," said Rowlett, "like Ruey Cason, John Lykes, and the Bridges boys. It all meant a great deal to me." Unfortunately, it appears that the first Florida football teams don't mean a great deal to the university.

These men sweated and bled while playing under the "University of Florida" name, so their games should be counted by the school instead of merely dismissed.

During the Gators' one-sided 18–4 run against Georgia from 1990 to 2011, Florida followers have often been quick to instruct us Bulldogs fans to *stop living in the past*. Evidently, part of the University of Florida's documented football *past* never actually occurred.

DEFENDING THE SEC

When Florida entered its regular season finale of 1962, besides the Georgia faithful, perhaps no one had ever rooted harder against the Gators than the Penn State Nittany Lions.

Penn State had finished its regular season with a 9–1 record and was ranked 9th nationally in both major polls. However, when the New Year's Day bowls handed out their bids, there was none extended to the Nittany Lions. Instead, the eastern power had to settle on a December 29 date in Jacksonville's Gator Bowl—the same bowl game it had played the year before in an easy victory over the SEC's Georgia Tech.

Penn State's bowl opponent would depend on the winner of the upcoming Florida–Miami (Fla.) game on December 1. The

Gator Bowl had decided if the Hurricanes were victorious, it would likely invite ACC champion Duke (8–2 record) to face the Nittany Lions. However, a Florida win would mean the Gators were in, despite having lost four games during its season.

To the chagrin of many, especially Penn State, Florida defeated the Hurricanes by a scant two points, and the Gators were thrilled to be headed to, or more like *backing into*, the 18th annual Gator Bowl. The Nittany Lions, on the other hand, felt like they had been dealt a slap in the face.

Nevertheless, Penn State may have taken home the Lambert Trophy as college football's best eastern team that year, but it would be denied its second consecutive Gator Bowl championship. Led by bowl MVP Tommy Shannon, who completed seven of nine passes for two touchdowns, and a stellar defense, which yielded only 139 total yards, Florida played its "best 60 minutes of football all year," according to head coach Ray Graves. Penn State was upset by a score of 17–7, giving the Gators a major boost to its mediocre program and a lift to the Southeastern Conference in general.

Florida's "monster" defense was given credit as a major factor for the Gators' shocking victory. Featuring five men on the line and four linebackers, the newly formed defensive formation was designed by assistant Gene Ellenson specifically for the Gator Bowl and installed and perfected in just eight bowl practices.

The monster defense and quarterback Shannon may have won the ballgame for Florida, but it was something else which was the team's so-called inspiration—what it rallied around—

although we would hope the Gators wouldn't take too much pride in it today.

To defend "the Southeastern Conference versus the East," according to Graves, Florida altered its helmet design just for the game by moving the jersey numerals—the Gators' customary helmet logo at the time—from the sides of its helmets to the front and replaced the numerals with logos of a Confederate battle flag.

"We stressed [defending the SEC] by putting the Confederate flag on their helmets," said Graves following the victory. "The boys felt like they were playing for the whole conference."

Nearly 50 years later as Florida prepared for its Gator Bowl appearance against Ohio State on January 2, 2012, the University of Florida's official team website reminded viewers of the Gators' proud victory over Penn State in 1962 and their psychological ploy in its *Gator Bowl Memories* feature: "The Gators took the field with Confederate flag emblems on their helmets as a not-so-subtle reminder to the Northerners that football, indeed, was played in this part of the country."

We certainly understand that Florida's embarrassing helmet stunt was from a half-century ago and also during a time when no team from the SEC had been integrated. In addition, Florida players would later say that the new logo was not meant as any kind of racial slur but a display of regional pride. Even today, some of us Bulldogs fans see nothing wrong with the Confederate flag, believing that its true meaning—one of respect, southern pride, and a communication symbol during the Civil War—has been misconstrued.

Regardless, when Graves and his Gators entered the 1962 Gator Bowl, they faced a Penn State team with a number of African Americans on its roster. For the first time a Florida team would be competing against black players, and instead of wanting to "defend the SEC," the Gators should have been aware of the cultural and racial implications at the time and that the Confederate flag even then, like today, was considered by some as a symbol of hate.

Moreover, the official site of the Gators should not be reminding its readers in 2012 of what we assume many Florida fans would like to forget about their team's past.

GATORADE

Thank goodness for the 1965 Florida football team and a few of the university's researchers from the time. Because of them, there have been far fewer athletes affected by the heat and heat-related illnesses; these much-appreciated Gators are the reason for the acclaimed sports drink of Gatorade.

In the spring of 1965, an assistant coach approached Dr. Robert Cade, the university's kidney disease specialist, asking the reason why so many Gators players were "wilting" toward the end of games in the Florida heat. In response, Cade and other researchers formulated a new beverage to help counteract the players' debilitating dehydration better than just plain drinking water.

The new drink—Gatorade—was presented to head coach Ray Graves, who agreed that the researchers could try out the concoction on his Gators, but only the freshman team.

Legend has it, the first on-the-field tests of Gatorade came in a scrimmage between the freshmen squad, or the "guinea pigs," against the superior Gators' B team.

"At the end of the first half, the B team was ahead 13–0. They pushed the freshmen around pretty good," Cade says. "In the third period, the freshmen, who had been given the solution, came out and began pushing the B team around. They scored two or three touchdowns in the third period and five or six more in the fourth period."

Florida Gators football players down Gatorade on the sideline during a game in 1968. Gatorade was touted as the secret to the team's success, especially in performing well in the fourth quarter, despite a lot of evidence to the contrary.

Coach Graves was instantly sold on Gatorade and asked the researchers if they could supply enough for the entire Florida varsity to use in its upcoming game against heavily favored LSU. The very next day, Florida came from behind in the fourth quarter in 102-degree heat in Gainesville to upset the Tigers 14–7. Apparently, the Gators had been filled with Gatorade in the second half, whereas LSU had wilted down the stretch. At that point, according to the drink's official website, "the Gators began winning…outlasting a number of heavily favored opponents in the withering heat and finishing the season at 7–4."

With Gatorade in hand, it only got better for the Gators. In 1966 they achieved a regular season record of 8–2 while earning the reputation as a second-half team. Prior to Florida's first-ever Orange Bowl appearance that season, the *Florida Times-Union* summed up the Gators' newly found success and their secret remedy with the headline: "One Lil' Swig of That Kickapoo Juice and Biff, Bam, Sock—It's Gators, 8–2."

In the Orange Bowl, the Gatorade-filled Gators defeated Georgia Tech, finishing its season with a school-record-tying nine victories. Word soon spread about the University of Florida's balanced carbohydrate-electrolyte beverage and how the magic potion brought instant fortune to its football team. And, as they say, the rest is history: "Orders from other college football programs across the country soon followed, as playing without Gatorade on your sideline began to be likened to playing with just 10 men on the field."

Let us first start off by saying that your average Bulldogs fan does not dislike Gatorade simply because it was created by

a group of Gators. Most of us like the drink, in fact, probably just as much as the next guy. We've even used it once in a while for alternative purposes, like dumping it on our coaches following a big victory. However, the Gators tend to often exaggerate their football history, while we Bulldogs usually will call a spade a spade.

In 1965 "heavily favored" LSU was actually just a three-point favorite over the Gators. Also, Florida did not rally in the fourth quarter to defeat the Tigers as the story goes; the Gators didn't score a single point in the final quarter and actually never trailed the entire game.

As far as Florida "outlasting a number of heavily favored opponents" that season, in fact, the opposite could actually be said. Following the victory over LSU, the Gators did not win a single game as a decided underdog while actually losing two games when ranked in the top 10 to unranked teams—Auburn and Miami (Fla.)—who would both finish their seasons with subpar records.

The 1965 Florida football team would actually end its season with an overall record that was a little worse than the Gatorade-less Gators from the year before.

Granted, the following season of 1966 was a banner year for Florida. However, if one considers the first three Gators teams that were drinking Gatorade, including the '66 Orange Bowl champions, and compares them to the three Florida football squads *prior* to the drink's creation (1962 to 1964), each group of Gators lost the exact number of combined games: 10.

As far as the '66 Gators earning the reputation as a second-half team, any "reputation" certainly wasn't earned in Jacksonville, when Florida blew a 10–3 halftime lead to Georgia and was outscored 24–0 in the second half (17–0 in the fourth quarter). We guess the Gators forgot to drink their Gatorade during the final two quarters, especially the top Gator—quarterback Steve Spurrier, or "Superman" as he was then known.

Constantly harassed and repeatedly sacked while throwing three interceptions in the second half against the Bulldogs, instead of Gatorade, Superman must have come in contact with some kryptonite.

BULLDOG-TURNED-GATOR

Perhaps the only thing stronger than the hatred many Georgia followers have for Steve Spurrier is the Evil Genius' contempt for the Bulldogs. But where did Spurrier's presumed scorn for our team stem from? Why all the snide and ridiculing comments about Georgia and its coaches over the years? What is the reason for the called flea-flickers and end-arounds when a number of Bulldogs-Gators games were already well decided?

Most of us have always assumed Spurrier's beef with the Bulldogs was simply because of the defeats he endured as Florida's quarterback in 1964 and particularly in 1966 to Georgia. However, the supposed truth goes much further than that.

Gene Ellenson was an All-SEC tackle as a Bulldog, a member of Georgia's 1942 national championship team, and a Battle of the Bulge hero from World War II. After an assistant coaching stint at Miami (Fla.), he became Georgia's top candidate to fill

the head-coaching position left by Wally Butts in 1961. In fact, UGA President Dr. O.C. Aderhold reportedly went so far as telling Ellenson the job was his to lose…but lose it he would.

Before his hiring became official, Ellenson, who was known for his motivational speeches, spoke a little too much to a Jacksonville newspaper, indicating several changes he would make if he became the Bulldogs' head coach. With that, according to author Jesse Outlar, "Ellenson had talked himself out of one of the most sought after jobs in football."

So it was off to the University of Florida for Ellenson, where he would serve as a defensive assistant for almost the entire Coach Ray Graves era of 1960 to 1969. Against Georgia in 1968, in an attempt to shake things up with a struggling team, Graves had the ingenious idea of swapping coordinators— defensive coordinator Ellenson suddenly was the offensive coordinator. Graves' move more than backfired as the Gators were trounced by the Bulldogs 51–0.

In that game, the Bulldogs comfortably led 48–0 with more than five minutes to play. Georgia had reached Florida's 5-yard line, where it faced fourth down. Coach Vince Dooley decided to call upon reserve Peter Rajecki—a German-born, barefooted kicker, and the school's first soccer-style place-kicker— to attempt his first-ever field goal as a Bulldog. Rajecki made the 22-yard attempt.

As the story goes, the successful field goal meant much more to the Gators, Ellenson, and eventually Steve Spurrier, than simply another three points for the Bulldogs. Spurrier, who was then playing in the NFL for the San Francisco 49ers,

was told of Georgia's "running-up-the-score" maneuver by Ellenson in a phone conversation. Spurrier was furious and vowed then, if he ever got the chance, he'd run the score up on the Bulldogs just like they had done to his Gators.

In his first year as Florida's head coach in 1990, Spurrier brought in Ellenson to deliver a motivational message at the team meeting the Friday night before the Georgia game. The Bulldog-turned-Gator speaker stressed taking charge of one's own fate and not letting outsiders control it. The motivated Gators responded with an easy victory over Georgia, where Spurrier got his chance to run up the score, and sure enough he did in a 31-point victory. A year later, it was the same as the season before—Ellenson spoke to the team on Friday, urging them to go to "another level." The Gators would hold a late, comfortable lead over the Bulldogs the next day. Yet, it was not quite comfortable enough for Spurrier, who didn't let up for a second straight blowout win for Florida over Georgia.

So, more or less, that is supposedly the reasoning behind Spurrier's hate for Georgia while at Florida. However, there is a bit of information the Gators tend to leave out when recalling the story. Let's just say that for many attending the Georgia-Florida game on that rainy day in 1968, it was rather obvious that the Gators collectively did not put forth their best toward the end of the game.

Dooley was not one to run up the score during his 25 seasons as the Bulldogs' head coach. Further, he certainly hardly questioned an opponent's effort, if ever, besides this one example. Dooley said after the game, "I really believe Florida's effort was not at its maximum.... I believe you had a [Georgia]

ASSISTANT COACHES AT BOTH GEORGIA AND FLORIDA

John Donaldson (UF): 1960–63
(UGA): 1964–68, 1971–72

Def. Backs, Head Frosh. Coach
Off. Backs, Recruiting Coord.,
Head Frosh. Coach

Sterling Dupree (UF): 1948–49, '61–63
(UGA): 1950–60, 1964–76

Backfield, Head Recruiter
Off. Backfield, Recruiting Coord.

Joe Kines (UF): 1979–84
(UGA): 1995–99

Linebackers, Def. Coordinator
Def. Coord., Asst. Head Coach

Fred Pancoast (UF): 1964–69
(UGA): 1970–71

Off. Ends, Backs, and Coord.
Off. Coord.

John Rauch (UF): 1952–53
(UGA): 1955–58

Quarterbacks
Quarterbacks

Perron Shoemaker (UF): 1949
(UGA): 1951–56

Ends
Ends

Ted Twomey (UGA): 1931–37
(UF): 1946–49

Ends, Line
Line

Barry Wilson (UGA): 1968–73

Frosh. Asst., Head Frosh. Coach,
Def. Ends/Linebackers

(UF): 1996–97

Special Teams, Linebackers

football team after the third quarter that was really keyed, against a team that was giving less than maximum effort."

Therefore, it appears that an assistant's hard feelings for his alma mater and a head coach's vengeance against the same rival results from not necessarily Georgia trying to run up a

score, but perhaps something else, namely the Gators simply not playing to "another level" in the 1968 game.

Besides, what would Spurrier and the Gators faithful have preferred Dooley execute on fourth down from the 5-yard line and with more than five minutes remaining in the game?

Run a Spurrier-like end-around with a wide receiver?

ABOUT TIME!

When the Gators discuss the history of their football program, there's a very good reason why it might often seem the sport did not begin at the University of Florida until the 1990s.

Coach Steve Spurrier's resounding victory over Georgia on November 9, 1991, was much more than a second consecutive rout for the Gators over the Bulldogs in Jacksonville, it was a historic moment Florida football had never experienced in its long history. The Gators' 45–13 win clinched at least a share of an SEC championship—the program's first conference title in its nearly nine decades of playing football.

Prior to Florida's championship in 1991, 10 different teams from the Southeastern Conference laid claim to a combined 69 conference titles since the SEC's inaugural season of 1933. Even Mississippi State had captured one conference championship during that time, Kentucky had two, and there were even two schools who were no longer conference members—Georgia Tech and Tulane—that had won a combined eight titles.

Through 1990, Georgia claimed 10 SEC titles, and a total of 12 conference championships in its history, while Florida had won zero and none.

To that point, only two schools that had ever been members of the conference—Vanderbilt and Sewanee—like Florida, had also never won the SEC. However, the Commodores had 13 conference titles from their time in the Southern Intercollegiate Athletic Association and Southern Conference to their credit, while the Tigers had won four championships. Poor Gators—at the time, they sat all alone at the bottom of the league without a single football championship to their name.

Prior to Coach Ray Graves' arrival in 1960, for the most part, the Gators had hardly ever even contended for a conference title. In his first few seasons at Florida, Graves admitted that he felt no particular pressure to win the league. Nevertheless, that attitude from the Florida faithful would soon change as Graves and his successor, Doug Dickey, would come close to winning an SEC crown on several occasions. However, as Graves once told the *St. Petersburg Times*: "There was always just one game that kept us from the championship. They were all weird games with the Bulldogs."

Through the decade of the 1970s, five times the Gators entered their game with Georgia in early November undefeated in SEC play, but five times a Bulldogs victory would ultimately cost Florida a championship. This included the 1976 meeting when Florida held such a commanding lead over Georgia that "we were in the locker room at halftime getting measured for our [championship] rings," joked Scot Brantley, a Gators linebacker from the time.

Also, there were back-to-back occasions in 1968 and 1969 when Florida did not enter the rivalry game undefeated, but a victory over Georgia would have eventually given the Gators a share of the SEC title. Instead, a loss and a tie, respectively, to the Bulldogs left Florida on the outside looking in.

In 1980 a new Florida head coach, second-year man Charley Pell, endured another near-miss for the Gators against the Bulldogs, resulting from a 93-yard, game-winning touchdown pass from Buck Belue to Lindsay Scott. Without the miraculous play, Florida would have won the game and would have finished its season with a 5–1 conference record and a share of the SEC title along with Mississippi State and nemesis Georgia.

Four years later, Pell would begin a trend at Florida, where even when the Gators won the SEC championship, or at least finished first in the conference standings, they really had won nothing at all.

(And this is the part we Bulldogs really hate to recount; we don't like to hear of any program cheating. Notwithstanding, you know what they say about cheaters never winning, and they certainly shouldn't reap any rewards.)

Only two games into the '84 season, the NCAA charged that Florida committed 107 rules infractions related to the recruiting of football players. Violations included a direct payment of nearly $1,000 by Pell to one of his players and the head coach's controlling of a $4,000 slush fund used for illegal scouting and supplementing assistant coaches' salaries. Pell would admit, among other things, he knew of and took part

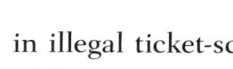

in illegal ticket-scalping to channel money to his players, in addition to authorizing a scheme to spy on opponents to steal their game-day strategies.

The NCAA, whose investigation of Florida lasted nearly two years, would eventually place the Gators on probation for three years, later reduced to two, with no televised games, no postseason bowls, and scholarship reductions.

In mid-September, Pell was fired after the school revealed its head coach had repeatedly lied to the university's attorney during the course of the NCAA investigation.

Amid the controversy, interim head coach Galen Hall remarkably led the Gators to eight consecutive victories, including a 25–17 win at Kentucky that apparently clinched an SEC football title for first time in Florida's history. That day in Gainesville, students jammed city streets, throwing packets of sugar during an all-night celebration in anticipation of the Gators playing in the Sugar Bowl that January 1.

The Gators returned home to a pep rally attended by 22,000 at Florida Field. During the celebration, then school president Marshall Criser named Hall the permanent head football coach and announced that a four-year contract had been negotiated. Criser said to the celebratory, emotional crowd: "You want Galen? You've got Galen."

Speaking of emotion, less than five years later, Criser's successor, interim president Robert Bryan, would admit that Hall was hired merely "on a crest of emotion, on a wave of emotion."

Four days after the victory over Kentucky, the Southeastern Conference's Executive Committee prohibited the Gators from playing in a postseason bowl game. Just over four months later, the same committee ruled in a 5–1 vote that Florida had been punished enough for its recruiting violations and would be allowed to keep its first SEC title. However, just one month later, or 193 days after the championship had been won on the field at Kentucky, league presidents of the 10 member schools voted 6–4 to recall the title the Gators chased for more than 50 years.

It was believed that Georgia was one of the six schools, along with Vanderbilt, Tennessee, Mississippi, Kentucky, and LSU, which banded together to strip the 1984 crown from Florida.

In 1985, for the second year in a row, the Gators had the conference's best record, but once again, there was no championship for Florida because of its NCAA violations.

Four years later, in 1989, and while Florida's basketball program was being investigated for drug use and allegations that coaches paid Gators players thousands of dollars, head football coach Hall resigned midway through the season amid charges he made unauthorized payments to a player and to his assistant coaches in violation of NCAA rules. Hall, who had stated, "we have got to run a clean program…which we will do," when he had been named interim coach in 1984, admitted that he helped out a player who faced a court order arising from non-payment of child support, while an unidentified graduate student told university officials that Hall had him deliver money for the player in a sealed envelope.

STATS WE HATE

Georgia-Florida Comparison, 1990–2011

	Florida	Georgia
Overall Winning Pct.	.774	.686
SEC Winning Pct.	.787	.606
Bowl Appearances	21	18
SEC Championships	8	2
National Championships	3	0
Series Wins	18	4

For the second time in five years, a Florida head football coach had been forced to resign in the middle of a season, and because two major rules violations had been committed within five years, there was the possibility of the NCAA ordering the "death penalty." This would have resulted in shutting down the Gators' football program for at least a year.

At that point, things had gotten so out of hand that even Charley Pell was "very surprised and very disappointed" in his former school. "I'm disappointed for the team," said Pell following Hall's resignation. "I'm disappointed for the Florida people and the university."

Florida football would avoid becoming just the second football program to ever receive the death penalty, but a month into the 1990 season, first-year head coach Steve Spurrier still found himself engulfed by the ghosts of Gators past. Because of the major rules infractions during the Hall coaching regime, the

NCAA declared Florida bowl-ineligible, while the SEC maintained that a school which isn't eligible for postseason play isn't eligible for the conference title, either.

That season the Gators finished atop the SEC standings, but for the third year in the previous seven, the SEC football title did not go to Florida, even though it finished with the best record in the conference.

After the NCAA had penalized the Gators in 1990, Coach Spurrier foreshadowed, "If we just do it the right way, if I am able to coach a little ball...it will work out here."

GATORS BOOKS WE HATE

Gators: The Inside Story of Florida's First SEC Title by Steve Spurrier and Norm Carlson

Urban's Way: Urban Meyer, the Florida Gators, and His Plan to Win by Buddy Martin and Urban Meyer

The Gators: A Story of Florida Football by Tom McEwen

University of Florida Football: Yesterday & Today by Pat Dooley

The Steve Spurrier Story: From Heisman to Head Ball Coach by Bill Chastain

Go Gators! by Arthur Cobb

University of Florida Football Vault by Norm Carlson

What It Means to Be a Gator by Mark Schlabach

After decades of subpar teams, a number of near misses, and a few conference-best-but-ineligible Gators squads, it *would* finally work out at Florida under Spurrier. After the Gators won their first SEC title in 1991, four in a row would soon follow from 1993 to 1996, culminating with a unanimous national championship in '96.

How ironic is it that it took seemingly the most evil, sneaky, and hated head coach of them all to finally remove the Gators from their cheating ways and deliver the program to multiple championships?

As mentioned earlier, while a cheater may never win, you know what they also say when it comes to nice guys and finishing last.

6

WE HATE UF, GAINESVILLE, AND GATOR NATION

Growing up, I thought I wanted to be a lawyer. But I realized that if I became a lawyer, there's a good chance I would end up practicing my trade inside of a courtroom. At that point, I'd be known as a litigator. And well…it just didn't set right to have folks knowing me as being ANY sorta gator.

—Joke passed along by Bulldogs fan Casey Dalton

UNIVERSITY of FLORIDA

In 1905 the Buckman Act consolidated the four colleges of the University of Florida at Lake City, the East Florida Seminary in Gainesville, the St. Petersburg Normal and Industrial School in St. Petersburg, and the South Florida Military College in Bartow to form the "University of the State of Florida."

Located in Gainesville, the school officially changed its name to the "University of Florida" in 1909, tracing its founding date back to 1905. However, in 1935, the founding year was traced back even further to 1853—the year classes began at the East Florida Seminary, the oldest of the original institutions that eventually merged to create the University of Florida.

Confused yet?

In just over 100 years, the university's enrollment has grown from approximately 100 students in 1906 to currently around 50,000, making the school the sixth largest single-campus university in the United States as of 2012. However, many of

FLORIDA

TOP UF ALUMNI

The University of Florida Alumni Association boasts the school has nearly 350,000 alumni on record, residing in all 50 states and more than 100 different countries. Gator alumni include multiple Nobel Prize winners, over 125 Olympians, and countless governmental officials.

Here's our all-time list of the top UF alumni, or ex-Gators who at least attended a few classes while at the school:

Cam Newton and **Gene Chizik:** Both Newton and Chizik briefly played football at the University of Florida. Newton rushed for four touchdowns as a backup quarterback in six combined games in 2007 and 2008. Chizik's bio claims he played for the Gators in 1981 at linebacker, although there is no record of him lettering. Regardless, the two would eventually team together—Newton at quarterback, Chizik as head coach—to deliver a national championship in the 2010 season for another hated rival of the Bulldogs—Auburn.

Darrell Hammond: After majoring in broadcasting at UF, Hammond would become a famous actor and comedian. He is best known for his celebrity impersonations as the longest-tenured cast member of *Saturday Night Live.* In 2011 Hammond revealed that throughout his lengthy time at *SNL,* he was drunk, medicated, cut himself backstage, and even once had to be removed from the studio and taken to a psychiatric ward.

Corrine Brown: Congresswoman Brown of Florida's third congressional district spoke in front of the House of Representatives

the campus' facilities and buildings have not kept up with the drastic increase in enrollment, remaining outdated, shabby-looking, and devoid of character.

The University of Florida seems to always place highly in academic rankings among other institutions. But the school

chamber in March 2009 to commend the Florida Gators on their victory over Oklahoma to win the national football championship. Dressed in an orange-and-blue silk Gators robe, the 1971 master's graduate of the university wanted to "gradulate" the team and "Corch Urban Meyers." Brown's babbling nonsense became a YouTube sensation while leaving all who heard the speech wondering how the heck she ever got elected—"Go Gator!"

Vernon Maxwell: In 1987 "Mad Max" led the Florida basketball team to the program's first-ever NCAA Tournament and eventually became the Gators' all-time leading scorer. However, the tourney appearance was later vacated and Maxwell's records erased when he admitted to accepting cash payments from coaches and snorting cocaine prior to games. Following his days as a Gator, Maxwell's madness continued, running in the stands to punch a fan while in the NBA, allegedly knowingly infecting a woman with herpes, and being arrested for violation of probation charges related to failing to pay child support.

Charley Eugene Johns: Although Johns attended UF for only a few months, he did the university proud by becoming Florida's 32nd governor in 1953. Johns would then lead a campaign at his old school, and other universities in the state, to persecute African Americans, Jews, homosexuals, and liberals.

Honorable Mention: For the UF alumnus and editor of *UF Today*—an alumni publication of the University of Florida—who mistakenly featured Johns in a 2005 article listing the school's most outstanding alumni.

FLORIDA

is more well-known for its partying, being dominated by fraternities and sororities, and extremely focused on its football program. And for those students who do attend class, many instructors are renowned for being rather inaccessible.

Following their freshman year, most students move off campus into the city of Gainesville. And before signing any kind of lease, at least the more astute students will make sure to look into the good possibility of pest issues and/or maintenance problems that apartments and condominiums in Gainesville are notorious for having. In short, for any potential University of Florida students, if you drink a lot, want to be part of the large percentage of undergraduates who go Greek, and don't mind simply being just another number, this school could be your perfect fit!

Remember, college is supposed to be the very best years of your life, so choose one wisely.

GAINESVILLE

Question: *If there's a car containing a Gainesville resident, a UF student, and a Florida Gators football player, who is driving the vehicle?*
Answer: *A cop.*

Gainesville, or the "armpit" of the state of Florida, as referred to by some, was incorporated nearly 150 years ago and currently has approximately 150,000 residents.

You'll hear many say that Gainesville is a "true college town." In other words, nothing really makes the city special besides it

being the home to a large university. And you've already been informed on how unbearable the school can be, so we recommend visiting Gainesville at your own risk.

The city's crime rate is rather high, there's a problem with homelessness, and for the Gainesville residents who do own homes, property taxes are among the highest in the state. On a lighter (or higher) note, at one time the city held the Gainesville Hemp Festival, and continues to be celebrated by the

WEIRD FLORIDA LAWS

Planning on heading down for the Cocktail Party? Be careful when crossing the Georgia-Florida border. These strange-but-true state laws are still on the books in the Sunshine State. You've been forewarned...

- Women may be fined for falling asleep under a hair dryer, as can the salon owner.
- Penalty for horse theft is death by hanging.
- A special law prohibits unmarried women from parachuting on Sunday or she shall risk arrest, fine, and/or jailing.
- It is illegal to sing in a public place while attired in a swimsuit.
- It is considered an offense to shower naked.
- Having sexual relations with a porcupine is illegal.
- Men may not be seen publicly in any kind of strapless gown.
- You are not allowed to break more than three dishes per day, or chip the edges of more than four cups and/or saucers.
- It is illegal to fish while driving across a bridge.
- When having sex, only the missionary position is legal.
- You may not fart in a public place after 6:00 PM on Thursdays.
- You may not kiss your wife's breasts.

FLORIDA

recreational drug culture for its growth of a particular potent type of marijuana—"Gainesville Green."

Still, Gainesville has been ranked in the past as one of the better cities in the state, and even in the entire country, including by a worldwide television channel in 2007 as one of the "best places to live and play" in the United States. However, it's our guess that whoever conducted this survey got their hands on some Gainesville Green prior to releasing its rankings.

THE SWAMP

Thank goodness, this is one subject we Georgia fans know very little about. Our Bulldogs have been forced to play at Florida's Ben Hill Griffin Stadium just twice in their football history: the first time in 1931, when the stadium was known as "Florida Field," and then 63 years later, when it was better known as "the Swamp."

Prior to 1933, the Bulldogs and Gators had yet to decide on Jacksonville as their permanent meeting place. Up to that point, Florida had been fortunate enough to visit Athens on four occasions while Georgia once reluctantly made the trip to Gainesville for the Gators' Homecoming of 1931.

According to newspaper reports, the Bulldogs' initial visit to the University of Florida actually wasn't as bad an experience as expected. "There seemed to be almost as many cars from Georgia jamming the streets as there were Florida cars," according to the *Florida Times-Union*. A crowd of 22,000— the largest ever at the time to see a sporting event in the city— packed the stadium to witness Georgia pound its host 33–6.

Florida coach Urban Meyer shakes hands with painted, dead-eyed Gators fans after a hard-fought 41–3 victory over perennial powerhouse Louisiana Tech on September 10, 2005 in the aptly named "Swamp." Photo courtesy of Getty Images

Still, it was said the Gators fans in the stands were gracious in defeat and accommodating to their visitors.

Boy, how times have changed…

From its humble beginnings to the present, Ben Hill Griffin Stadium has had its fair share of expansions and renovations, while currently seating 88,548 as of 2012. In 1971 Florida was

the last of the handful of SEC schools to install AstroTurf; it only took the Gators almost 20 years before they realized their unwise decision. It required a genius, and an evil one at that, in Steve Spurrier to insist the turf be removed for natural grass, and not long afterward, the head coach gave the stadium its famous moniker.

The Swamp is known for being one of the loudest and most intimidating stadiums in all of college football. Of course, most anybody disorderly to begin with and drinking cheap beer all day, like many Gators fans on game day, would be rather raucous. At one time, spectators were allowed to leave at halftime and could later re-enter the stadium. Considering the Florida fan base, this was yet another poor arrangement by the school—one that was eventually and thankfully banned.

Over the years, there have been a number of bewildering tales from the Swamp, most of which involve overzealous Florida spectators. One of the most astounding was how, during a game, a Gators fan dumped a cup of urine on Vicky Fulmer, wife of former Tennessee head coach Phillip Fulmer.

While the old Gator Bowl was being renovated for the NFL's expansion Jacksonville Jaguars, the Bulldogs made their second trip to Gainesville in 1994. Just a few days prior to the game, Georgia safety Will Muschamp, who lived in Gainesville as a youngster, said of the Swamp: "It's loud and those people are fanatical down there."

Nearly 20 years later, an experience at the Swamp is every bit of how Muschamp described it. More so, according to most

Bulldogs who've made the visit, it will make one ever so grateful our annual game with the Gators is played in Jacksonville.

WE ARE GATOR HATERS
(AND FOR GOOD REASON)

> *For my son's first trip to Georgia-Florida in 2003, there was much adventure prior to the game for a nine-year-old (scalper arrests, broken bottles, a sea of Florida fans in jean shorts, etc.) and the Dawgs ended up losing a close game. On the way back to the car, a Gators fan—a grown man—actually started walking backward in front of my son, taunting, "Hey, boy, get used to it. This is what it feels like to be from Georgia."*
>
> *His Gators buddies laughed and pulled him away, but the gift was already delivered. My son is currently contemplating what college to apply for and is considering a number of schools. The University of Florida is not on his list. Immediately after his run-in with the Florida fan eight years ago, he vowed then he would always be a "Gator Hater."*
>
> —A Proud Father (2011)

We totally understand that every fan base, even our own at Georgia, has its bad apples. Also, we generally would not paint one school's fans with a broad brush. However, the account above is an example of what nearly all of us have been exposed to, while very tame compared to what most Bulldogs fans have experienced when dealing with members of Gator Nation.

Georgia first became accustomed to the Florida fans' unruly behavior a little more than 80 years ago when the Gators

finally defeated the Bulldogs in football. As Georgia was winning the first seven games of the series, we heard little from the Florida faithful. Just when we began believing the rivalry could be a civil one, the Bulldogs had to slip up and lose to the Gators in 1928.

At Savannah's Municipal Stadium, Florida was leading 26–6, and fortunately for the Bulldogs the game was drawing to an end. Suddenly, a Gators fan from the stands fired a pistol into the air. Believing the shot was the contest's final gun, Florida supporters first swarmed onto the field to tear down both goal posts and then incited a number of fist fights with Georgia fans. When order was finally restored, the game resumed, and a number of Gators followers were taken away by the police.

Over time, Gators fans have evolved to be regarded as among the most insane, disrespectful, and rude in all of college football. See for yourself. Look up "SEC's worst fans," or the like, online and you'll likely find Florida atop the rankings—a position many of them actually take pride in.

For those of you who follow the NFL, an encounter with Gators fans is often something on the order of going to an Eagles game in Philadelphia. Expect a fan to get in your face, for you to be ridiculed, and at least one Gator to try to start a fight with you. And if Florida fans ever had the chance to boo and throw snowballs at Santa Claus, like Eagles spectators did at Philadelphia's Franklin Field in 1968…let's just say it's a good thing it rarely snows in Gainesville.

But at least Eagles fans are dedicated. With a new head coach and a nationally ranked team, the fair-weathered Florida

faithful didn't even sell out the Gators' 2011 home season opener, breaking a streak of 137 consecutive home sellouts dating back to 1989.

SOURCES

BOOKS

Barnhart, Tony, and Dooley, Vince. *What it Means to be a Bulldog: Vince Dooley, Mark Richt, and Georgia's Greatest Players*. Chicago: Triumph Books, 2004.

Burns, Robbie. *Belue to Scott!* Macon, Ga.: H&H Publishing Company, 2010.

Conley, Cale. *War Between The States*. Atlanta: Gridiron Publishers, 1992.

Garbin, Patrick. *About Them Dawgs! Georgia Football's Memorable Teams and Players*. Lanham, MD: The Scarecrow Press, Inc., 2008.

Garbin, Patrick. *The 50 Greatest Plays in Georgia Bulldogs Football History*. Chicago: Triumph Books, 2008.

Garbin, Patrick. *Then Vince Said to Herschel... The Best Georgia Bulldog Stories Ever Told*. Chicago: Triumph Books, 2007.

Martin, Charles E. *I've Seen 'Em All*. Athens, GA: The McGregor Company, 1961.

McEwen, Tom. *The Gators: A Story of Florida Football*. Huntsville, Al.: Strode Publishing, 1974.

Outlar, Jesse. *Between the Hedges: A Story of Georgia Football*. Huntsville, Al.: Strode Publishing, 1973.

Seiler, Sonny, and Kent Hannon. *Damn Good Dogs! The Real Story of Uga, the University of Georgia's Bulldog Mascots*. Athens, GA: Hill Street Press, 2002.

Smith, Derek. *Glory Yards*. Nashville: Rutledge Hill Press, 1993.

Thilenius, Ed, and Jim Koger. *No Ifs, No Ands, A Lot of Butts: 21 Years of Georgia Football*. Atlanta: Foote & Davies, Inc., 1960.

NEWSPAPERS, MAGAZINES, AND JOURNALS

Atlanta Journal-Constitution
Explore (University of Florida)
Florida Times-Union
Gainesville Sun
Macon Telegraph
Orlando Sentinel
Red and Black (University of Georgia)
St. Petersburg Times
South Florida Sun-Sentinel
Sports Illustrated
Tampa Bay Times

WEBSITES

About Them Dawgs! Blawg (www.patrickgarbin.blogspot.com)
College Football Hall of Fame (www.collegefootball.org)
ESPN.com
Georgia High School Football Historians Association
    (www.ghsfha.org)

OTHER SOURCES

1943 University of Georgia *Pandora*
2011 Florida Football Media Guide
2011 Southeastern Conference Football Media Guide
Georgia Football Media Guide (1949–2011)
"Georgia vs. Florida, November 6, 1976." ABC-TV. 1976.
Rivalries: The Tradition of Georgia vs. Florida (video). New York:
    Hart Sharp Video, 2003.